MW00559724

THE UNVEILING

THE UNVEILING

A MOTHER'S REFLECTION ON MURDER, GRIEF, AND TRIAL LIFE

RUTH MARKEL

A POST HILL PRESS BOOK

The Unveiling:
A Mother's Reflection on Murder, Grief, and Trial Life

ISBN: 978-1-64293-957-6
ISBN (eBook): 978-1-64293-958-3

Interior design and composition by Greg Johnson, Textbook Perfect

This is a work of nonfiction. All people, locations, events, and situations are portrayed to the best of the author's memory.

Post Hill Press
New York • Nashville
posthillpress.com

Published in the United States of America
1 2 3 4 5 6 7 8 9 10

To my daughter, Shelly,
for her love, support, and dedication
to keep the light bright in our lives.

To my grandchildren,
Michal, Ari, Roni, Benjamin, and Lincoln,
who have the courage to make
what looks impossible, possible.

A special mention to Phil and Ian
who share this tragedy and journey.

Contents

Introduction

By 6 a.m. on the morning of September 26, 2019, it was already ninety-one degrees, another hot and humid autumn day in Tallahassee, Florida. I was getting dressed to attend the trial of two of the people accused of killing my forty-one-year-old son, Dan Markel. Even though the weather was oppressive, I put on my usual business uniform of a black jacket and black pants. I glanced in the mirror. I looked the same as I have looked for the past seven years, ever since Dan died. Haunted. Defiant. Devastated. Battle ready. I remembered I had to take a warm shawl with me to the courtroom, as the Leon County courthouse is always frigid. I checked my reflection one last time and asked myself these questions: *Will I be comfortable sitting for hours in these clothes? Do I look appropriate for the jury, for the media, for Dan? How am I going to react when I watch the defendants walk into the courtroom for the first time? How will I deal with reporters following my every move? How did we get here? Will Dan ever receive justice?* At this moment, I don't have a clue.

The Unveiling references my lowest emotional moment—going with my family to the cemetery to see Dan's gravestone for the first time, nine months after his death—and, like the act of lifting the cloth that revealed the writing carved on his tombstone, this book will expose what it feels like to be living what I call the "trial life." It is, in effect, a series of unveilings.

To date, one defendant has turned state's evidence, cooperating in exchange for a lesser sentence. Another has been found guilty of committing Dan's murder and has received a life sentence without parole.

He has lost the appeal of his verdict. A third is being retried in 2022 after a mistrial. Others who were once members of my own extended family have been allegedly implicated in the case but have yet to be charged. With the many inevitable postponements on the way to these new proceedings and the likely appeals if there are guilty verdicts, my own life sentence offers no likelihood of parole.

You might wonder if Dan may have done something to put himself in jeopardy. He didn't. My son was never involved in any criminal activity, and he didn't engage in dangerous behaviors or live recklessly. Instead, Dan was an upright, thoughtful citizen. He was a devoted father and a loving son; a dedicated, revered law professor; a prolific, well-known scholar; and a wonderful uncle, brother, and friend. He lived a law abiding and productive life dedicated to teaching and helping others. Dan himself was adamantly opposed to the death penalty, a view he addressed strongly and repeatedly in his work; he favored the justice of legal retribution. His death was felt by people in far-flung places around the world, and for those of us closest to him, it brought life's normal progression to a complete stop.

There is so much I have learned to lean on to survive my new shadow-existence of what is trial life. My book will delve into the extreme juggling act my family and I have been obliged to perform while grieving a terrible and violent loss. Each chapter will describe my experience, from learning about Dan's murder to the pretrial experience and our days in and out of the courtroom, as the case wound its way through the criminal justice system. I have learned a great deal about the machinations of a murder case, the elements that the families of victims can bring to investigations and cases, and the very public and proactive roles thrust upon us as we seek justice. The financial and psychological burdens are staggering, shattering, irreversible, and permanent.

Besides sharing my experience and knowledge for interested audiences as well as fellow victims' families, I also wrote this book is to highlight the issues and problems surrounding the legal rights of grandparents in Florida.

Until now, I haven't told my story, but I have decided to open up my life and my heart to describe the difficult moments that my family and I have experienced as we became connected to one of the most notorious crime stories of the past decade. In the following chapters, I will give the heart-wrenching details of the murder itself as well as the trial of the killers. And beneath those headlines, I will also discuss what life has been like for me—the unimaginable experience of being the mother of a murder victim.

As the evidence unfolded and we have moved forward in our quest for justice, I have learned extraordinary lessons and gained invaluable insights. Many have been rude awakenings; others, as we found a community in our grief and advocacy, have offered unexpectedly beautiful and affirming moments. In this book, *The Unveiling: A Mother's Reflection on Murder, Grief, and Trial Life*, I hope to uncover and share hard-learned lessons, which were imparted to me while waiting for hearings, trials, mistrials, and appeals.

In addition to telling my and my family's story, I will write about my experience of the trial life to dispense any wisdom and insights I have gleaned along the way and to emphasize how people can show support and offer empathy to others left bereft. Helping living victims of violent crimes, or indeed anyone navigating the trials of life, including trauma of any kind, is a cherished goal of mine. I want to make sure that other grandparents do not find themselves in the same situation as I and Dan's father are, grieving the loss of contact with grandchildren. I want to inspire people to find a purpose in their lives and to use their grief and loss, however they show up and in whatever context, to make a real difference. And most importantly, I want to guarantee that Dan is never forgotten by his children, our family, the legal community, and the world at large. He contributed so much during his far too short time on Earth. Continuing to contribute, even after his death, would be very much in character for Daniel Eric Markel.

Part I

DISBELIEF

CHAPTER 1

The Murder

The revelation of Dan's shooting and the realization that I was now embarking on an entirely new and alien way of life.

My son, Dan, and I had a ritual. He would call me in Toronto from his car while he was driving home from work. We would talk until he started pulling into the garage of his house in Tallahassee. "I'm almost there," he would say in a certain tone, a signal that we needed to wrap things up. Dan and I always had a lot to say to each other, but both of us were also efficient conversationalists. Usually, upon entering the garage he would say goodbye. We could always pick up our conversation another day.

As a mother and son, we were very close, and he was called "Danny" when he grew up in Toronto. Starting when he left home for college at eighteen, Danny (who then preferred to be called Dan) would reach out to me to share his thoughts and experiences. Whether he was studying in Cambridge, Massachusetts, or Cambridge, England; living in Israel; clerking for a judge in Arizona; working for a Washington, D.C., law firm; or teaching as a law professor in Florida, where he had settled with his wife and family, he always stayed in touch. When he traveled abroad, Dan would describe in animated detail the landmarks he had visited, the regional delicacies he had eaten, and the people he had met across North America, Europe, and the Middle East. From an early age, he sent his family and close friends long, long emails, which probably marked the beginning of his writing career. He kept us up to date on his latest paper to be published in a law review and on speeches he was making at criminal justice conferences about procedure, punitive damages, or the constitutionality of discretionary sentencing. I was always fascinated how Dan could express himself in a variety of styles; he was adept in academic and legal language, but he could also write in accessible prose. When he was just twelve, we talked about his dreams of studying to be a rabbi. Later, he became interested in becoming a lawyer, or better yet, in bringing his combined skills in teaching, communication, and fundraising to the role of dean of a law school. Dan confided in me during the breakdown and eventual end of his marriage to Wendi Adelson, a fellow lawyer. He kvelled with pride about his two little boys, Benjamin and Lincoln. And he let me in on his budding relationship with a new girlfriend, a professor at New York University in Manhattan.

Usually when Dan called, I was at home in Toronto, not far from the house in North York where his father, Phil, and I had raised him and his older sister, Shelly. Sometimes, Dan would be driving home from the law school campus at Florida State University (FSU) after finishing a day of teaching criminal justice. Sometimes, he'd be coming back from the gym. The only time he wouldn't call me was when he was alone in the car with the boys. He adored being with his sons and wanted to give them his undivided attention during every minute they shared. Even when I was visiting and the four of us were in the car together, Dan would shush me if I talked while the boys were speaking or listening to one of their CDs. "Wait," he would say to me. "We're coming up on Lincoln's favorite song!"

There was nothing unusual about the call he made to me on July 18, 2014—at first, anyway. I was in Montreal that day to celebrate my uncle Lazar's ninety-seventh birthday. Lazar, my mother's brother, had taken a paternal role toward me after my own father died suddenly of a heart attack when I was only nine years old. Single and childless at the time, he acted as a father to me and my older brother, Bob, for a good fifteen years and only married once he was sure we were taken care of and happy. Lazar and I had planned a get-together with Bob, his wife, Carolyn, and other friends to celebrate; his birthday party would be part of a Kiddush luncheon the next day to be held after services at Lazar's synagogue. I had flown in early to spend some extra time with him and would be staying over with him and his caregiver, Kris, at his apartment. Soon after I got there, Dan called my cell phone to wish Uncle Lazar a happy birthday. He loved Lazar and often kept him apprised of his latest accomplishments. Then Dan asked to speak with me again. When Lazar handed me back the phone, I noticed that Dan's tone had changed. It was far less joyful.

He was upset with his ex-wife, Wendi, which wasn't unusual. After seven years of marriage and the birth of their two sons, they had been through a contentious divorce that had been finalized a year earlier. Her desire to relocate from Tallahassee to Miami to be closer to her family was a longstanding issue between them. Dan had considered commuting or getting a different position at one of the universities in South Florida, but Miami was a ten-hour drive away, and the position he was interested in wasn't available there. In June 2013, Leon County Circuit Court Judge Barbara Hobbs denied Wendi's petition to allow her to move to Miami with the boys. The Court ordered that the Former Wife, Wendi, did not meet the burden of proof that a relocation was in the best interest of the minor children.

Once they had separated, it became clear that Dan and Wendi had very different parenting styles. For example, when it was Wendi's turn to have the children as part of their shared custody agreement, Dan would ask to speak to the boys by phone at night and would often go to their daycare center to have breakfast with them. But when Dan had the boys, he felt Wendi was unreachable. He would attempt to reach her so the boys could have contact when they were away for extended periods, but she was often unavailable.

In addition to where they would live, another of Dan and Wendi's issues concerned the children's religious education. Dan was determined to raise them as traditional Jews who kept kosher and were educated in the faith. He was angry that Wendi had filled out an application for their oldest, Benjamin, to be enrolled in a nondenominational charter school kindergarten without consulting Dan first. He had a lot of questions about the education Benjamin would be receiving there, so the school had arranged a phone meeting between Dan and one of the teachers that morning, right after his conversation with me. That day, Dan had to cut our conversation short a few minutes earlier than usual before pulling up to his garage. "Ma, I have to take this call," he said. "Talk to you later."

* * *

After Dan hung up, I left the apartment and spent the day crisscrossing town. Going back to Montreal has always been special for me, as the city is my childhood home. After my father died, my mother ran the family business, manufacturing ladies' clothing with her brothers, and we grew up among our extended family of cousins, aunts, and uncles. The joy of being raised this way is one of the reasons I believe in the value of close families, and Dan inherited this passion for family.... Maybe it was one reason why he was so resistant to Wendi's wish to separate their own family.

That afternoon, I had lunch with an old friend at a favorite bistro and made other brief visits. It was a joy to be in Montreal and reminisce. I made a few phone calls and went back to Lazar's before 5 p.m. to help set up for Shabbat dinner. It would just be the two of us, along with Kris, who wasn't Jewish but had learned the practices for Lazar's sake. At 5:30, even though the sun wouldn't be fully set for a few hours, we decided to light the candles and say the blessing early—Lazar didn't need a late night before his birthday celebration in the morning.

Kris lit the candles and the three of us prayed together: "*Baruch atah, Adonai Eloheinu, Melech haolam, asher kid'shanu b'mitzvotav, v'tzivanu l'hadlik ner shel Shabbat.* Blessed are you, Adonai our God, Sovereign of all, who hallows us with mitzvot, commanding us to kindle the light of Shabbat." The landline rang, and Kris went into the kitchen to answer it. "It's Phil," she called out to me. Phil, Dan's father, was calling from Colorado, where he was visiting friends. He was always concerned about my uncle, so that wasn't strange, but I was surprised that he wasn't calling my cell phone. Then I heard his voice; normally more even-keeled, he sounded extremely tense.

"Are you sitting down?" Phil asked. "Go get a chair."

His voice was alarmed and very clear. "Something terrible has happened."

He'd never spoken to me like this before. I did as he asked and sat down.

"Danny's been shot," Phil said in a shaky, frightened voice.

I went completely numb, and suddenly understood that phrase you always hear—an "out-of-body" experience. What I was feeling was completely real and completely unreal at the same time. The sensation I experienced as I heard Phil's words was terrifying and utterly alien. I felt as though a large sinkhole had started rupturing in the floor of the apartment, and that some destructive force was pulling me toward the opening. It took all of my strength to keep from falling in.

"What do you mean? I spoke with Dan this morning and so did Lazar," I replied. "He told me that he would call me back, and he always does."

"He was shot in his car in the garage at his house a few hours ago," Phil said.

Shot in his garage. Right after I spoke with him. Apparently, someone had followed him into the garage as he parked his car and fired at him twice. I needed to find him, to talk with him. I felt completely unmoored. I needed Danny to tell me what happened.

"How is he?" I asked. "Why hasn't anybody called us until now?" This was so sudden. "Could it be a mistake?"

Phil told me that the police had had a hard time finding us and only reached him by looking him up on Facebook. Then he told me that one of the bullets had lodged in Dan's brain. The friend Phil was staying with in Colorado was a doctor who told Phil right away that there was no chance that Dan would make it after sustaining that kind of injury. If Dan survived, he would be a vegetable.

Shooting. A vegetable. Hearing those words made me think my whole world was turning upside down.

Kris came back into the kitchen. She had left while Phil and I were speaking. I don't know what my face looked like, but it must have been clear to her that something was terribly wrong. Dinner was ready on the dining room table, and the Shabbat candles lit, just as if it were a normal night. I left the kitchen and walked over to my uncle, who was sitting at the dining room table. At that moment, my task was one of the hardest things I ever had to do in my life—I had no idea how many more hard things I would soon have to do. I sat beside Lazar, put my hand on his shoulder, and leaned forward.

"Lazar," I said. "It's Danny. Danny's been shot. In the head." I couldn't bring myself to tell him that Danny was going to die.

Uncle Lazar stared at me, taking in the news. He didn't say anything at first. Then he raised his fist slowly and slammed it on the table, laying it with an intensity that continues to burden my life in the most previously unimaginable ways to this very day. It was with the force of a younger and very angry man, and a message that shook me.

"*Machatunim*," Lazar said in Yiddish. "*Machatunim*."

The in-laws. The in-laws.

* * *

He was talking about the Adelsons, Wendi's family. I didn't want to encourage these accusatory thoughts of Lazar's. He was upset enough as it was, so I just sat with him quietly. I'm not sure if we ate or what we ate, but it was a very short and extremely solemn dinner. I felt as though I was moving in slow motion. All I could do was watch Kris as she passed food and cleared away the dishes.

The phone rang again, and I got up from the table. The call was from the Chabad Rabbi, Schneur Oirechman, in Tallahassee, one of Dan's many rabbi friends. Somehow, Dan's university colleagues and the authorities had been able to track him down, as well as some other friends of Dan's, earlier than they had reached Phil and me. The rabbi had been at the hospital, saying prayers over Dan to give him a Jewish version of last rites. The rabbi told me, "The doctors said that Dan's not going to make it past one or two in the morning." I couldn't believe it. It sounded so final. All I could do was wait for the phone call. Tallahassee was more than 1,400 miles away. I'd never be able to get to Florida by then.

The rabbi put one of the ER doctors on the phone with me. The doctor explained that surgery was required to take out the bullet in his head. He said nothing about saving him; he didn't even put it out there as an option. I thought to myself, "*They don't perform unnecessary surgery on a patient who is certainly going to die unless they need evidence of foul play.*" This would be my first experience of evidence gathering, a process that would be part of the criminal exam and would continue from that day on. It was my first glimpse into the life that awaited me. In those first moments, I was already introduced to the language of criminal investigations. Now I had another reality to grapple with, not just the one of losing my son.

This was the moment when I first realized that this was not the normal loss of a son, not a normal death...whatever can be considered normal in the face of such a tragedy. It could be a *murder*. This had never been part of my vocabulary. Who would think of murder? The sinkhole opened even wider, and my body felt as if it were falling and failing. Who would shoot Dan, my baby boy? He was the youngest, and I had a flashback of his childhood. In the flashback, Dan was eighteen months old, running through the house with a mop and pail—his favored toddler toys. Now he was dying. I needed to tell other people what had happened. I don't know how I made it through those calls with Shelly and her husband, Ian, or with my brother, Bob, and his wife, Carolyn. When I reached her, she immediately started sobbing and hung up the phone. My numbness had started. Bob called back five minutes later and asked me, "Did you tell Lazar? Did he understand everything that you said? Did he understand that Dan was shot?"

"Yes," I said flatly. "Unfortunately, he understood everything."

For the next several hours, I paced up and down the main hallway of Lazar's apartment, from the front door to the master bedroom and back again. I couldn't stop. As I walked, I tried to look at the vivid Judaica paintings and evocative watercolors Lazar had collected on his visits to Israel and hung on the walls of his home, wondering if I would find solace or meaning in them. Instead, the shapes and colors blurred together, and my eyes refused to focus. My mind was trying to absorb what was happening, but I couldn't process the information. *Danny. Gone.* That was unthinkable to me. This was too sudden. I was in a shock and a daze.

In my work, in a crisis, I was always known as "Ms. Fine." In fact, my predisposition to coolness in hot situations informed my career. I was an expert in emergency preparedness and disaster planning; my specialty was training and consulting with companies, schools, and houses of worship to deal with the potential of everything from fires to bomb threats. I had always relied on my hard-headed efficiency and problem-solving skills. But this was one emergency I was not prepared for. I couldn't think ahead to my next footstep, let alone any of the steps toward burying my son.

At 2 a.m., the hospital called to say that Dan had passed away; the gunshot wounds were too severe for him to have any chance of recovery, and the hemorrhaging in his brain had proven fatal. I couldn't think or feel anything; I was frozen. I started packing to leave on the first flight out.

Before being picked up at 6 a.m., I woke up my uncle to tell him that Dan was dead. Lazar started shaking and crying uncontrollably. "Call me from Florida," he said, tears flooding his eyes. "I wish I could be there." As I looked at his stricken face, I realized that I still hadn't cried. The sight of Lazar shivering like that was awful; it has stayed with me ever since, and I will never get over it. This was the beginning of his undoing. I would soon lose my surrogate father, Lazar, and my son within three months. More devastation would enter my world.

All I could do was concentrate on logistics and small tasks before me. One foot in front of the other. My son-in-law, Ian, had arranged for his father, who lives in Montreal, to take me to the airport. Ian had also booked my flights, met me at the Toronto Pearson airport, brought me home to grab some clothes and my passport, and then drove me back to Pearson to meet Shelly and fly to Tallahassee. Ian stayed home in Toronto to take care of his and Shelly's three children. I was walking like a zombie, but Shelly had pulled herself together and was anticipating all that we needed to get done. Before we boarded the plane, she turned to me and said, "Mom, we had better call the synagogue people and Dan's friends to make a memorial for tomorrow. They'll want to do something. We have to give them at least a day to get it together."

Shelly was right. Dan belonged to Congregation Shomrei Torah in Tallahassee, a small, conservative synagogue that was lay led. This meant that Dan and other dedicated members of the shul organized religious education and events and took turns leading the services. There was no head rabbi to help assemble people to mourn Dan. I was catatonic. So, my daughter, Shelly, reached out to Sam Kimelman, Dan's close friend and fellow leader at the synagogue, who had also been Dan's accountant. Sam and the rest of the shul community were way ahead of us and had already started planning a gathering for the following morning, barely twenty-four hours after Dan had been shot.

Twenty-four hours. Twenty-four hours before, I had been talking to Dan. Five minutes later, he had been ambushed. I felt very badly for the teacher he had been speaking with when he was shot, but selfishly I was grateful that I hadn't been on the line myself. *What would I have done? How could I have ever forgotten the awful sounds I would have heard?* If we had been speaking while this happened, I would have felt as though I was sitting right next to my son in the passenger seat—too powerless to save him.

I stared straight ahead for most of the flight. I didn't even allow myself to start asking the typical questions: *Why Danny? Was this a robbery? Was it a disgruntled student? A colleague? Who could hate him so much to do this?* Right now, the one thing that kept running through my mind over and over was *What am I going to say to his children?*

David and Mona Markell, friends (but no relation) of Dan's, picked us up at the Tallahassee airport along with Phil, who had flown in from Colorado on an earlier plane. David, a fellow law school professor at FSU, and Mona, an actuary, had been with Dan in the hospital room, and stayed most of the evening, along with a few other university friends. I still don't know if anyone was in the room with Dan at the time of his death. It's terrible to think of him being alone.

The Markells waited in the car as we checked in at our hotel, then took us back to their house for dinner. I don't remember much, but I know they coddled us, fed us, and told us what they knew: *Danny was on a ventilator. He was not conscious when the doctors took him to surgery; when the nurses brought him back to the room, he didn't move at all, and his head was bandaged. They stayed until after the surgery and left around 10 p.m.* Through my haze, I thought, "Danny has such good friends." Back at the hotel, I continued pacing for hours until I finally fell into a brief, restless sleep.

The memorial was scheduled for noon. At 9 a.m., investigators from the Tallahassee Police Department (TPD) came to our hotel to meet with us. As we sat around a long table in the hotel's nondescript conference room, Craig Isom, the TPD's lead detective, gently started telling us what he and the other investigators had been doing in the hours since Dan's death. He made it clear that they were approaching the situation as a criminal case and viewed Dan's house as a crime scene. Despite this brief period, they had uncovered a good deal of information. They had already interviewed some of Dan's friends and had started inspecting his house and office, removing computers and papers they thought might be important, like his life insurance policy. They were following the money right away.

Then they told us what they had learned about the attack: Danny had been on the phone with the charter schoolteacher. The teacher told the police that Danny had suddenly said, "There's someone next to me," and then he heard a gun go off twice. Danny was shot at intermediate range through the car window and had been hit once in the forehead and once in the left cheek, causing major bleeding and shattering his eyeglasses. The teacher had called 911. One of Danny's neighbors, who had also heard the gunshots and thought he had seen a white or silver Prius peel out of the driveway, dialed 911 as well. He called them over and over when EMS didn't show up for about twenty minutes. While other neighbors and the local media were concerned that this was a random burglary, Isom told us that there were no signs of a break-in and that nothing inside the house appeared to have been touched. The police already knew it was a murder. The police described the head injury in full, and no details of the scene were left out.

These were things that no parent should ever have to hear. Years later, when it came to watching the visual depictions during the trial, I would be unable to remain in the courtroom to see the criminal evidence. For now, they asked us a lot of questions, took notes, recorded us, and listened to every word we said. I was able to give my answers in a relatively calm tone because I still had not fully accepted that Dan was dead. I wasn't in shock. I was in an out-of-body experience. I hadn't descended into proper grief yet. Other people might have been in hysterics, but I was experiencing a strange reaction: I just answered the questions, teary-eyed, but I was able to respond as if it was all so rational, as if these questions were like any other questions. People would ask me questions about Dan all the time, so I was used to talking about him, but not with the police. I always remembered the description of the bullet in his head, but I never wanted to see the crime pictures.

Then the police shifted gears and started asking who might have wanted Dan dead. I sifted through my memories, grasping for clues. Something suddenly occurred to me.

"A few weeks ago, I read something on Dan's blog," I said. "He was having some sort of angry exchange with somebody who accused him of editing the comments section, or something like that. Check the blog. Check the internet. Check his profile."

Dan was a great debater, and he could be very opinionated. He had strong feelings about a number of issues, such as the death penalty, which he vehemently opposed, and he made no apologies about arguing his point of view on any forum. I felt this could be a lead. I wanted to provide any insights I could. "Danny would have been very helpful with solving a mystery like this," I thought to myself. "If he only was here."

The police mentioned people in Dan's orbit, perhaps jealous women or angry colleagues. They weren't ruling out strangers with road rage or others he might have encountered by chance. I couldn't recall any additional incidents or disagreements that might have provoked a violent reaction. "Any other thoughts?" Isom asked.

My mind was reaching for other viable explanations, but I couldn't bring myself to think about it too much. All I really wanted was to get together with Wendi, Benjamin, and Lincoln in person. I knew it would be painful, especially since I could so vividly see a young Dan in my grandsons' faces, but I felt that being surrounded by family would comfort me. And I wondered, "What must she be going through?" I wanted to support her with the boys, to be there as they absorbed as much as little kids could about their dad being gone. I felt many similarities to my young grandchildren as I had already experienced the suddenness of the early death of my father. I was also facing this trauma as an adult woman, and I had very strong maternal feelings of caring I'd inherited from my mother. Despite suffering throughout her life as a widow, she always put her children first and never veered from her dedication. This was in my DNA and dominated any feelings and thoughts, even in this horrific moment.

After almost three hours of debriefing and questions, the detectives drove us in a squad car to make sure we were at the synagogue before twelve. I wished I was feeling more relieved that the questioning was over, but I wasn't. It had only just started. I must have known subliminally that, from this point onward, my life would be transformed into a never-ending series of personal and criminal questions, gathering evidence, investigations, hearings, and trials. My time and life were now intertwined with law enforcement, criminal talk, and legal thinking.

My thoughts and eyes could have barely prepared me for the synagogue attendance. The synagogue parking lot was completely filled with cars. Many people attended from the Tallahassee community. I was in awe to see how many people attended from other communities, including Orlando and Jacksonville.

Even though there had not yet been time for an official announcement or obituary, Dan's circle had kicked into high gear, taking charge and contacting everyone they could think of by phone and social media. Seeing what these devoted friends had managed to pull together for my son provided a very brief moment of solace. That generosity of spirit would continue from our friends and family for years to come. I had no idea how much the support would mean to me going forward.

The synagogue had folding chairs covering every square inch of available space. More than two hundred people came from all over Florida. Along with other congregants, Sam Kimelman organized the speakers, the prayer order, and the hymns. I caught a glimpse of Wendi and her family in the back of the shul, with four-year-old Benjamin standing near her family and three-year-old Lincoln in her arms. I couldn't wait to get close to them. It felt awkward that they were not in the front.

The congregation grew quiet, and several people got up to speak, eloquently describing the difference Dan had made in their lives as a colleague, a professor, or a friend. Alex Greenberg, a veterinarian, talked affectionately about Dan's frequent visits to see him and his family at their home just over the Florida/Georgia border. They would talk about all sorts of subjects during those weekends, but Alex was amazed that Dan never spoke about his successes, or about his standing in the legal field. He felt that Dan may not have been humble about sharing his opinions as he taught in class or wrote online, "but he was humble about himself." Jeremy Cohen, an executive at a marketing firm, said that Dan was well known for being a hugger, a warm person, and that he had himself been drawn back to the Jewish faith after watching Dan teach his little boys about the importance of belief and tradition. Tamara Demko, one of Dan's law school classmates, spoke about all of their adventures together at Harvard, her visits with Dan when he first moved to Tallahassee, and his love for his sons. Shelly spoke briefly about the horror of this moment and more fully about Dan having a hundred best friends and about his love of his sons and his community. Then I surprised myself by standing up to speak.

I had barely been able to articulate more than a few sentences in the past two days. Yet something was nagging at me. I wanted to use the moment to tell the boys what their father would have wanted for his sons. I motioned for Wendi to come forward. She brought Lincoln to the stage, while Benjamin stayed at the back with his grandparents, Donna and Harvey. When I spoke, it was directly to the boys. "Benjamin, Lincoln, your father loved you both so much," I said. "And he wanted more than anything for you to have Jewish roots, understanding the tradition of Shabbat and holidays and to be close to your family."

Then I went in a different direction and spoke to everyone. "My five grandchildren mean everything to me. But when any of them asks me to buy them pretend guns or other police toys, I say, 'No. We don't play with those kinds of things.' We come from Canada, and we don't encourage guns as gifts. We know that guns are dangerous, that terrible accidents can happen with them, and that they should not be used for problem-solving. I couldn't help myself. Wendi stood holding Lincoln, listened until I was finished, and then carried him back to her family. She didn't say anything.

After the liturgy for Dan ended, it seemed as if the entire congregation swarmed around us. Everyone wanted to talk. No one was ready to leave. It felt painful to break up the community that had come together for Dan.

Along with their condolences, people started voicing their opinions about who they thought could have perpetrated this terrible deed: who did it, who didn't do it, and when the police might catch the killer. Everyone wanted to play detective and help us solve the case: *"I heard there were students out to get him." "What if it was a jealous ex?" "Is the killer still out there? Should we all be scared?"* The theories were coming thick and fast. Shelly, Phil, and I listened to their conjecture, answered what we could, and nodded our heads blankly. We still had not hugged or kissed our grandchildren.

Then Tamara, the friend from law school who had spoken about her friendship with Dan, came over to us, very eager to talk. "I taped the whole service for Dan's girlfriend, so don't worry—I'll make sure she gets it," she said breathlessly. "Danny and I were very close."

Wendi was completely buffered at the synagogue, held close by her family and friends, and we didn't get a chance to talk to her or exchange condolences. There were so many people in the shul, so many who wanted to share, to connect. Plus, I knew we would be able to catch up at her house later that evening, where I would finally be able to see the boys. Before we left, Wendi's mother, Donna, walked up to us, weeping almost uncontrollably. "We'll make sure the boys have roots," she said between sobs, referring to the content of my speech, "I promise." They were fine words. In retrospect, those words would become even more telling.

As we walked out of the synagogue, a large gathering of the media was waiting to take our pictures and ask us questions, but the police, who had provided security during the service, whisked us quickly away. The local newspaper, *The Tallahassee Democrat*, ran huge front-page headlines about Dan's death, and there were plenty of other reporters, print, broadcast, and internet, who were anxious for the real story—we had that in common. In these early days, the press in Florida generally remained on the side of deference, and respected limits. We were a grieving family. We were too absorbed in the details of Dan's death to pay attention to them anyhow. But a sign of things to come was coalescing in Toronto. A neighbor told me later that the media had descended on the street where I lived in Toronto, pursuing my neighbors to ask them everything and anything about Dan. It was a fool's errand: Dan hadn't grown up in that house, and those neighbors didn't know him at all. By this time, Toronto and the whole world knew about the slain Canadian-born professor murdered in Florida.

In Tallahassee, the detectives led us from the crowd in front of the synagogue to an unmarked police car so they could drive us over to Dan's house for more questioning. I felt actual terror at the thought of being inside my son's home and of looking through his belongings, and that he was not there. Even worse, he was not coming back. I was not ready for this reality.

On the way, Detective Isom and his team were honing in on specifics. "Did Danny have a will?" Isom asked, turning to face us from the front seat. "We did a thorough search through the house and found a life insurance policy, but no will and testament. Any idea where it is?" He explained that one of the threads they were pursuing was "the money." I knew that Danny didn't have any gambling issues or loan sharks coming after him, so I wasn't sure what "the money" meant. Then, even in my stupor, I said, "I know where to look."

When I visited Dan a few months earlier, I had given him my own serious papers, including my life insurance information, and noticed that he placed them in a particular spot in his bedroom. Dan kept his papers and books in what I would call orderly piles. It's how he organized himself. There were a lot of them: a pile of his lecture notes and piles of university papers, of banking information, of personal papers, and numerous stacks of books. If my documents were exactly where he had put them when I was with him, the rest would surely be nearby.

Dan's house was on Trescott Drive, in the tree-lined Betton Hills neighborhood of Tallahassee. As our police car turned the corner, I saw Dan's house for the first time since the killing. It immediately looked different to me—this home that had been filled with so much love and life was now dreadful with tragedy. The police pulled into the driveway. Dan's house was a contemporary split-level decorated in a style I would joke with him about and describe as early twenty-first century preschool. Dan had designed the entire first floor, with its huge open-plan kitchen/living room, to be supremely child-friendly for Benjamin and Lincoln. Dan didn't just have toys and games for them everywhere—he had attached a long clothesline across the entire ceiling, from which he hung all the boys' artwork. It was so touching. Walking up to the front door, that banner was at the front of my mind. Would seeing the row of crayon drawings and finger paintings lovingly displayed make me break down?

As we opened the front door and walked in, I took a quick, harsh intake of breath. I did not collapse. But in truth, it felt even worse than I had imagined. My soul was screaming: *Why isn't he here?* And I felt the indescribable sadness of knowing my son had breathed between these walls just days before. What had Dan touched before he left the house on Friday? Could I find anything still warm from his fingertips? I looked up and saw the clothesline filled with the boys' drawings and collages. You could even see the Lego construction—a massive project that Benjamin started on the dining room table nearby. I had some strange feeling of trespass. *Would Danny want people going through his papers?* But I soothed myself by remembering that Dan had always welcomed his family into his home and that he would have wanted us, his family, to be the ones handling his private stuff.

He was right: I desperately wanted to be with my family and for us to be able to grieve together. We were somewhat immobilized and so sad, and there was too much to be done. I was starting to learn that in the business of murder, closure is a very far-off horizon. I was fortunate to have people like Craig Isom around who could usher us onto the proper paths. He was just the first in a network of those who would help us navigate the criminal justice system.

Phil and I went into Dan's bedroom, where the piles were just as I had remembered them. We stared at them for a while, unable to touch them. We were so tired. It would be too much for us to deal with that day.

"Oh, there's Danny's *siddur*," Phil said, noticing the Orthodox prayer book on top of one of the stacks. I told Craig Isom that we were not ready to look though all of Dan's important financials. Instead, Phil, Shelly, and I decided to spend our few hours at Dan's house that day, gathering his most meaningful belongings, the things often related to Jewish ritual life that would have been most important to *him*. It wasn't a practical plan; it just felt necessary. We searched for his *kittel*, the white gown worn to lead a Passover Seder or by a religious bridegroom on his wedding day. We knew that Dan would want to be buried in his wedding kittel, so we looked around and found it in a drawer, along with his *tefillin* (the small black leather box with straps that Orthodox men wear on their heads during prayer) and his *tallit* (prayer shawl). If Dan had been able to make such wishes, we knew he would have passed these cherished possessions down to the boys, and with them a sense of his connection to the Jewish faith. Not wanting to leave these precious emblems of our son's spiritual life in the empty house, we took them back to the hotel. The papers could wait for another day. And I could not wait another moment to get to Wendi's, to finally see the boys.

Wendi lived in a rented house about a fifteen-minute drive from Dan's. I'd never been there before, but at first glance the interior looked familiar enough since it was filled with much of the furniture that she and Dan had shared when they were married. That being said, the house was a rental, and upon closer inspection, it very much looked like it. There wasn't much decoration, and there weren't many toys in the living room—no kids' blankets or "soft stuff," as Dan liked to call the boys' stuffed animals. Wendi's place was neat and tidy, verging on empty. It felt very different than Dan's house, where it was clear from the playthings everywhere that two little kids lived there happily.

Wendi's mother, Donna, greeted us warmly but was very busy talking to the guests who were there. She had gone into full hostess mode, cooking, serving, and cleaning. As uncomfortable and in shock as I was, Donna's behavior appeared normal. People had dropped off meals and sweets, and Donna made no effort to respect the Kosher laws that we all knew were so important to Dan. Harvey, Wendi's father, said a meek hello to us but kept moving, even though he looked as though he didn't know where to go.

Since arriving in Tallahassee, this was the first time I had properly seen Wendi face to face. I wanted to sit down with her for a moment to find out how she was doing, to understand how much the boys knew about what was really going on. But Wendi was surrounded by friends at all times, just like at the synagogue, and didn't break away from them to talk to us. Why? Why? I noticed that, from time to time, she would disappear into her bedroom with a friend for long stretches of conversation. During one of the few moments I was able to speak with Wendi in passing, I asked her if she knew whether Dan had a will, and if so, did she know where it was. "No," she replied, and kept walking. It was awkward. We felt like intruders.

Shelly and Phil had spotted Benjamin and Lincoln at the arts-and-crafts table adjacent to the kitchen; the boys were drawing with colored pencils, so they went over to join the children, helping them draw and color. Harvey also seemed lost and couldn't connect, not with the playgroup of Shelly, Phil, and the boys or with the other visitors. When a small group of family friends waved him over to join them, he didn't respond. I was sitting in a chair and was not engaged in the play activities, still in disbelief.

A few hours later, Shelly, Phil, and I got ready to leave Wendi's house and return to the hotel. Family friends had offered to drive us back. We had another appointment with the police scheduled for early the next morning and arrangements to take care of at the funeral home. As we were leaving, I told Wendi that we would like to see the boys after those meetings at around noon, and she agreed nonchalantly. I said I would call when we were done to firm up the plans and wished everyone goodnight. We hugged the boys goodbye, not knowing this was our last family visit in Tallahassee.

When morning came around, I found I couldn't quite comprehend that my son had been shot dead, or that I was on my way to more meetings with the funeral home and the investigators. At the police station, we were introduced to Sara Latorre, our first official victim support advocate from the TPD, a capable and compassionate young woman. We would learn that victim support workers and advocates were critical to families like ours, who were not familiar with the process, providing invaluable emotional support and practical guidance as we faced this crisis. Sara was the leading support person who helped us find resources and fill out innumerable forms. She answered stupid questions without any judgment. She accompanied us through many of our criminal proceedings. I don't know how we would have gotten through those first few days without Sara Latorre and Craig Isom.

We went to the university that day. In those first critical hours after we had arrived in Tallahassee, colleagues, faculty, and friends from FSU had helped to drive us around the city, made sure we got fed, and set up a meeting with the school human resources office to start the process of untangling Dan's assets at the school, such as his 401(k). I knew they were doing this for Dan, but they couldn't have been kinder to us. The FSU administrators, faculty, staff, and friends provided us with light and guidance. We needed and received all of the support, information, and logistics to face this nightmare.

It was a difficult morning, but I got through it knowing that we would soon be spending time with the boys. I called Wendi to make sure that noon was still okay.

"It's not," Wendi said. "The boys are really busy."

"Okay," I said. "How about 1 p.m.?"

"Not today, Ruth," Wendi said. "It's not a good day."

I couldn't believe it. What a punch to the gut! I was feeling terrible already. This was my only connection to Dan. I felt the boys needed us as well. It was summertime. Benjamin and Lincoln weren't old enough to go to school, and I couldn't imagine that they had a lot of plans. However, I figured they might be feeling emotional and unsettled, so I tried not to make a big deal out of it—the "Ms. Fine" part of my personality was coming out.

"Tomorrow then?" I asked, trying to keep my extreme disappointment out of my voice.

Wendi said yes, we would speak in the morning.

When I got off the phone, my daughter, Shelly, was furious, furious enough for the three of us. "What the hell? Unbelievable!" she said angrily. "These boys are just babies! Where could they be going at twelve o'clock in the afternoon? What could be so important?"

I agreed with her, as did Phil, but short of storming over to Wendi's house uninvited, we didn't have much choice but to wait. It was crazy and unbearable, but Phil and Shelly were having none of it. We calmed down and got back to the grim tasks we were busy with. After all, we would see the boys tomorrow.

When I called early the next morning, Wendi said Benjamin and Lincoln were still busy, but she put them on the phone with us. I was so happy to hear their voices and excited we had connected. All I wanted to do was hold them. We expected to see them at noon and went back to the dreaded tasks. We returned to Dan's house to face the challenge of going through his possessions. Combing through them was unspeakably painful, and we were frustrated that, after looking everywhere, we did not find Dan's will. We collected his clothes and housewares and called his close friends to ask each of them to come by and take what they wanted. Then we packed up the children's toys to bring them over to Wendi's. Dan had a house full of playthings—and Wendi's place looked like it needed some.

After we had gathered up everything, I decided to try Wendi again. "We found so many of Linky and BenBen's toys at Dan's house," I said, "and we'd like to bring them over."

Wendy didn't even pause.

"Unfortunately, you can't see them," she replied. "I was so worried about their safety—and mine—that we left the house and drove back to Miami right after we saw you."

I was stunned. They were in *Miami*?

"But Wendi, yesterday you said Benjamin and Lincoln were too busy to see us."

"I know," Wendi said. "I wanted to tell you, but I couldn't. You know, for safety's sake. I'm sure you can understand." In fact, the police had been careful to tell us that, even though they had provided security at the synagogue, they had no concerns about the safety of Wendi, the boys, or us. Now my blood was boiling. I was stunned and wobbly on my feet.

Wendi, Donna, and Harvey had just packed up the house and left! The cars must have been crammed full, so they could take everything on the seven-plus hour drive to Miami. *Did they leave in the middle of the night? Early on the morning after the memorial and the lasagna? How did the boys feel? Would they ever know how much we loved them and wanted to grieve with them? Who would ever do this to us?*

Nobody else—not the police or any mutual friends—was aware that Wendi and the boys had left town. Dan had been shot on Friday, died on Saturday, memorialized on Sunday, and by Monday his children and their mother had up and moved to Miami. I now understood why there had been so few of the kids' belongings in Wendi's house: when I saw it, they were halfway out the door. *How could they have packed so fast? Did they know this would happen?*

Now I was aware why I never had a moment alone with Wendi. We had been deceived and were just pawns on a chessboard.

Phil, Shelly, and I wanted to delve into this craziness and were in disbelief and shock, but there was no time for reflection or philosophy. There were real deadlines and important things to do. There was too much to arrange before we took Dan back to Toronto to be buried: We had to make arrangements to transport his body internationally, plan a funeral in Toronto, get all the records from the hospital and the university, and give more interviews to the police. We also had to hire an estate attorney and deal with taxes, beneficiaries, and insurance. I was still trying to approach every new meeting and every new situation in this terrible business of death as if I had my act together. "Once I get through this, once we take care of Dan, we will have a moment to breathe," I thought.

But I wouldn't be able to catch my breath for years.

In an instant, my life had completely, irrevocably changed. Not only was there the horror of outliving a son, I'd also fallen down a rabbit hole from which I would never emerge.

I'd also need to become an expert in issues of murder, fluent in the language of crime. I would discover that evidence is everywhere, and for me, privacy was nowhere. From that day forward, every detail of my family's life would be filtered through law enforcement. My son was gone. Someone had killed him. And with the murder went the rest of my life as I had known it. Ease was over. The road ahead, only difficult. Nothing would ever be private.

On a very emotional level, I had to bring Shelly's children in Toronto to experience a family death, funeral, and burial at their young ages of eight, eleven, and fourteen years old. Cemetery visits would become a part of their life, as had been the case for me.

Turbulent times had just started. We would share this madness with other families who had become victims of sudden death from murder and violence—in the hope I could offer these families compassion and be their trial guides. I made the choice to lift the curtain on being a victim.

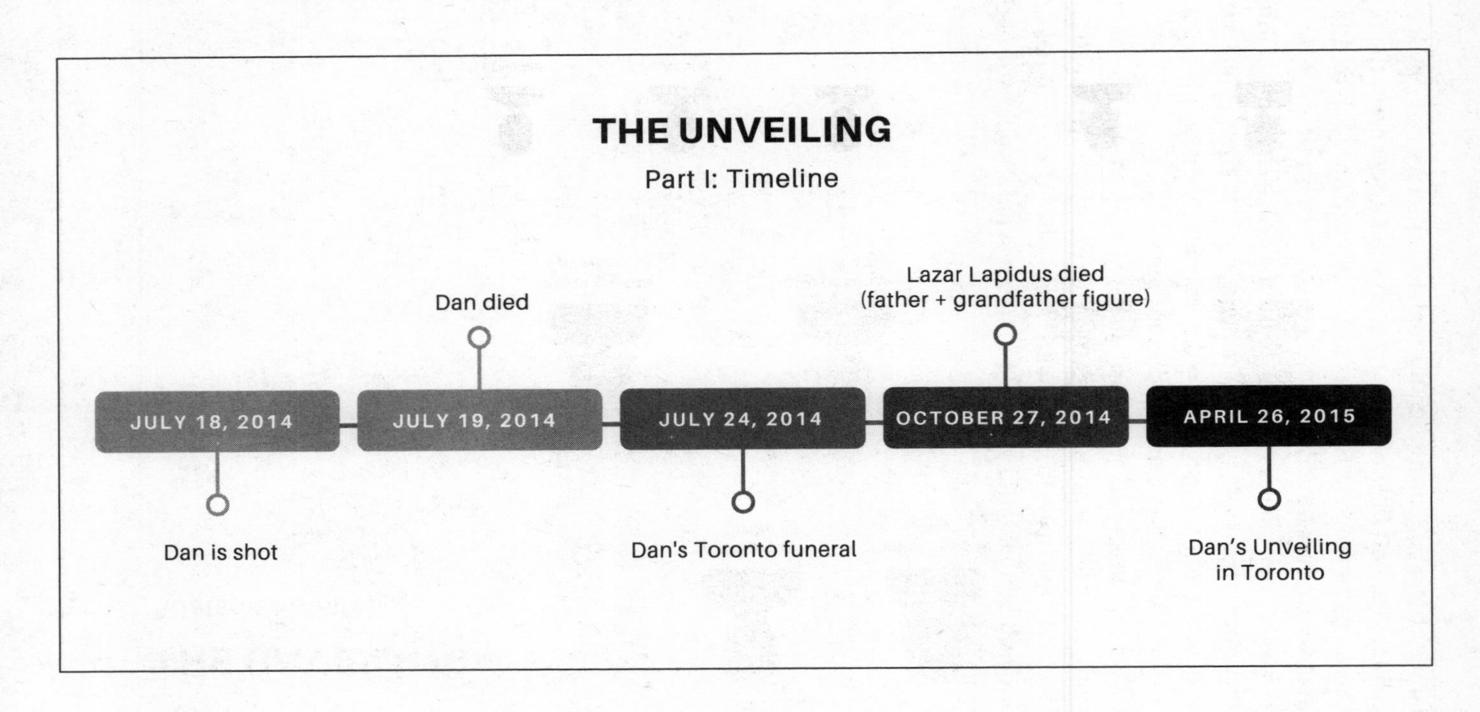
THE UNVEILING
Part I: Timeline
JULY 18, 2014
Dan is shot
JULY 19, 2014
Dan died
JULY 24, 2014
Dan's Toronto funeral
OCTOBER 27, 2014
Lazar Lapidus died
(father + grandfather figure)
APRIL 26, 2015
Dan's Unveiling
in Toronto

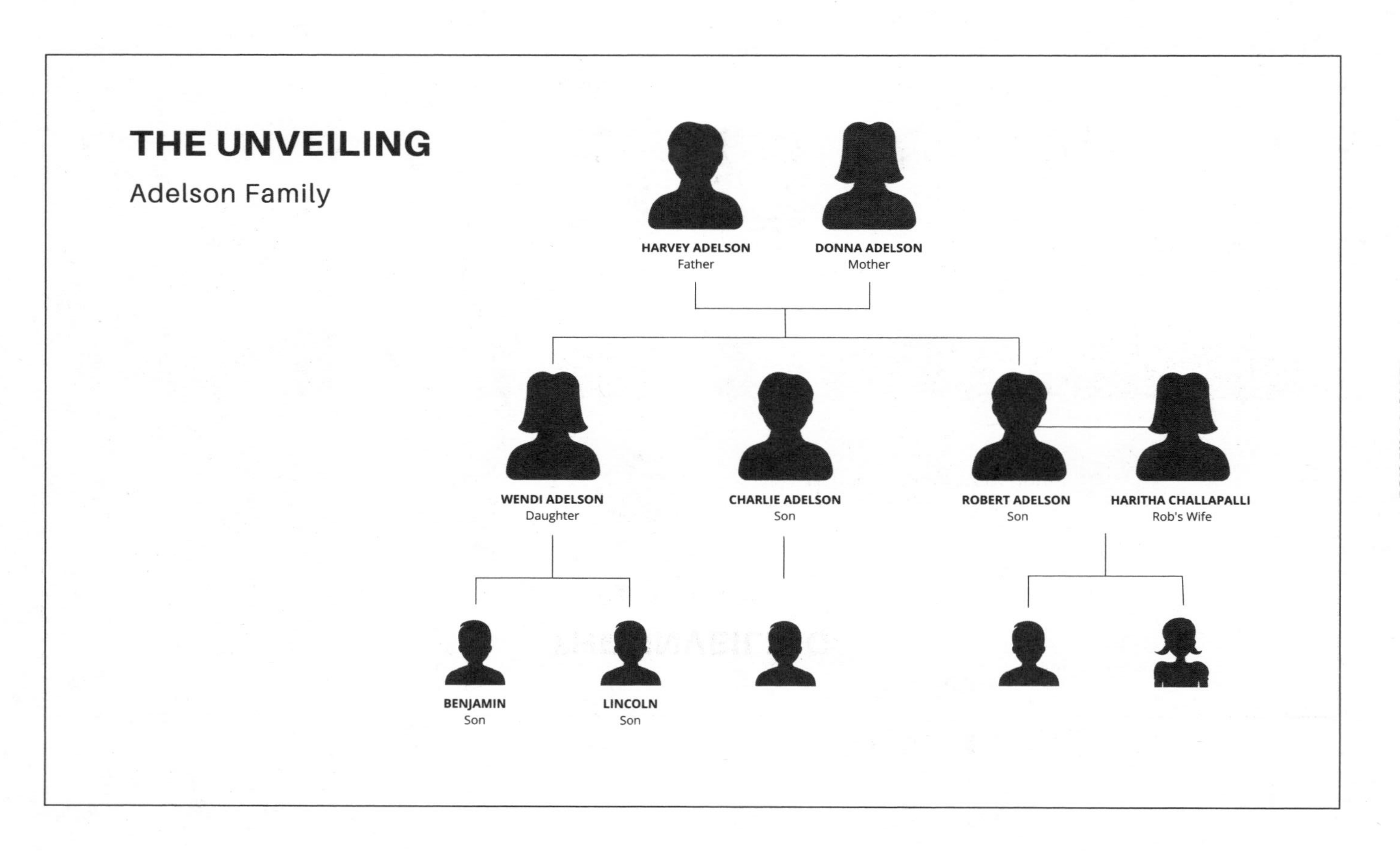
THE UNVEILING
Adelson Family
HARVEY ADELSON
Father
DONNA ADELSON
Mother
WENDI ADELSON
Daughter
CHARLIE ADELSON
Son
ROBERT ADELSON
Son
HARITHA CHALLAPALLI
Rob's Wife
BENJAMIN
Son
LINCOLN
Son

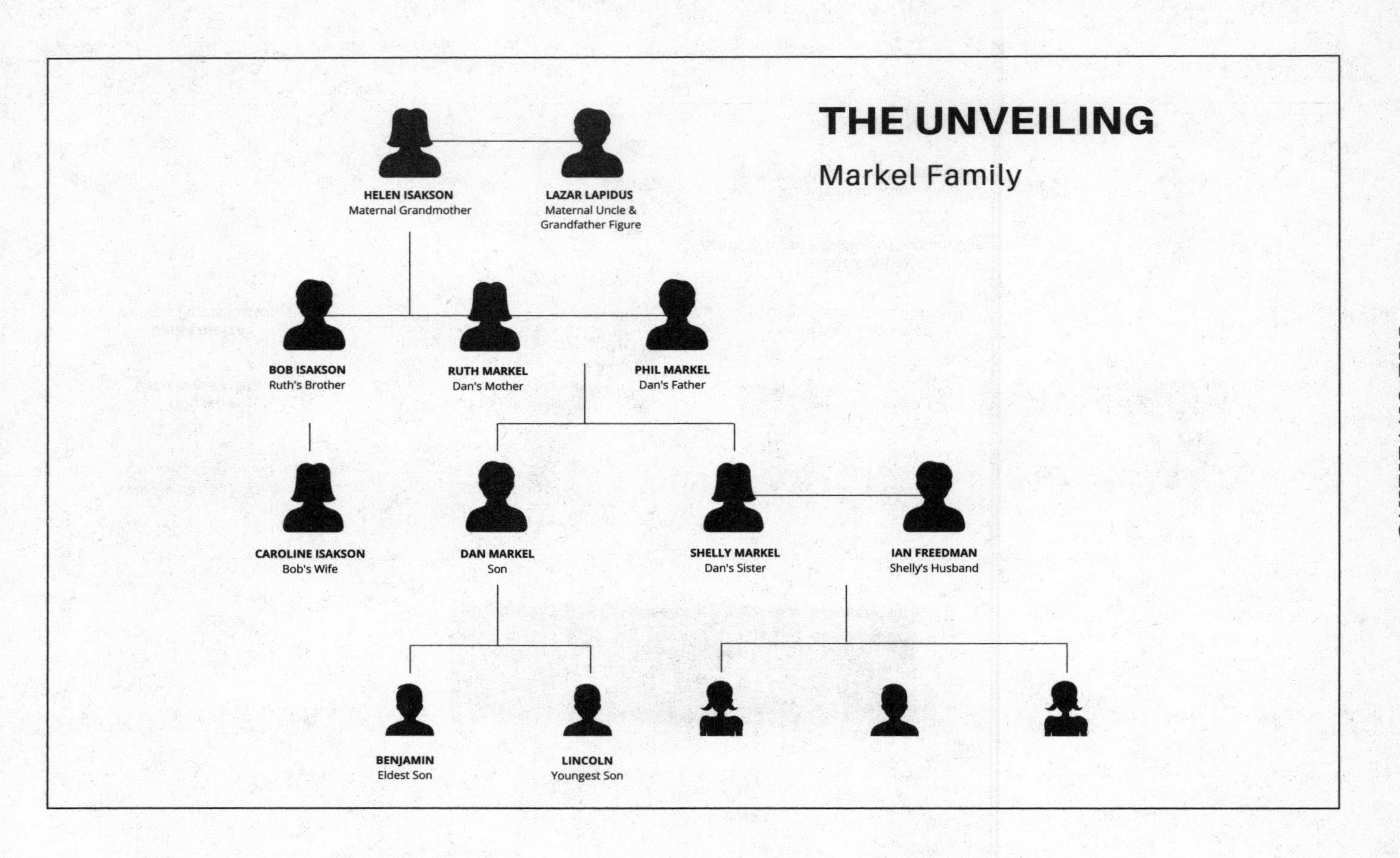
THE UNVEILING
Markel Family
HELEN ISAKSON
Maternal Grandmother
LAZAR LAPIDUS
Maternal Uncle &
Grandfather Figure
BOB ISAKSON
Ruth's Brother
RUTH MARKEL
Dan's Mother
PHIL MARKEL
Dan's Father
CAROLINE ISAKSON
Bob's Wife
DAN MARKEL
Son
SHELLY MARKEL
Dan's Sister
IAN FREEDMAN
Shelly's Husband
BENJAMIN
Eldest Son
LINCOLN
Youngest Son

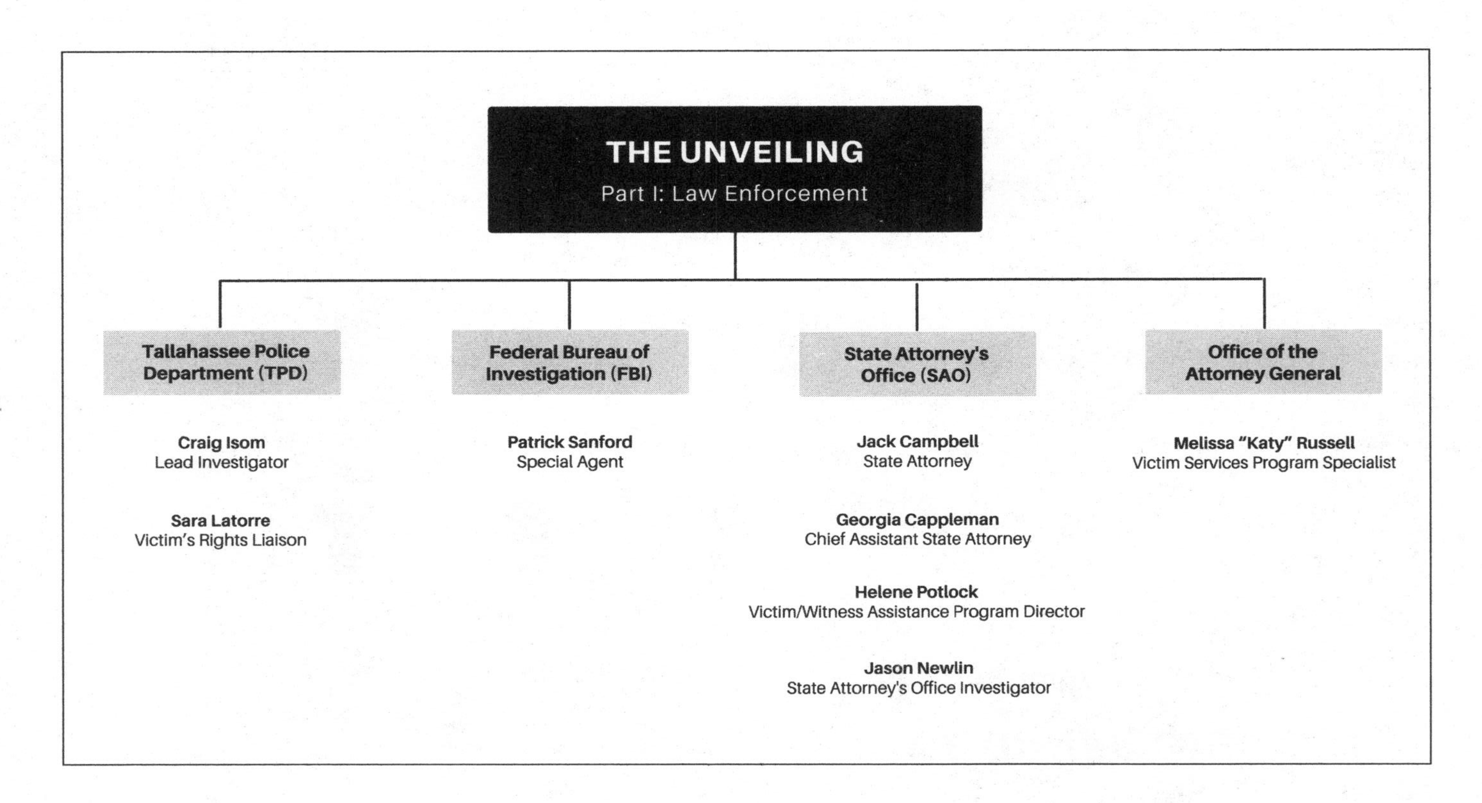
THE UNVEILING
Part I: Law Enforcement
Tallahassee Police Department (TPD)
Craig Isom
Lead Investigator
Sara Latorre
Victim's Rights Liaison
Federal Bureau of Investigation (FBI)
Patrick Sanford
Special Agent
State Attorney's Office (SAO)
Jack Campbell
State Attorney
Georgia Cappleman
Chief Assistant State Attorney
Helene Potlock
Victim/Witness Assistance Program Director
Jason Newlin
State Attorney's Office Investigator
Office of the Attorney General
Melissa "Katy" Russell
Victim Services Program Specialist

CHAPTER 2

Danny and Wendi

Dan is buried in Pardes Shalom Cemetery in Maple, Ontario. In one fell swoop, my son, a brother, and the father of two young boys was killed. My Danny. It is still unthinkable to me, the heartbreak overwhelming every single day. I brought my son into the world on October 9, 1972; I tossed the first shovel of earth onto his coffin on July 24, 2014. Since then, my life has been a tapestry of pain, horror, anguish, and ultimately, a quest for justice.

After the death of a loved one, you are supposed to face the loss, the void. You are meant to experience grief and maybe achieve closure if you are lucky. They say, with grieving, there are "steps." But when you lose a child, life's progression comes to a complete stop. Joy ends. Spontaneity ends. The lightness of life ends. And grief never ends. For me, closure is a word in a dictionary; "normal" is something I feel I will never experience again. At the time of this writing, it's been more than seven years since Dan was murdered. The legal process that unrolls after a murder—the investigation, the arrests, the courts, the trials as well as the endless, endless, endless *waiting*—has taken over my life, coating it with anxiety and misery and trauma and ensuing poor health. And most of those involved in Dan's killing have yet to be brought to justice.

You might as well know this now: I have also been barred from seeing my grandchildren. My son has been killed, and I have not seen Benjamin and Lincoln in more than five years—the walking, talking evidence that Dan lived on this Earth, the people he made whom I love so much, who live with the horrid legacy of a murdered father, who deserve to know their father's family. The last time I saw the boys was in April 2016, and they were both under ten years old. It's hard enough to mourn for my son, but when you lose touch with grandchildren, you are experiencing another major emptiness. My "Canadian grandchildren"—Shelly's three—were often with me when we visited or hosted the Florida cousins. They were also cut off. Their grandfather Phil was cut off from the boys, as well as their Aunt Shelly and Uncle Ian, and their three cousins.

My life as a grandmother was yanked away from me, despite my unrelenting efforts to maintain connections with them. Phil and I have been denied any and all visits with Benjamin and Lincoln, and direct lines of communication between us have been blocked. In fact, Benjamin and Lincoln have been completely cut off from their father's entire family. They do not know Shelly and her children, now aged twenty-one, eighteen, and fifteen, and sometimes I wonder if they even remember who I am. If they saw Phil walking on the street in Miami, would they know he was their grandfather? It's like a family photograph has had half its people cut out of it, not least Dan. We miss the children's songs, their voices, their toys, and their laughter.

I was blessed with two great children and five grandchildren. Shelly, who lives in Toronto, was very protective of younger Dan and always shared his visits to Toronto, with their children playing together. Along with her husband, Ian, their lives were turned upside down.

Dan's older relatives could also not comprehend this tragedy. My maternal ninety-seven-year-old uncle Lazar had a special bond with Dan and suffered greatly from Dan's murder. He gave up and died only three months after Dan's murder. Of course, there are many more individuals, including Dan's girlfriend in New York, whose lives were devastated as a result of this crime.

Dan knew that everyone loved him.

Part of my job with this book is to put the picture back together, to claim what is right, to claim *my rights*, as the mother of a slain son, and what is right for Dan, who dedicated his career in law, essentially, to making things right.

Dan was an ambitious boy. We moved from Montreal to Toronto when he was five years old. He left Toronto at the age of eighteen to attend Harvard University and never returned. He received his undergraduate degree from Harvard and continued his studies at the Hebrew University of Jerusalem, then moved to England, where he earned a master's degree in political theory from Emmanuel College, Cambridge, in 1997. He returned to Harvard for law school and graduated in 2001. He became a law clerk to Senior Judge Michael Daly Hawkins, United States Court of Appeals for the Ninth Circuit. Dan had a passion for travel and lived in many cities, including Montreal, Toronto, Boston, London, Jerusalem, New York, Phoenix, San Francisco, Miami, Tallahassee, and Washington, D.C. He made friends and meaningful connections with people wherever he went and stayed in touch. Dan's first full-time job was as an associate with the law firm Kellogg, Huber, Hansen, Todd, Evans & Figel in Washington, D.C., a firm excelling in litigation, including commercial, appellate, and intellectual property.

It was when he was in Washington, D.C., that Dan met Wendi Jill Adelson, a law student living in Miami, Florida, on a Jewish dating site, JDate. They fell in love in 2004 and were married in February 2006. In 2005, while they were seriously dating and talking of engagement, there were many back-and-forth trips from D.C. to Miami. Dan decided to leave the D.C. firm, so he could spend more time with Wendi in Florida. He had always had aspirations to be a professor. He joined the faculty of FSU in 2005 so that Wendi could complete law school in Miami. Dan was recommended for tenure in 2009 at FSU and became a very sought-after legal author and speaker. He also cofounded an extremely well-known and well-used blog called *PrawfsBlawg* for law professors, which has hosted hundreds of contributors. Naturally, we were very proud of his accomplishments.

Wendi received a bachelor of arts from Brandeis University in 2001. She later went to the University of Cambridge and received a master's in philosophy in 2004. She completed her law degree at the University of Miami School of Law in 2006. Wendi worked at FSU College of Law as a clinical instructor for over three years. She also worked as an immigration lawyer after they were married and living in Tallahassee.

Donna, Wendi's mother, was not pleased that Dan left a very established firm in D.C. to pursue an academic career. It was well known that the prestige and earning in this boutique firm were bigger than in academia.

Between Dan and Wendi, issues in the marriage were evident from the start—even before the start. The Thursday prior to Dan and Wendi's wedding in 2006, Dan came to Miami, where Phil and I were staying at my uncle Lazar's condo in North Miami beach. We went on the balcony facing the ocean and had a long talk, and he asked us not to mention that he went to Harvard at the various parties we were about to attend prior to the wedding. "Why?" we asked. Dan said he did not want Wendi to feel inferior around his friends. We never spoke of Harvard at these parties. Phil and I chose to be silent at the large gathering on the Saturday night before the wedding where there were many toasts and speeches. I think Dan must have also spoken to close friends about this issue, guiding them to avoid much talk about his accomplishments. There were few toasts for him, but many for Wendi.

Dan and Wendi were soon established in Tallahassee. They had two sons: Benjamin in 2009 and Lincoln in 2010. It is hard to capture in words the joy and excitement I felt when Dan became a father and I a grandmother. I found even more wonderment in watching Dan raise his sons: he was a present, devoted, loving, supportive, selfless father who always acted with his sons' best interests in mind. Dan regularly visited the boys' daycare during his pickup and drop-off times. Sometimes, he led holiday programs for all the children there. When I was with Dan in the car, he always played the children's music. We were never allowed to have "adult conservations" or even talk when their favorite song was playing. Ben and Lincoln loved their father. He was their hero.

Some of the early indicators of problems within the marriage had to do with Judaism. Wendi and Dan came from different Jewish backgrounds. Wendi's family was affiliated with the reform practice. We leaned toward the conservative synagogue. Dan had strong traditional Jewish interests and often joined Orthodox services, which were more observant. After the boys were born, Dan, who was always more observant than Phil or me, wanted to keep a kosher home. This meant not eating pork, shrimp, and certain other kinds of meat and seafood. In the early years of their marriage, Dan and Wendi had worked out a kitchen where Dan had kosher meat and ate on different dinnerware; most of the time, they ate vegetarian before the children were born. Dan and Wendi arranged to bring things like tofu hotdogs or falafels to the boys' daycare, so that Lincoln and Benjamin would not feel left out when non-kosher meat products were served to the other children. Each parent cooperated with this plan. They also had regular Friday night dinners to welcome the Sabbath, and Dan often took the boys to the synagogue (Wendi would join them for special events).

Wendi's parents, Donna and Harvey, were very disruptive about the kosher issue. They went out of their way to disrupt the dietary restrictions the boys had; they introduced them to cheeseburgers at McDonald's, a violation of Jewish dietary law (which also forbids the mixing of meat and milk products like cheese in the same meal). On one of my visits, the boys wanted McDonald's, and before Dan answered, I said, "Great idea, we can go to McDonald's for milkshakes and fries," which would keep the meal kosher enough by leaving the meat out. Dan said, "What a great idea," and we went to McDonald's. Phil and I did not keep a kosher home, but we respected Dan's wishes for his kids. Donna never stopped questioning us as to why Dan was more observant about Jewish dietary laws than the rest of his family. It irritated her.

But Dan's observance was a lovely thing. He'd been interested in Jewish practices since the age of twelve. Dan had always sought out Shabbat services in the various cities he'd lived in. In Dan's words, he was "pro-Shabbat." On Friday nights, he did all the blessings, no matter what house or city he lived in. And he had a strong leaning and feeling toward attending synagogue services. But he was hardly a religious fanatic. For him, the Sabbath, the kosher home—these roots were about maintaining a sense of meaning, structure, continuity, and holiday celebrations. Dan liked tradition and a sense of belonging to the Jewish community. These traditions were less important, if important at all, for Wendi's family.

Big Issue #2 between Dan and Wendi was their adopted home of Tallahassee. Wendi disliked Tallahassee, while Dan was becoming increasingly established at FSU, attending regular social events and participating in various academic committees. He and Wendi frequently hosted others at their home. Dan was on the board of Shomrei Torah Synagogue, and he was also involved with the Chabad community in town. Dan volunteered to participate in the Chabad community to ensure that they had enough people for smaller Jewish holidays, such as Sukkot, and he and the boys were regular attendees at events hosted by the city's reform synagogue, Temple Israel. His life in Tallahassee was full of community and fulfillment. That being said, Dan was very geographically and psychologically mobile. He was prepared to move to other cities across the States, provided he and Wendi had work. Wendi would only move to warm states as well as Washington, D.C. In reality, because she had young children, the only place she really wanted to live was in Miami, where her family was.

To make matters more complicated, Dan's career had taken off. As an academic speaker, he was in demand and frequently needed to attend conferences out of town. Wendi felt "stuck" and frustrated with Dan's travel, which required so many trips away from home. After Wendi graduated law school, Dan secured a position for Wendi at FSU as a spousal hire. But rather than making Wendi feel valued, this may have had the opposite effect, making her feel less empowered than if she'd found a job in her own right.

Like many young working couples with very young children close in age, home life could be a struggle. Wendi expressed some difficulties balancing a full-time job and the responsibilities of home life. Dan did many chores, shopping, and daycare, but when he was away, the household and childcare routines became more stressful for Wendi. In private conversation, I told him to get more support for him and Wendi, such as hiring a cleaning service and/or babysitters, who only did minor chores. Wendi already seemed to have sensitivities about her own capabilities in the home. She had a major role model in Donna, a stay-at-home mom when the children were young, who did everything and did it well.

Although Wendi never said it out loud to me, there was resentment. In 2011, Wendi published a novel titled *This Is Our Story*, a thinly veiled account of her marriage as well as her fight against human trafficking. Wendi's depiction of her fictional character's, Lily's, marriage mirrored what we would later learn were her feelings in her own: her fictional Lily felt trapped in a small Florida Panhandle town while her bumble-prone professor husband, Josh, brought little excitement to her life. Ultimately, Lily left her husband along with their child—shortly after the publication of her book, Wendi did the same.

Wendi often stated that Dan never read her book. Recently, I learned from one of Dan's close friends that he did read Wendi's book and despite his awareness of her depiction of his character in the story, Dan even promoted it heavily throughout his circles, including to readers of his popular blog, *PrawfsBlawg*. Nevertheless, Wendi maintained that Dan had ignored her work.

Once the children were born, Donna began to campaign for them to leave Tallahassee. I am reminded of the late Princess Diana in her interview with Martin Bashir when she said, "There were three of us in this marriage, so it was a bit crowded."[1] Donna and Wendi had always been very close. When Wendi first went on JDate to find a suitable match, it was with Donna by her side, mother and daughter scrolling together. Donna liked to be involved in every aspect of her daughter's life.

Cracks in Dan and Wendi's marriage started to become more obvious to us by 2011. Dan was away in Israel for most of the month in December. As soon as he left, Dan learned that Donna fed the boys shrimp and pork, two obviously non-kosher foods.

Phil and I arrived in Florida soon after that for the December vacation. One day, we met Donna and Harvey for brunch with Dan, Wendi, and the boys. The mood was tense. Dan and Wendi left early to give the boys their afternoon nap. Dan also seemed anxious and said he had an upset stomach. Once Phil and I were alone with Donna and Harvey, Donna zeroed in on me.

"Why is Dan more observant than anyone else in your family?" she grilled. It wasn't the first time. I explained, again, that Shelly and her family have a kosher home as well. Donna remained frustrated about the Jewish dietary practices.

The interference that Dan perceived became increasingly troublesome to him. Dan told me that Donna's involvement was too much for him, especially after the birth of Lincoln, their second child, but I felt it wasn't my place to intervene.

Today, I debate the merits of sharing my opinion about another's relationship versus biting my tongue. I always took on an active listening style and was supportive of Dan. Perhaps I should have suggested he be more forthright with Donna. I still kick myself sometimes, wondering

---

1 Holly Christodoulou, "'IT WAS VERY CROWDED' Martin Bashir Princess Diana interview: When was it and why is it controversial?" *The Sun*, November 19, 2020, https://www.thesun.co.uk/news/4095068/martin-bashir-princess-diana-panorama-interview/.

if I could have made a difference. Magical thinking is sometimes desirable, especially from a mother.

After the tense December vacation in Miami with us and Wendi's parents, Dan and Wendi returned to Tallahassee and began the process of marriage therapy. The marriage was now "officially" rocky. Wendi felt that Dan was not proud of her accomplishments. This was not true; he took a lot of pride in her success and was publicly, often gushingly, admiring of her.

We frequently received emails from Dan talking about Wendi's accomplishments. Dan wrote on February 8, 2005, "Wendi has an op-ed in today's *Miami Herald*. Go her."

In this period, when Dan and Wendi were in therapy, there was increasing interference from Donna and Harvey. I spoke to Dan often during this time. While he was earnestly approaching counseling with the hopes of making their marriage work, he talked of how Wendi seemed to withdraw more from the marriage. By the time I visited Tallahassee in the spring of 2012, a coldness between them was palpable to me. By August, when Dan and Wendi came to Toronto for a visit with Benjamin and Lincoln, I felt a lot of tension. While in Toronto, Wendi said she had to go to New York to apply for a Human Rights Watch interview, which should have taken one day. But while in New York, Wendi decided to take a few extra days to stay and visit a very close female friend whom she often confided in. Dan, who saw some "writing on the wall," became quite upset and took more private time than usual at our vacation home in Ontario. Phil and I became more involved with Benjamin and Lincoln in all their daily activities, such as baths and meals. We visited with Shelly's family often and kept the boys busy with their cousins at the beach.

But Wendi was planning a separation. She had been for some time. We didn't know it, but in Florida Donna and maybe others were busy making moving arrangements in Tallahassee and renting a separate house for Wendi. By the time Wendi returned from her multi-day interview in New York, something was different. We went to Montreal for a family celebration of my uncle Lazar's ninety-fifth birthday. He was the grandfather and father figure for the whole family. Wendi attended, but she had a sugary smile on her face.

I could tell something was not right. My inner thinking was that a separation was coming. Dan had a temporary moment of hope when a few months prior, he felt an improvement in the marriage. Wendi seemed more pleasant. But we now know that this was exactly the period in which Wendi had applied for the Parent Education and Family Stabilization Course, a requirement under Florida law for separated couples. She had also emptied the safety deposit box in that period. During the trial for Dan's murder, specific emails from Donna to Wendi from this timeframe had surfaced, with Donna telling Wendi that she could do all the things necessary because she is a good actress.

In "The #1 Story In Miami In 2019: Dan Markel's Murder Was A Contract Hit,"[2] Steve Miller, a writer for *Miami New Times*, would later describe what was really going on during the summer of 2012.

It turns out that Wendi, Donna, and maybe others used this time to orchestrate the marriage's separation. They were acting together, planning Wendi's extraction from the marriage behind Dan's back, while Wendi kept up a ruse of working on their relationship.

For Dan's family and friends, it was a wrenching experience to see the couple come apart. Ben and Lincoln were still only preschool age, and from where we stood, their parents' separation seemed like a storm—very ugly and dramatic. Dan described it as a "Pearl Harbor style" separation—a surprise attack that shook his world and changed everything. Following his murder, much has been reported in the media about the marital breakdown.

* * *

"Pearl Harbor," as Dan called it, occurred while Dan was in New York, preparing to give a lecture. Wendi called to tell Dan that she was leaving him. He did not realize then that she'd already left, taken the children and their belongings, and emptied more than half of the house, including the ketchup in the fridge. Dan canceled his lecture, called us, and got a flight back. He called us again from the airport, and we stayed on the phone with him on his ride home. He sounded horrified.

---

2 Paul Caron, "The #1 Story In Miami In 2019: Dan Markel's Murder Was A Contract Hit," TaxProf Blog (blog), December 17, 2019, https://taxprof.typepad.com/taxprof_blog/2019/12/the-1-story-in-miami-in-2019-dan-markels-murder-was-a-contract-hit.html.

We were on the phone with him the whole time as he walked through the house. His voice was shaky and anxious as he saw that Wendi had taken much of the furniture from the living room, master bedroom, and dining room. The children's bedroom was upstairs. When he got there, he started to cry and broke down. The boys' room was totally emptied. There was no evidence of their toys, room decoration, or clothing. Wendi had even removed the beds. Dan looked in the closet. The only clothes that remained were all toddler sizes the boys had outgrown. Dan cried out, "My boys' home is gone." Luckily, we were scheduled to come the next day for the Jewish New Year. When Phil and I entered the boys' room, Phil noted that even all the wall plaques of alphabets and animals had been taken down, leaving just the nails in the walls.

After the initial shock of seeing the children's bedroom had worn off, Dan thought he'd better check the bank account and investments. He did, and half was gone. He later learned that Wendi had emptied the safety deposit box weeks before. He then went back to the master bedroom on the main floor, and there were divorce papers on the marital bed, including a child custody arrangement that favored Wendi. During that discovery, Dan experienced a feeling of sudden shock: *Where were the kids? Where had they gone?* He pulled himself together and said he had to get off the phone and find the children. I was devastated by hearing this and witnessing Dan's trauma and felt his pain.

Phil and I were both left in extreme distress. Thank goodness I was packed for our visit to Tallahassee because I could barely think. I have often been criticized for too much advanced planning, but this time my overplanning and fastidiousness were very convenient. We kept the phone free in case we heard back from our heartbroken son. The next day, Wendi met Dan in a restaurant with friends, there as witnesses, to show him the boys were safe. Custody arrangements were not in place yet, but Dan had the boys for the next few days.

When we arrived in Tallahassee for the Jewish New Year, we quickly went to Dan's house and saw Benjamin and Lincoln. Dan was pale; Benjamin was warm and friendly, but Lincoln looked flushed and anxious. We all went to the synagogue the next day. Tallahassee is a small community, and the bad news of Dan and Wendi's breakup had already spread. Dan and Wendi were a charming and very social couple. Dan shared his traumatic story with select friends and received support. The holiday did not feel like a celebration, but more so a challenge for survival. We tried to create some kind of normalcy for the boys—we took them to Target and outfitted them from head to toe with new clothes; we also bought toys and beds for their rooms. By the time Phil and I left Florida, the upstairs looked remade. All that was missing was a cohesive family with two parents in the same home.

Dan wanted to make amends with Wendi. He said he wanted to keep on trying, and we did not interfere. He soon had another out-of-town speaking engagement and dropped the children off at daycare, where Wendi would pick them up. He asked Wendi where the children would be staying, but for two weeks, Wendi refused to tell him the new address of the rented house. Dan quickly filed for fifty-fifty custody and was successful.

The boys' daycare became the pickup and drop-off point for the children. However, a battle arena developed around coordinating the children's visits and communications to the children when it was each parent's turn. Dan and Wendi had very different styles and interests of communication to the children on the off days. Dan wanted as much opportunity as possible and even had breakfast at the daycare on his off days. He also wanted to speak to the children according to the court's allowances. Clashes on childcare arrangements were frequently resolved through lawyers and parenting coordinators.

Other situations became exacerbated. Dan heard from the boys that Donna had been talking badly about him, and that she had been feeding them bacon and shrimp. In addition, Dan heard from the daycare center that Donna told the daycare to give the boys regular hotdogs, not tofu, which made their meals unkosher at school. This was a huge offense for a grandmother to make and represented not only her lack of respect for Dan's parental and religious preferences, but what seemed like her desire to instigate a conflict or drive a deeper wedge. Her goal was seemingly accomplished: tensions were exacerbated. Needless to say, there were numerous court documents during this period. Donna and Wendi continued to pressure Dan to allow Wendi to leave Tallahassee, hoping that, through the courts, the children would be permitted to move back to the Miami area.

Before the dissolution of the marriage occurred, I was very close with Dan. Now we were even closer, and Dan had started to tell me where all his assets were at the university, such as pensions, and what Wendi had taken. He also frequently discussed their disagreements about childcare arrangements and visiting the daycare. There were very lengthy phone calls to try and help him solve many of the issues related to the children. I was incredibly sad after these calls and felt troubled. It was a very difficult time.

Wendi had prepared a petition for her to move with the children back to Miami. A hearing was held by Leon County Circuit Court Judge Barbara Hobbs. Wendi had advocated for the relocation to South Florida to provide more stability and consistency as well as a better quality of life for the children by increasing their access to her close family. Also, Wendi had been offered a job in Miami as an attorney, where she could earn substantially more in salary and year-end bonuses. This job was better than her current one at FSU.

The court hearing in June 2013 was a major roadblock. Dan had prepared a motion, witnesses, and arguments to battle the move. His efforts were all unnecessary; Wendi's request was denied in a few hours. Dan was elated from the results.

The situation intensified, as numerous attempts by Wendi to relocate to South Florida were blocked. Donna felt caged in and continued sending Wendi strong emails. Donna would try anything to gain control over the children and get them away from Dan. Donna became obsessed with her hatred of Dan and kept on coming up with new plots for Wendi to move to the Miami area. We would later see an email Donna had written on June 25, 2013, which encouraged Wendi to use her "acting skills": "Tell Dan that the children will be baptized in the Catholic church as long as he wants you to remain in Tallahassee." In one particularly unhinged email, Donna referred to dressing the children in "Hitler youth" costumes to upset "Jibbers," the name she and Wendi used derogatorily to refer to Dan.

She advised Wendi to tell him: "You wanted me in Tallahassee, my children to fit into this bible belt." Donna even documented to Wendi how the family was prepared to offer Dan $1 million to allow Wendi to move to South Florida, using a split of funds between Wendi herself, her parents, and her brother Charlie.

* * *

After eighteen months of trying to settle, Dan and Wendi were granted a divorce without a trial in July 2013. As the documents show, Dan and Wendi had fifty-fifty custody of the children, a lump sum of $120,000 was allocated to Wendi in addition to the funds that she had already taken, and Dan was also to pay $841 a month for child support. There continued to be unresolved conflict over Markel family heirlooms that Wendi had never returned to Dan, as well as Dan's discovery that he believed Wendi had failed to disclose the true sum of her funds as required by the court. Also, Wendi's desire to move to Miami remained an ongoing theme.

The children told Dan that Donna had been bad-mouthing him and calling him "stupid." Dan got fed up and put his foot down. In March 2014, Dan filed a motion to prevent Donna from having unsupervised time with his sons to protect them from "disparaging comments about their father." This was another ugly and stressful period. A court hearing was scheduled to occur in 2014 to address these issues, but that hearing was delayed and ultimately would never happen. Dan would be murdered before it could.

The Marital Settlement Agreement (MSA) dated July 30, 2013, signed by both Dan and Wendi discussed various parenting provisions, and made clear that no such disparagement, or alienation, would be acceptable.

Dan's motion included reference to this, stating:

> **Section 2.1E of the MSA requires, in pertinent part that "Neither party shall at any time disparage, criticize, belittle, or otherwise ridicule the other parent in the presence of the minor children. Each party shall instruct the children to love and respect the other parent, and shall promote a loving and caring feeling for the other parent."** [emphasis supplied] **Section 2.1K of the MSA requires, in pertinent part, that "Each party shall encourage a feeling of affection between the minor children and the other party. Neither party shall do anything to hamper the natural development of the minor children's love and respect for the other party."** [emphasis supplied]
>
> <u>By Flouting the Right of First Refusal the Former Wife Creates Conditions for Mr. Markel to be Disparaged In the Presence of the children by their Maternal Grandmother.</u>

"On three specific occasions in November 2013, the children informed Mr. Markel: 'Abba (Dad), Grandma says you're stupid.' When queried as to why Grandma (the maternal grandmother) would say such things, the children replied jointly that it's because 'she says you are trying to take her 'Sunshines' away from her.'"

"In December 2013, Lincoln, the younger son, further stated to Mr. Markel, in front of the Former Wife, 'Abba, Grandma says she hates you.' The children were sitting with their grandparents at that time."

"That the children have heard disparaging statements from their maternal grandmother about their father is especially concerning in light of the fact that, as mentioned above, the Former Wife leaves the children unsupervised with her parents in violation of the court-ordered right of first refusal [she was supposed to call Dan to give him the chance to be with the children prior to hiring a babysitter, but she had not always done so]. Mr. Markel is concerned that continued exposure to such negativity forms the foundation for parental alienation. Mr. Markel is puzzled by the maternal grandmother's behaviour as he has been supportive of the children's relationship with the maternal grandparents. Regardless of the rationale, the maternal grandmother's dislike of Mr. Markel must not be displayed in the presence of the children."

"The Former Wife is obliged to prevent disparagement of the children's father. The fact that the reports arose after the children spent substantial time with the maternal grandparents, either alone or with the Former Wife, is circumstantial evidence that the Former Wife has breached her contractual obligations in this regard."

In the meantime, Dan had met a new girlfriend in New York during his monthly consultations with the legal academic community. He fell in love again—with a lovely law professor at New York University School of Law. Wendi had also been dating again, and ultimately formed a relationship with a social work professor, Jeffrey Lacasse. Dan had really turned the corner; his career was stable, and he had found new love. I rejoiced to see him happy again. In 2012, he came to Toronto with Benjamin and Lincoln for the Bat Mitzvah of his sister Shelly's daughter. It was so great for all of us to feel like we could breathe again and enjoy a family celebration, what we call a *simcha*. I was sure we had come through the bad weather. We were on the other side. Little did I know that on the horizon, a hurricane, an earthquake, a storm I never could have imagined was looming.

Danny and Wendi

Danny and Wendi

CHAPTER 3

Grief

I was a child of tragedy. My father died suddenly of a heart attack when I was nine years old. My mother, thirty-eight years old and with little means of self-support, went out to work. It was 1954, and back then it was uncommon for middle-class women to work full time. My mother became a rare example. And soon, she also became something even more rare: a mid-century female successful in business. My mother looked like a young Nancy Reagan. She was a model of mastery and determination and grew her ladies' clothing manufacturing company with her two brothers. I often feel I owe my career to her. She was involved in banking and union relationships. She often talked about payroll, cash flow, and other issues of business and money—in an effort to teach, she hid nothing. I treasure this fact, and so I started building my own successful management consulting firm, dealing with large corporations and hospitals. I was very well groomed from watching my mother deal with money issues and negotiation. Even in my first career in social work, I had a large private practice and an entrepreneurial mindset. I began to see myself as a "second-generation" woman executive. I later wrote books on women's advancement and negotiating skills, a career advantage I learned from my mother.

When my father died, many family members swooped in to help my mother, my brother Bob, and me. Harry, my mother's older brother, became a ballast with Sunday morning visits after piano lessons. My father's extended family was also very close to us, operating like a clan to support my mother. They never abandoned me or my brother, trying to create as much normalcy as possible.

But it was my maternal uncle, Lazar, my mother's younger brother, who stepped in the most. Lazar was a father figure to me in no uncertain terms. When my father died, Lazar was still unmarried (he later married, when I was twenty-two). Lazar treated Bob and me like his own children. He had already lived an incredible life: he was born in Lithuania and survived the Holocaust through the efforts of a Catholic family who hid him for two years in their barn. The family, Maria and Antanas Cesnavicius, later adopted Lazar, giving him their family name and a false passport. Together, they went to Germany six months before the war ended. Lazar stayed in Berlin until 1949. My mother was not a Holocaust survivor and came to Canada at fifteen years of age. She married my father, and they both sponsored Lazar to came to Canada. He had remained in Europe after the war and needed a sponsor to come to Canada for immigration purposes. My mother had grown up with Lazar and was so pleased he would be joining their family in Canada.

He kept very close contact with this family who later moved to Hamilton, Ontario. My uncle never forgot the family who saved him and honored their memory in Israel. We visited the Yad Vashem Holocaust History museum on a family trip to Israel. It was there that Uncle Lazar had honored their memory by documenting their efforts and had their names included among the Righteous Among the Nations from Lithuania. This is an honorary title given to citizens of other countries who risked their lives to rescue Jewish people during the Holocaust. My youngest granddaughter was underage, but the guide took her to see the names. It was a special moment for all of us. Lazar was the epitome of positive thinking. It would take him a long time before entertaining any negative thoughts. He taught me to "never give up."

Because of my family's great efforts, Lazar's in particular, my childhood was filled with children's activities, camp, competitive swimming, ballet, and piano. I had many friends and all kinds of hobbies. When a father was needed, Lazar accompanied me and my brother with my mother to family dinners, school events, and summer camp visits. All of our friends saw Lazar as a dad to us.

Still, even with all this support, my life was different from that of my peers. We had a housekeeper who lived with us for a few years because my mother worked. I ate lunch with another friend in elementary school because her mother, who was divorced, also worked. During that period, most children would walk home for lunch that their mothers had prepared, but my mother and hers worked. We'd keep each other company instead.

I also had biannual visits to the cemetery with my mother to visit my father's grave. We recited a special prayer of Kaddish, and the clergy recited Kel Maleh Rachamim. This prayer is often recited at funerals, unveilings, Yizkor (remembrance services), and special memorial services. Many times, parents today ask at what age their child should visit the cemetery. My experience has led me to believe a child over the age of five or six can understand death and benefit from the rituals surrounding it, especially for a close family member.

My father and Dan were nearly the same age when they died: my father forty-two and my son forty-one. So now I am both a child and mother of early death. And what has become clear to me, through both instances, is that while death is grief, it is also work.

My life story of early death, which could have prepared me for this experience of sudden death, shock, grief, visiting cemeteries, resilience, and personal strength, was very different from what I experienced with Dan's murder. As an adult, I continued to visit my father's grave with my mother even after I moved away from Montreal to Toronto. What I never thought during these cemetery visits was that I would need them later, as a mother.

My life is now the center of a tragedy, filled with a shooting, the death of my forty-one-year-old son, still my youngest child, from murder. The trauma is all being relived again due to the criminal justice process and trials. My life has changed in a way that I will never fully understand. This death, Dan's murder, is incomprehensible and final.

The only familiar reality of Dan's death from my previous life is that we again experienced *shiva* (Jewish mourning for seven days), rabbi involvement, and cemetery visits. My life is filled again with upheaval, this time being much harder despite the help from people stepping up and offering support. This state of being is permanent and everlasting.

So, as a mother with a lost son, I have engendered a shift from grief to advocacy. My primary grief is, of course, in losing Dan. But the second arrow of my grief is in the subsequent alienation from Dan's two young sons, Benjamin and Lincoln, with whom I seek reconnection. Grandparent visitation has been the focus of my advocacy. I will discuss more details on the subject later. I am working on a bill in Florida to expand existing law and provide grandparents with greater access to courts to petition for visitation with grandchildren in extraordinary circumstances. My ethos when it comes to this topic has been ingrained in me from childhood by Uncle Lazar: "never give up."

* * *

In mid-April 2014, Dan and the boys came to Toronto for Passover. After the trauma of Dan and Wendi's divorce, including my own maternal pain from seeing my son's suffering and that of Benjamin and Lincoln, it felt like the worst was over, like we were reaching a new, happier family plateau. And already, he and the boys were coming to Toronto more freely. I felt we were moving toward a new reality! Dan was very family oriented and loved bringing the children to Toronto, especially on holidays.

I remember the children wearing masks at the Seder to tell the story of the plague in the tale of the Exodus. The Passover Seder is probably the most well known and beloved of Jewish home rituals. Many Jews have cherished memories of family Passover Seders. The word *seder* literally means "order." And what the order refers to is the telling of the story of the Jews' Exodus from slavery in Egypt. It is believed that the obligation to tell this story has been observed by Jews ever since the actual Exodus itself. As Jews, we see the scriptural command to tell the story of the Exodus to us as a positive commandment, a *mitzvah*, a good deed. For families, it is often a time of coming together in peace.

But only several months later in July 2014, these sweet memories felt like something from another life. My son was murdered. At the age of forty-one. In his garage. Benjamin and Lincoln's new world was fatherless. My new world was as the mother of a slain professor. Phil had no living son, Shelly no brother. Suddenly, Dan was gone, and we were all "homicide survivors."

Never had I imagined that I would be a "homicide survivor." In addition to being a homicide survivor, I am also now a "victim in the criminal process." I have "victims' rights" as I enter into the world of criminal investigations and the court systems of Florida. Under Florida law, victims of crime have the right to be treated with compassion and dignity and are protected from harm and intimidation and informed about the stages in the criminal justice process.[3]

I began the grieving process, which has no end and no normalcy. I felt numb after the shock and was in disbelief. Because Dan's death was so sudden, it was hard to comprehend, which soon prompted questions: *How did this happen? Who would do this? Why did this happen?*

I did not experience many of the well-known symptoms associated with grief and shock, such as changes in appetite, self-destructive behavior, crying, mood disturbances, and sleep disturbances. During the first week, I did pace throughout my house in the night and early mornings. I really need my sleep to cope, so I was fortunate this did not last long.

I was in a daze, and when I got out of it five weeks after the murder, there was much to do. I am not the only homicide survivor. Phil, Shelly, and her family as well as Benjamin and Lincoln, are all homicide survivors. This also includes Dan's girlfriend and many other family and friends. Our immediate family was disrupted. I became removed from everything and shattered. My life as I knew it felt like a personal earthquake.

Coincidentally, as mentioned earlier, my professional profile includes expertise in emergency preparedness, a service I offer to schools, companies, and government offices to help them plan for unexpected catastrophes, from shootings to earthquakes. Yet, no amount of training could have prepared me for what had happened to Dan. Living with the murder of my son and its aftermath has been and has continued to be a "life sentence" for me.

Sometimes, it still feels surreal. At those times, almost like a movie on repeat, the mind can't help but recount the events of that terrible day and the nightmare that followed.

At this time, no suspects had been identified by authorities. Many media outlets were beginning to put together assumptions of their own. Over the course of that weekend, the story of Dan's case greatly

3 "Your Rights as a Victim of Crime." Accessed December 9, 2020. http://www.sa15.state.fl.us/stateattorney/VictimWitness/indexRights.htm.

evolved. Many news stories speculated whether it was possible that Dan had been shot during an attempted home robbery, with some community members noting that there had been a series of burglaries in Dan's neighborhood in the months prior. At the time of his death, I was still in Montreal and traveled to Florida the morning of July 19, only twenty-four hours after the shooting.

It wasn't until July 21 that the robbery hypothesis and all others involving random acts were put to bed. The TPD released a statement in the early afternoon stating that Dan's murder appeared to have been targeted—that Dan was the "intended victim." Now some wondered whether the shooter was a student or colleague who had a beef with Dan over marks or even opinions. Some of the content posted on his well-known blog, *PrawfsBlawg*, had received some criticism in the past. Could the murder have been on ideological grounds? I was still so overwhelmed and had not yet focused on the motive or speculated on the murderer.

The TPD soon created a dedicated tip line for the case. This number was spread throughout the Tallahassee community, with many media and news outlets encouraging anyone with any information to call. The TPD made attempts to locate witnesses within the area during this time, asking everyone—from delivery drivers to pedestrians who had been near Dan's home between 10 a.m. and 12 p.m. on July 18—to call the tip line with any information they had. A reward of $1,000 for information that could lead to an arrest was offered by Crime Stoppers. Dan's friends later offered a $100,000 reward, which was organized with the TPD.

With only minimal details being released about Dan's murder, social media erupted with speculation about neighborhood incidents. People in Dan's Betton Hills neighborhood and academic community worried about their safety. Once it was released that the murder had been a targeted one, the articles and media coverage on the story only intensified. Dan's murder became newsworthy in Canada, Israel, and England, as well as the United States.

Many memorials were held for Dan after the murder. Shomrei Torah, Dan's synagogue in Tallahassee, held a memorial service for him that attracted more than two hundred mourners, including synagogue members, family, friends, and many students and colleagues from FSU. Phil, Shelly, and I attended.

Shelly gave an excellent speech on Dan's childhood and life. There was also a flurry of articles from students, other academics, and admirers. There was not one that detailed Dan's murder before describing his amazing academic achievements and what a great friend and father he was.

PrawfsBlawg, the influential blog Dan cofounded, posted a heartfelt entry on July 19, 2014, which speaks to the stunned confusion we all felt at that time. "We write this together, all of us, as a community," wrote *PrawfsBlawg* colleague Paul Horwitz. "Our friend Dan Markel has been taken from us, suddenly and terribly. His law school, the FSU College of Law, will issue an announcement in due time. We do not have all the details, but our understanding is that Dan was shot and killed. Painful as it is to say that, and as little as we know, the early news reports left enough room for speculation that it seemed necessary to say that much. The terrible, senseless nature of his loss makes it all the harder to bear."[4]

For another law blog, *Above the Law*, David Lat wrote: "But Dan was much more than the sum of his resume items. I was one of his students the first year he taught at FSU. He was a fantastic professor. Here is what Professor Michael McCann shared with me: I appreciate you writing on Dan's death. Your story captured the horror of what's going on. Like everyone else, I'm stunned and shocked and desperately trying to figure out how this could happen. I've known Dan for almost 10 years and we were co-authoring a forthcoming sports law article in the Harvard J. of Sports and Entertainment Law. Thank you for writing about him and bringing national attention to his life. He was a remarkable guy and a true pioneer in both the legal academic and the blogosphere. His legacy will only grow as more and more legal commentary takes place on-line rather than in print."[5]

* * *

I often still think of my last phone call with Dan, on that Friday morning in 2014, just minutes before he was shot. He was coming back from

---

4 Paul Horwitz, "We Have Lost Our Beloved Friend, Dan Markel," *PrawfsBlawg* (blog), July 19, 2014, https://prawfsblawg.blogs.com/prawfsblawg/2014/07/we-have-lost-our-beloved-friend-dan-markel.html.

5 David Lat, "Professor Dan Markel: Some Personal Recollections," *Above the Law* (blog), July 24, 2014, https://abovethelaw.com/2014/07/professor-dan-markel-some-personal-recollections/.

the gym. I was in Montreal. We had a normal talk: as usual, covering the boys, and weekend plans, and a bit of this and that. I often think that there was some luck in him being on the phone with someone else, not me, when the bullet hit. If I had actually heard my son being murdered, I don't know if I could have come back from that.

Then again, if you told me before that fateful day that Dan would be murdered and that I'd have to go on living, I would have thought that impossible, too—totally beyond me. Prior to that Friday morning, murder was not a word in my personal framework. In the early days and months after Dan's death, I felt like a woman outside her own body, in a daze, numb. This immediate grieving experience was then, over subsequent months and years, replaced with the torture of waiting for information, arrests, hearings, trial dates, and verdicts. It has now been seven years of this rollercoaster lifestyle as the mother of a murdered son whose case remains legally unresolved, of this life of navigating the justice system, of needing to do things like see my son's murderers in court and hear how bullets entered my son's brain. The fallout has been emotional exhaustion. Had it not been for those who stepped up and offered my family unbelievable amounts of support, I don't know where we'd be today.

There are no words in the English language describing a person who has lost a child. We have words for widow, widower, and orphan, but none for a parent who has outlived their son, their daughter. Life's progression comes to a stop when you lose a child. It feels like nothing is happening as it should, and everything is flipped upside down. Compound this hell with that of murder as a cause of death, and emotional shock turns to horror. I often think that I have been sentenced for life. That Dan's murder is also *my* life sentence: a void-like landscape of traumatic flashbacks, anguish, and prolonged anxiety. My hope is that things will get better when justice prevails. In the case of Dan, this has not happened yet.

My experience with trauma continues. Through my trauma, I recognize that all family members, friends, victims, and survivors are in pain and have unique reactions to the circumstances of their loss. One initial common experience shared by all is that your life is shattered. I now have a new identity: I have become known as the mother of the slain professor.

Prayers, events, and memorials continue all over the world, started by Dan's friends, family, and students. The unveiling on April 26, 2015, was the hardest thing for me to do since the burial of Dan. Similar feelings of intense loss resurfaced from the early days when we found out about the murder. It was like opening up the wound again.

* * *

I still remember giving birth to Dan and what it was like when he entered the world. He was born *big*—9.15 pounds—but he always had an easy temperament. But unlike most babies, Dan didn't sleep in the daytime until he was three months old. He woke up at 6 a.m. and stayed up until 7 p.m., almost like an older person with a job to do. He was just so alert, so high energy. These attributes were his enduring signature until the end of his life. He was a person who made life *happen*. He was very social and had friends all over the world.

I always saw so much of Dan in his kids, in Benjamin's inquisitiveness and in Lincoln, who was a lookalike of Dan. Benjamin was just turning five and Lincoln was almost four when their father was shot dead. Their loss is surely the greatest—they've lost love, roots, direction, commitment, and dedication. Dan's murder will bring the children lifelong and complex questions. Learning about "how" and "when" and "where" their father was killed will affect their mental life, family life, and well-being. At the time of writing, Benjamin and Lincoln continue to be cut off from their lineage, as they are not able to see me or Phil or any family on Dan's side—neither uncles, nor aunts, nor cousins—which adds more pain and loss for all of Dan's family and friends. They may not even know the names they were given at birth.

* * *

During this period, I could not shake the feeling that I was having an out-of-body experience, like I was living some other life, not mine. The chaos felt insurmountable. I cried in private. Around others, I was sometimes still numb. After the initial five-day stay in Tallahassee, we accompanied Dan's body back to Toronto for the funeral, which we had to organize. Then there were subsequent memorials at FSU; Harvard

University; Cambridge; New York; Washington, D.C.; Phoenix; California; and finally, Israel, where Dan had spent a year studying philosophy. We attended the FSU memorial in Tallahassee in September 2014, a major event with speeches, displays, university visits, and dinner.

Being busy with all this was, in a way, a welcome distraction. I felt wholly unprepared for the levels of loss, grief, and chaos I felt inside me. There is the famous Kübler-Ross model of grief after the passing of a loved one, which has it coming in emotional stages: first denial, then anger, then bargaining, then depression, and finally acceptance. In my experience, grief has been nothing like this. Closure does not exist when a death mingles with an unending trial and a life turned over to law enforcement and lawyers. Before Dan's death, I was a content person—I look at that person now and see how lucky she was.

That said, from the very first days, I found myself surrounded by friends, family, and other compassionate supporters. Some of the first advice given to me by a woman whose adult son committed suicide was to "take all the calls at the beginning, because the calls don't continue." This never happened in my case. In certain ways, I have even been unable to remove myself from the identity of "mother of slain professor," because the interest in Dan's case, not least from media, has been so ongoing.

In all this, there is no normalcy. In my case, experts might agree I suffer from what is commonly known as "complicated grief." Complicated grief can manifest as an ongoing inability to experience normal grief reactions. It can also come out as delayed grief, or chronic grief. Usually, complicated grief is associated with cases in which the death is sudden and the relationship with the deceased was close.

* * *

I recently learned that in the Jewish tradition, we have a distinction between mourning and grieving. Grief is a feeling. All people feel a loss. Mourning, on the other hand, is its own religious category, complete with rituals and responsibilities. Before Dan died, I was already familiar with many of these rituals—including cemetery visits, candle lighting, and prayer—due to the early death of my father. From my childhood, the day of Yahrzeit—a memorial day for the death of an immediate relative, observed on the anniversary of the death and iconic for the special long-lasting candles lit in honor—was an annual practice. Yahrzeit can also be marked by going to the synagogue or making a donation. It has been described by scholar Maurice Lamm as a tradition that is "commemorative of both the enormous tragedy of death and the abiding glory of the parental heritage." Lamm adds, "It is a day when one relives the moment of doom.... It is a day conditioned by the need to honor one's parent in death as in life."[6] Many also choose to light a Yahrzeit candle for twenty-five hours on one of the four holidays in which we recite Yizkor—these include Yom Kippur (the day of atonement), the harvest festival Sukkot, Passover, and Shavuot, a holiday that commemorates the giving of the Torah at Mount Sinai.

I am not the most observant Jew. But the traditions relating to death and the cemetery have become, over the years, a huge part of my identity, as a Jew and a woman. They have been a comfort to me, especially at family gatherings where the emptiness I feel from the loss of Dan is there, even more than usual.

And the usual? That's not easy either. In my day-to-day life, people often ask, "How many children do you have?" I answer by saying I have five grandchildren, three in Canada and two in the United States. For most people, this is enough. In very select situations, such as medical assessments, I will share about having lost my son to explain causes of stress. Usually, I wait until the appointment is over to let the person treating me know that my son was murdered, because it's always shocking to everyone. Even today, seven years later, I am still often asked impossible questions: *"What was it like when you got the news?" "How often do you still cry over Danny?" "What keeps you from just curling up in the fetal position and never getting out of bed?"*

At first, I was a bit puzzled by my coping mechanisms: numbness over crying, a feeling of being outside of my body over weeping. I thought something was wrong with me. I have since learned that there is neither a right or wrong way to grieve, nor a right or wrong way to feel. You have to find your own path through the ups and downs and

---

6 Maurice Lamm, "Yahrzeit: Memorial Anniversary," *Death & Mourning*, May 22, 2005, https://www.chabad.org/library/article_cdo/aid/281636/jewish/Yahrzeit-Memorial-Anniversary.htm.

hope that your personal ability to cope will bring you strength—and as close as possible to peace.

* * *

While Phil and I were getting used to life as the parents of a murder victim, Shelly took control of Dan's finances, a gargantuan task, on behalf of the boys. This was Dan's wish. Death can bring up all kinds of strange issues around money. I still remember when my mother-in-law died, the driver of the car taking us to the cemetery said, "I can't believe you are talking to each other." He explained that often the families he sees are already arguing about money on their way to the burial. With a murder, the burden to sort out finances becomes even more complicated. Breaking the law for money is not new, and people respond to the murder-for-hire jobs.

Within days of Dan's death, when his body was still at the local morgue, TPD searched his office and house for cash, and more importantly, for financial documents that might provide any evidence. They found a life insurance policy, but no will. I told the police I was surprised that we were getting into money so soon after my son's death. There was no burglary or any loan sharks or debt issues in Dan's life. The police explained that following the money trail could still be a very good way to provide solid leads in solving the case.

The police knew that Wendi asked about Dan's life insurance policy just days after the death. This set off alarm bells for investigators. During Dan and Wendi's separation and divorce, there was a lot of disagreement about money. Dan had taken a large life insurance policy around 2012 during the period when he and Wendi were in marriage counseling, and Wendi knew she was the beneficiary. Following the divorce, Dan changed all the policies, pensions, and investments so that Benjamin and Lincoln were the sole and equal beneficiaries. He did not have a will, but most of his assets had specific designations to the children or went to the estate. But the largest amount was the life insurance policy. Shortly after Dan's murder, Wendi was hungry to know who the beneficiaries were and kept on calling the insurance company for exact details.

During their search, the TPD found the insurance policy paperwork. They also went through all of Dan's piles of paper, at home and in his office. (Dan always arranged all his business in piles of paper, which looked like a mess to anyone but him.) After the first police search, Shelly and Sam Kimelman, Dan's accountants, combed the house again and found more financial documents.

Then came the issue of the estate. While Phil and I went to the funeral home to arrange the transportation of Dan's body back to Toronto, Shelly began interviewing Florida estate lawyers. The law faculty at FSU were very helpful to us and Shelly in these first few days. Manuel Utset, the assistant dean, Dave Markell, and the university's human resources department helped us navigate all Dan's holdings connected to the university, including his pension, health benefits, and insurance. The dean even canceled a major trip to be available for anything regarding Dan's case. Shelly ultimately hired a lawyer named Sarah Butters who at the time was with the Tallahassee firm Holland & Knight and has since joined the Ausley McMullen law firm. Shelly and Phil became Dan's personal representatives, creating an estate bank account, dealing with Visa card issues, and getting up to speed on all other personal and financial issues, such as creditors. Sarah Butters and Sam Kimelman worked on a plan relating to the mail and the taxes and the bills to be paid. It was an enormous amount of work—but typical of the complexities often faced by the families of those who have died suddenly. And with or without a will, "the business of death" is a normal activity for all families.

A GoFundMe page was started by Dan's friend, Tamara Demko, to get some immediate donations. We are so appreciative to Dan's family and friends for their considerations. The proceeds of the fund were later put in trusts for Benjamin and Lincoln. Wendi had tried to attain the GoFundMe donations directly, claiming to be Dan's widow, which added further grief and drama to the process.

Other than facing tragedy, my experience of suffering involved many other unthinkable heartaches. One trauma was cleaning out my adult son's home and office. The logistics of arranging to transport his body from Florida to Toronto under international law and Jewish burial practices were difficult.

We returned to Toronto a few days later for the Canadian funeral. Phil said the Mourner's Kaddish for Dan for thirty days. This prayer is said twice a day for all family members. It is said for eleven months for parents. The Kaddish was said at the funeral of which Shelly and I joined. During shiva, Shelly and other members joined Phil to say Kaddish at the synagogue in the mornings.

Along with the ritual of mourning, two other major impacts of death come into play—grief and the "business of death," such as estates, beneficiaries, wills, and financial obligations.

One major discussion involved Wendi directly. Wendi requested "upkeep," funds for expenses such as rent and food, from the boys' trusts. As I mentioned before, there were numerous other sources of funds, such as the pension and investments through the university. Wendi was also receiving $2,400 per month for each child from government social security because their father was deceased. Wendi also was entitled to take over the ownership of the house on Trescott, where Dan had lived. But almost symbolically, a few months after Dan's death, a tree fell on the roof, causing major damage. There were just so many complications, and issues concerning money began creating tensions between us and Wendi. Everyone walked on eggshells.

* * *

While all of the estate issues were happening, I wanted to continue seeing Benjamin and Lincoln. I visited Benjamin and Lincoln every few months with my Canadian grandchildren. In October 2014, I decided to take a preplanned trip, along with Shelly and her family, from Toronto to Florida to visit Wendi and the boys. It was my seventieth birthday present to myself. We stayed in Orlando and drove to meet Wendi and my grandsons at the butterfly conservatory in South Florida. When Wendi showed up, it was not just with the kids, but also with Donna, Harvey, and other friends. I realized that, since Dan's death, she still hadn't been alone with me.

Benjamin and Lincoln were happy and excited as they looked at the amazing tropical insects and watched butterflies hatch. I then noticed that the Adelsons would not leave me alone with the children for even a minute, hovering very closely at all times. Even when Benjamin gave me my first long hug since his father's death, the Adelsons were standing nearby and monitored the encounter. At one point during this outing, Donna came up to me when I was sitting alone and said, "Who would have done such a thing in broad daylight?" I was already sad while watching the children; I did not want to talk about murder.

Prior to our leaving, I wanted a quiet moment with Wendi to discuss the unveiling. Harvey quietly came over to eavesdrop on the conversation. Wendi had not attended the funeral in Toronto, and I felt that I wanted to give her and our grandsons an opportunity to attend the unveiling. We then said our goodbyes, and I returned to Orlando with Shelly and her kids. I was feeling strange and uncomfortable. It was hard for me to say goodbye.

* * *

With all this going on, another complication had emerged from the emergency response to the 911 call put in by Dan's neighbor, James Geiger, after the shooting. After James heard a shot, he called 911. There is a full record of this 911 call. James had walked over to the driveway and discovered Dan in a pool of blood. To the 911 dispatcher, he emphasized, "You need to send an ambulance in a hurry. He is still alive. He is moving." James was very distraught about how long it took for an ambulance arrive: nineteen minutes. The neighbor was a force in expressing his frustration with EMS.

Soon, the media in Tallahassee brought major attention to the long ambulance wait, and there were many criticisms piled on the Consolidated Dispatch Agency (CDA), the company in charge of sending the ambulances out. An advisor informed us that we had a fiduciary responsibility to Benjamin and Lincoln to sue the agency. On the recommendation of some of Dan's colleagues, we hired Eric Abrahamsen as our lawyer on the case. It took over a year to reach a settlement with the CDA. We ended up claiming $40,000 from their liability insurance to avoid further litigation. The money was paid into Benjamin's and Lincoln's trusts.

Besides my grief over the loss of Dan, I was very concerned that not only was Shelly's life disrupted by losing her brother, but she was also burdened with all the financial complications. In the division of labor we had set up following Dan's murder, it was Shelly who had assumed the stress and annoyances of dealing with the financial arrangements:

she was designated as the custodian of his funds. This was not easy; the administrative responsibility alone was emotionally taxing.

Shelly had a full plate as a mother of three children: Michal, who was fourteen at the time; Ari, then eleven; and Roni, then eight. Shelly was also very active in the Jewish community, graduated in law, and earned an MBA. Ian originally worked as a lawyer but later became a business executive. Shelly and the family have been very blessed with Ian's contributions as well.

So for Shelly, the burden is still ongoing. Every year, she needs to deal with financial, tax, and estate matters. Shelly will also need to handle Benjamin and Lincoln's trusts. Her husband, Ian, has been a great support through all this.

My first degree is a master's in social work. Over my career, I have worked with families who have lost children, usually to illness, like cancer. Bereavement of a death of a child is long term. Now, it was my turn to face major loss, and I wondered if I had the strength to use any of the methods I'd studied and taught and apply them to myself and in my own community.

In Toronto, I'd always been Ruth Markel, a successful businesswoman and author. Now, I was Ruth Markel, whose son was killed in his garage from a gunshot to his brain. The first time my family had to stand up for the Yizkor on Yom Kippur, the memorial part of the service where bereaved families remember and bless their dead, it was very heart wrenching. Since I was nine years old, I had been standing for various family members, including my parents. But this was the first time Phil, Shelly, and I stood up in a very public place and identified ourselves as the family grieving the murder of our son, our brother. In the Toronto community, Dan's case was by then well known, which made it feel harder and very visible.

Dan's birthday was also around this time (October 9, 1972), which created emotions that were even stronger. I was coming out of my initial state of numbness, into reality, and now encountering some of the deepest feelings of sadness I have ever known. My experience was no longer "out-of-body." This period was the beginning of my realistic grief journey. There was no tombstone yet, but I had already started frequently visiting the cemetery. These visits were very private and reflective moments for me. Each visit felt more tormenting than the last, like hammering another nail into Dan's coffin. I would ask myself, "How did this happen? How come I am here?"

* * *

After the earlier arrangements of the death, funeral, and burial, the next big emotional turmoil was the unveiling.

In the Jewish tradition, there is the "unveiling." Once a Jewish tombstone is placed, there is a specific service for removing a cloth covering it. I called this book *The Unveiling: A Mother's Reflection on Murder, Grief, and Trial Life*, not only because the unveiling of Dan's tombstone was the most difficult moment for me after the murder, but also because the removal of the cloth symbolizes what I want to show: the real story that goes on behind the scenes and behind the headlines for families who are victims of crime and violence. In my family's case, we continue to face hearings, trials, mistrials, and then even more delays due to COVID-19. Like the act of lifting the fabric that reveals the writing carved into a tombstone, this book will expose what it feels like to be living the "trial life."

When Dan was killed, I had had little experience with murder. In my sheltered mind, people familiar with murder lived in a world far outside of my own. Now, I am one of those people. And in this existence, standard words describing criminal proceedings, such as "investigation," "evidence," "hearing," "verdict," and "sentencing" take on enormous emotional significance. Words like "adjournment," "mistrial," "appeal," and "postponement" can feel like personal affronts. Commonplace setbacks become devastating while incremental gains carry the magnitude of tremendous victories.

But it was the tombstone that would not let me forget that Dan was gone forever. I visited Rabbi Aaron Flanzraich at the Beth Sholom Synagogue in Toronto. Shelly and her family are members there and attend frequently. Rabbi Aaron, as he is known, had officiated at the funeral and had been very supportive of me. Phil and I had already selected the cemetery plots before the Toronto funeral back in July 2014. At our synagogue, the Beth Emeth, Pearl Grundland, the executive director, treated us with great compassion, as did the Beth Emeth leadership. We now faced the unveiling, and we had to choose the tombstone. Phil and

I chose one together. We explored several monuments before deciding on a light brown granite stone. For my family, the tombstone inscription was something we approached with great focus, like a work of art. We needed to figure out what to say but also wanted to write something that really reflected Dan. Common inscriptions, such as "loving father, son, brother, and friend, always cherished," were not enough. We went through numerous drafts and consultations with friends and the monument designer. We wanted to get so much on the stone that we needed to make sure there was room. Our final inscription reads as follows:

"In loving memory, of
DANIEL ERIC MARKEL beloved father,
son, brother and friend.
October 9, 1972 – July 19, 2014.
His children were his world.
His family, friends and community his pillars.
His academic work his passion.
His light above so bright, that it will never be extinguished."

Anticipating and planning for the unveiling takes time. Due to the Canadian winters, we planned the unveiling date for April 26, 2015, which fits with the North American practices for conservative and other Jews who sometimes wait up to twelve months. In Israel, some religious groups chose the day right after shiva or within thirty days. For me, the date of the unveiling came after some memorials, the Jewish holidays, and Dan's birthday in October. Many people tell you that the first time you experience certain events is monumental. For me, our first Yizkor (remembrance service) after Dan's death; Yom Kippur 2014, when people mourn and others stand up in the synagogue for special prayers of Kaddish; and Kel Maleh Rachamim, a prayer that was chanted by the chazan (clergy), were all epic.

Nothing could have prepared me for the emotions I experienced prior to the unveiling. The reality of planning for this moment was difficult. I was no longer in a haze, like I was during the funeral. The weeks prior to the unveiling were my deepest feelings of sadness. I was not numb. Selecting the actual tombstone brought me back from my "out-of-body experience."

It took a few months for the tombstone to be ready. Once it arrived and was set in place, I went back to the cemetery numerous times to get used to the monument, to break down my fear. I felt I needed to practice seeing the tombstone covering Dan before the unveiling. I was an emotional wreck. I've always felt that as a woman, I am well endowed with coping skills, but I had never been challenged like this before.

On one of my visits to the cemetery with my friend Arthur, I placed small rocks on the head of the tombstone, which is a Jewish tradition, a custom more than a law. This tradition was well described in a *Sun Sentinel* article by Rabbi Marc Gelman and Monsignor Thomas Hartman on September 15, 2018: "Placing pebbles on a tombstone is… widely practiced and for relatively the same reasons that headstones are placed. From the time Jacob set a stone at the burial place of his beloved wife, Rachel, on the road to Ephrat/Bethlehem (Gen. 35:20). Since then, setting tombstones over graves (in Hebrew, they are called matzevot) has been a custom revered by Jews. The stone is a sign that the living remember the dead. The pebbles on the stone are like the stone itself; they are signs that this is a pious family who visits the grave of their loved one."[7]

On these visits, the fabric cover still hid the tombstone. Of course, I knew what lay beneath the cloth, but I wasn't prepared for the reaction I'd have when the cover was removed.

In the meantime, I had made myself very busy in planning for the unveiling ceremony. Friends helped a lot. Harvey Silver, another friend, had already taken me to see the rabbi, the caterer, and the synagogue event planner. It is customary to serve refreshments after an unveiling, and the event is usually held at the house of one of the mourners. We decided to hold the event at our synagogue. My ninety-seven-year-old uncle Lazar had died in October 2014, barely three months after Dan died. There had just been so much trauma. Maybe this was why I wanted the event at the synagogue, so Dan's friends and family could share this tradition together. Phil felt the same—that this should be a larger event rather than a small family gathering. There were so many close family members, friends, and colleagues who were supportive to

7 Rabbi Marc Gellman & Monsignor Thomas Hartman, "Honoring Dead with Pebbles on Tombstones," *South Florida Sun Sentinel*, September 15, 2018, https://www.sun-sentinel.com/news/fl-xpm-2006-07-29-0607270825-story.html.

us, but over and above that, we all needed to coalesce over Dan, to bring meaning to his memory in the face of a senseless killing. I felt that if we could provide some kind of comfort for our community of mourners, I wanted to do that. It may not have been a conventional thing to do. Shelly kept on asking, "What is this, a Bar Mitzvah?" But Phil and I were sure. For weeks, we checked with each other: "Did you invite this person? That person?"

* * *

I felt terribly sad and full of pain as my wound was reopened. It was April 26, 2015. The ceremony at the tombstone began with Shelly's eldest, my granddaughter Michal, beautifully singing the song of "Eli, Eli," based on the poem written by Hannah Szenes, a Hungarian Jewish resistance fighter. Shelly spoke many meaningful words, shared memories of Dan, and thanked everyone for keeping Dan's memory alive. There was a large turnout. The rabbi spoke, and we unveiled the stone. When it happened, my pain felt almost insurmountable. I never wanted to return to that place again, and yet, I never wanted to leave, because leaving would mean leaving Dan forever. All of my memories of Dan's life came back, from childhood to adulthood. Each person present reminded me of another period of his life, and another, and another. It was unbearably sad.

I always had an honest relationship with Dan, and I knew that day that I would often return to visit him here in the years to come. Returning to visit him at the cemetery is my solace. It is where I would share the progress and accomplishments of his young sons, Benjamin and Lincoln, and report to him the difficult discoveries that will emerge over the course of the investigation into his murder. What I did not know on the day of the unveiling was just how soon I would be back at this solemn spot to give Dan bad news about his children and his ex-wife.

After the trauma of the gravesite unveiling, the post-unveiling service at the synagogue was meaningful, as the synagogue was well attended. In the end, the event that I planned resulted in a packed house. Dan's friends came in from Tallahassee; his childhood friends from Toronto were there, plus family from Montreal and the States.

Many of the guests were pale and flushed, with lots of tears and tissues as we shared a common sorrow. As I stood between all these people, I thought of the beautiful poem, read by Rabbi Aaron at the gravesite, trying to take its words to heart:

Do not stand
By my grave, and weep.
I am not there,
I do not sleep—
I am the thousand winds that blow
I am the diamond glints in snow
I am the sunlight on ripened grain,
I am the gentle, autumn rain.
As you awake with morning's hush,
I am the swift, up-flinging rush
Of quiet birds in circling flight,
I am the day transcending night.
Do not stand
By my grave, and cry—
I am not there,
I did not die.

Part II

REALITY

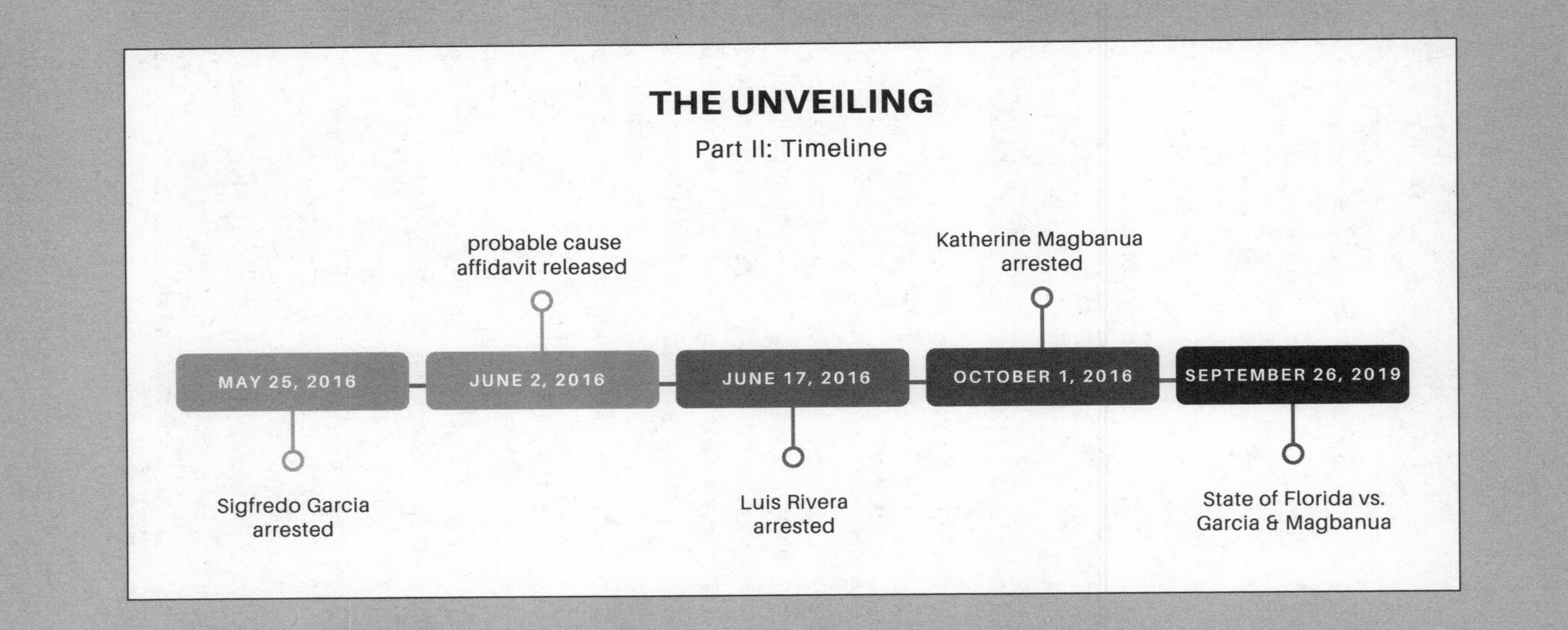
THE UNVEILING
Part II: Timeline
MAY 25, 2016
Sigfredo Garcia arrested
JUNE 2, 2016
probable cause affidavit released
JUNE 17, 2016
Luis Rivera arrested
OCTOBER 1, 2016
Katherine Magbanua arrested
SEPTEMBER 26, 2019
State of Florida vs. Garcia & Magbanua

CHAPTER 4

Arrests

The First Year: What Was Happening Prior to the Arrests?

Our family was consumed with questions about the legal case—specifically, who was the killer? Why did this happen?

We had informally organized tasks between us. I took on communication with law enforcement. My primary contact was Craig Isom, the lead investigator, who provided me with regular updates. I would share them on family conferences with our personal attorney Matthew Benjamin and other Gibson Dunn lawyers, including Orin Snyder. Phil and Shelly worked on the estate issue. Shelly also had the responsibility of all the investments and income tax follow-ups.

Our grief was complex, complicated by the daily reality of knowing that the murderer was walking free. Our social networks of support from family and friends had not diminished, and we never felt isolated—but even surrounded with support, the quiet moments of heartbreak and confusion left an undeniable mark.

The cloud of grief was particularly pronounced during the early period of the investigation. As Candace Lightner, the founder of MADD (Mothers Against Drunk Driving), writes, "Grief comes in three stages: the beginning, the middle, and the rest of your life." We were still in the initial period of devastation and hungry for news from the TPD. Often, there were leads and suspicions, but details were scarce as investigators rightly kept their process quiet.

Information on Dan's case dimmed in the media coverage for the next two years. There were still some published stories, but far less after the first few months following the murder. A year after his death, police released a photo of the Toyota Prius they believed was driven by the suspect.

As Dan's case remained a mystery, I found myself at the center of a large "murder community." Numerous people we know—and even strangers—wanted to offer their advice and help to solve this case. At times, I felt I was running a detective agency by myself. Dan's friends made epic gestures. Two of them helped finance the $100,000 reward for a tip leading to the arrest and conviction of those who committed the murder.

Our network grew as Dan's friends and fellow lawyers contributed advice and legal information. Many took on specific tasks; which included finding out about wrongful death suits, other civil actions, and lawsuits against the CDA. This support group offered opinions and suggestions every day of the investigation and sent books and articles to help. These gestures kept us going and meant more to us than our friends will ever know. Law enforcement was quite tightlipped in the early years, and there were no indications of any breakthroughs. There was some criticism of law enforcement initially, with the concern that nothing was happening or not enough was being done. Of course, nobody could know what investigators were working on behind the scenes.

In a July 2015 opinion piece in the *Tallahassee Democrat*, editors wrote, "Markel's murder represents a diminishment of our community on so many levels: as a father, educator, scholar, neighbor, congregant and human being. The loss is compounded by the frustration over the lack of progress in bringing his killer or killers to justice."[1]

Dan's best man, Matt Price, introduced me to his father-in-law, Abe Anhang, whose own son, Adam Anhang, was murdered by the woman he married—a rare female killer, Aurea Vázquez-Rijos, who plotted Adam's murder-for-hire. Abe has lived through the trial life for more than a decade, seeking justice for his son. He generously offered to share

---

1 *Tallahassee Democrat*, "Our Opinion: Dan Markel Deserves Justice," July 17, 2015, https://www.tallahassee.com/story/opinion/editorials/2015/07/17/opinion-dan-markel-deserves-justice/30314111/.

his experience and provide me with guidance, weighing in on concepts from coping with the media to prepping for the jury and counseling me to divide up tasks so that the burden didn't fall on only one person. I started referring to Abe as my "murder coach."

Abe, along with an extensive group of our friends and acquaintances, came forward to offer advice. I learned to be unafraid to harness the power of this circle of support.

As progress proceeded at a glacial pace regarding any publicly released information about breaks in the case, I learned to tolerate the hurtful actions of my former daughter-in-law for the sake of maintaining contact with my grandchildren. In fact, prior to the arrests I was visiting Benjamin and Lincoln, who were living in the South Beach area of Miami, where Wendi had decamped so quickly after Dan's murder. Getting to see them was worth every word unspoken, every question unasked, and every bit of swallowed pride it took to maintain a good rapport with their mother.

Nevertheless, in the alternative reality that had become my life, I began to realize that surprises are the only constants. I also learned that the heartache never ends. In September 2015, Wendi hurt us deeply by emailing me to tell us matter-of-factly that she had changed the boys' last name from Markel to Adelson the prior July, "for safety's sake," as she said.

The timing of her disclosure was no coincidence. We were scheduled to visit her and the boys the next day. The boys had recently started school, and their drawings already featured their "new" names, such as one we would see, hung on the wall, "Lincoln Adelson."

This was undeniably disingenuous—there was no safety issue for the boys that could relate to their last name. But that hurt would not be the last. The perception of her deceit was compounded when we discovered that she even had decided to remove Benjamin's middle name, Amichai, chosen to honor my mother. Changing their last names was also particularly hurtful to Phil, whose only son had kept his family name alive through his American grandsons.

Names had a lot of meaning to Dan. When Benjamin was born, Danny wrote this about his naming in a message to friends and blog readers, signed by himself and Wendi:

The name is powerfully special to us for several reasons. First, as many of you may know, Danny's Bubbie Helen, his grandmother, died just this past spring, after a rich and numinous life of 95 years. Bubbie Helen's Yiddish name was Khashkie, which was a diminutive of her Hebrew name, Khasia. That name Khasia means "Protected by the Lord", which is sometimes rendered as a sanctuary, a sacred place of calm and serenity. The name Amichai itself means "my people lives," and, like the name Khasia, it also includes the letter Khet. Knowing the unwavering commitment Bubbie Helen had to the Jewish people and the Jewish tradition, we think she would take great sanctuary, that is, great calm and serenity in knowing that her people, that is, our people, live on in the name Amichai. Secondly, the English rendering of the name Amichai begins with the letter A, which we use to recall Wendi's Papa Aaron, Harvey's beloved father, who died while Wendi was just a sophomore in high school.

As many of you know, the Hebrew name Amichai was the last name of the great Israeli poet, Yehuda Amichai, who died almost a decade ago. During the transformative year that Danny lived in Israel after college, Danny had the chance to meet with Yehuda several times informally, at parties, in Yemin Moshe, or on the bus, when they would serendipitously meet up en route to buy vegetables at the market. Amichai wrote poetry with an arch spareness, joyful affection for the human condition, and a deep and dry sense of humor. His poems and his personality are not only remembered but lived today, and with great fondness. We'd like to close by sharing a little bit from a poem called "Tourists," which evokes both Wendi and Danny's, and Amichai's love of the present moment, a love that helps us escape the dangers of being too contained and constrained by the dark memories of our people's often difficult and tragic past, a love that guides us toward the future with aspirations of connection and triumph.

Simply rereading Danny's words brings his presence right back into the room. The memory of Dan's deep intent in the naming of his children—the meanings he placed and the connections to the past he cared so much about preserving and honoring—was always a huge solace to those of us who mourned his death. His ex-wife's choice to change their last name and remove Benjamin's middle name felt inexcusable and heartless.

Another loss to mourn.

I have no idea how deleting someone's middle name helps keep them safe from harm, and she didn't explain. With Danny out of the picture, Wendi acted as though she was finally free to make choices for the children unfettered by his preferences.

Nevertheless, at that time, I felt I had to accept these very painful actions because I did not want to be cut off from the boys. Particularly as it was becoming clear that our former daughter-in-law and her family were taking steps to diminish the boys' memory of their father, including by removing his name from their own, it felt more important than ever for Phil, Shelly, and me to remain present in their lives.

That same month was also the one-year anniversary of Dan's murder. The police, who had been very quiet since my son was laid to rest, held a press conference where they announced the $100,000 reward (in addition to the Crime Stoppers reward) for information that could lead to an arrest and asked for the public's help. They had little else to report.

Shelly, Phil, and I tried to remain patient as the months ticked by. Wendi, Donna, Harvey, and Wendi's brother Charlie lawyered up, but unlike our team, their attorneys went public in print and on TV about Dan and the case, saying that the family had nothing to hide.

The Agony of Waiting

As we continued crawling through an atmosphere of uncertainty, foreboding, and inaction, we learned to draw upon a deep reservoir of patience.

Here's something I discovered about the trial life: it's an agony of waiting. Everyone involved in Dan's case tried to keep us up to date, but the detectives had scant or sensitive evidence to work with, and they couldn't share everything that they had uncovered. One of the TPD's only leads had been Dan's neighbor's belief that he saw a white or silver Prius pull out of the driveway soon after the gunshots were fired. I know they were searching for it, the proverbial needle in a haystack, but at that time they had uncovered no serious leads.

We lived in a perpetual seesaw of dread and hope. Even regular activities like grocery shopping, where papers and magazines are prominently displayed, brought with them an undercurrent of fear, along with a fervent hope for news. Every time I traveled to Florida, I consulted children's psychologists to understand how to talk to the boys about this tragedy.

One piece of advice I was given was to wait and not bring up Dan unless the boys did so first. The intention of this was to ensure the boys never felt uncomfortable around me. As a social worker I was already aware of the importance of listening to the children, to feel out what they were thinking or feeling. I would always choose my words according to the boys' ages.

I continued to take part in conference calls with our attorneys. I wanted it to be the last trip, the last consultation, and the last conference call. It never was.

In the months prior to the arrests, Craig gave some good news that he was working full time on Dan's case and there was a slight change of tone toward hope. In several earlier conversations with me, Craig had said they were working more in the South Florida area while looking at leads as far as New York.

I felt a change of direction, but my family and our team of advisors were more interested in facts and did not share my intuition that things had been progressing behind the scenes. It turned out they were *very* wrong.

Arrests & the Storm Behind the Arrests

I am often reminded of my undergraduate studies in psychology at McGill University. One of the long-lasting sociological models was conceptualized by Erving Goffman in *The Presentation of Self in Everyday Life* in which he described human interactions occurring in front and back regions. The front region is where individuals are interacting on stage in front of an audience. The back region is where individuals interact by letting their guard down, setting aside worries about their appearances and roles. The experience of going through the period of arrests has a strong affiliation in my mind to this reality of interactions in the front and back regions.

The front region is all the facts of the arrests, including all the press conferences and the criminal process. In the back region are the impacts and the developments behind the scenes. I have named this section, "Arrests & The Storm Behind the Arrests," with the arrests beginning on May 25, 2016. During this time, we were all moving along with the fast-paced legal development and major criminal drama. Yet there was much happening "behind" this experience that would take us quite a while to process.

Two years of excruciating anticipation were wiped away with one momentous phone call—and my trial life truly began.

On May 25 of 2016, I received a phone call from Craig at midnight to say that they had been gathering serious evidence and several important developments had occurred. They had picked up Sigfredo Garcia—the very first person publicly named by law enforcement as involved in Dan's murder.

I called Wendi in the morning to give her a heads-up that there would be a police press conference later in the day, possibly about an arrest. She proceeded to call me back several times, almost frantically, to get as many details as possible. I was in constant contact with Craig and was advised by him not to have any more communications with Wendi that day. It would be one of the last times I ever had an extended conversation with her.

In retrospect, calling Wendi to give her a heads-up was a result of my desire to maintain a working relationship with her for the sake of the two boys. I was trusting and cared so deeply for the safety of the children.

After a painstaking search involving footage from security cameras from Tallahassee's public bus system, GPS tracking from the SunPass highway toll network, security videos from a drive-through ATM, and a rental car contract, the police investigators traced the driver and passenger of a rented Prius. They had driven round trip from Miami to Tallahassee at a time consistent with leaving the crime scene. Cell phone records corroborated this timeline, placing two men from Miami in Tallahassee at the same timestamps as when the Prius had been there.

The news quickly spread: TPD had arrested a man named Sigfredo Garcia, whose friends knew him by his nickname, "Tuto." Later, it was announced that Garcia's accomplice was Luis Rivera, his childhood best friend.

The week was simultaneously the loudest and quietest we had experienced yet.

The news media coverage was limited for the first few days, as police kept information private to not jeopardize the ongoing investigation. There was lots of speculation, and we were caught in a high drama of bumper cars, going back and forth, and getting pushed around. The pace of news increased, and it felt like we were jumping through hoops.

The released information was quick and to the point. Garcia had been arrested for first-degree murder after nearly two years of investigation. He was arrested in Miami by the FBI, the Drug Enforcement Administration, the Hallandale Beach Police Department, the Tallahassee Police Department, and a full range of cooperating law enforcement agencies.

News about Garcia's life and history traveled from article to article, most of them highlighting his dark past. Christine Hauser from the *New York Times* reported on Garcia's criminal record with information from the *Tallahassee Democrat* on May 26, 2016, sharing how Garcia had been arrested multiple times in the past as both a teenager and adult on charges that included criminal mischief, assault with a weapon, car burglary, strong-arm robbery, and possession of cocaine.

This was a lot to digest—not just for our family but for so many. People were shocked, confused, baffled. A law professor was murdered by a lowlife who drove up from Miami to kill him? *Why? For what?*

On the same day, we heard from many of Dan's friends and family. Our personal support system worked and paralleled the criminal process. My murder coach, Abe, reminded us to "get ready with the photos of your son in better days," which would be all over the news. I am blessed with this outside influence.

It was at that time that Matt Price's wife wrote her father, Abe, telling him there had been an arrest.

Abe wrote to me:

Good morning Ruth,

Do you think they have the right man, and why he did it? How do you feel?

Abe

He continued his writing later at night:

We know the feelings. If they have the right man, it may take time but you have the knowledge it can only get better. Your heart yearns for closure while your mind searches for justice! If they got the right guy, they would get the rest—what is known in Italy as tracking "The intellectual author". In the US, the rest involved are called and charged as "co-conspirators". I have always believed that crime starts with one person and spreads.

You will soon be exposed to publicity. Remember, it can be your friend or your enemy! Truth be told, that will be up to you. If you ignore the press, they will find and make up their own stories; if you cooperate you may be able to put your spin on it! This is when it is about to happen.

All the best. If you want to talk, call me! Our next court date is two weeks away—June 9 when the trial dates of the whole family get set probably for the fall, when it will all end for us. We are in year 11, so in that respect you have been very lucky!

Abe

Abe was right. There was a media surge, and the Associated Press in Canada also noted the arrest in the murder case of the Canadian-born law professor. Some reports claimed that Garcia was arrested at least twenty-two times in Florida.[2]

As Chief Michael DeLeo of the Tallahassee police stated, "This is still an active criminal investigation."[3] Much remained to be revealed, and the anticipation of further arrests was noted. And the *Tallahassee Democrat* published an article on May 26, 2016, titled "Not Finished Yet: More Arrests Likely in Markel Case," supporting the suspicions of another suspect.

Wendi, on May 27, lauded the investigation and said "the arrests this week offered some closure for her and the children."

For my family, however, closure was far from felt.

2 Christine Hauser, "Florida Man Is Arrested in 2014 Murder of Law Professor," *The New York Times*, May 26, 2016, https://www.nytimes.com/2016/05/27/us/dan-markel-arrest-2014-murder-of-law-professor.html.

3 The Associated Press, "Florida Police Make Arrest in 2014 Slaying of Daniel Markel, Toronto-Born Law Prof," *CBC News*, May 26, 2016, https://www.cbc.ca/news/canada/toronto/florida-arrest-toronto-victim-markel-1.3602641.

The Probable Cause Affidavit Gets Released

In addition to all the excellent guidance from our lawyers at Gibson Dunn, such as their advice to not speculate in the press and allow them to do so on our behalf, we became news junkies, waiting for the next crisis and announcement. We became even more in-the-know about Florida and U.S. politics during that time.

That breakthrough was quick to come. The probable cause affidavit in the arrest of Garcia, who faced a murder charge in Dan's death, was unexpectedly—and perhaps inappropriately—released shortly after, on June 2, the day Garcia made his first appearance before the judge. I say inappropriately because at that point, there was still a concern that by releasing the documents that early, other possible co-conspirators could be tipped off about details that perhaps they'd be better off not yet knowing.

On June 2, 2016, there was another police update on the case. The press conference took place in the records rotunda of the TPD at 2 p.m. We learned more about evidence, such as Dan's prints, eyewitnesses, and even the Constitutional right to speedy trials. This meant that in most cases, the state of Florida would have to bring a defendant to trial within a specified time following an arrest. Our adrenaline was working hard; we were not exhausted but full of questions. We were told that we should be patient, polite, and grateful. We had to acknowledge that we might not get answers to all of our questions.

The *Tallahassee Democrat*, as reported by Sean Rossman, captured the story the same day, publishing the probable cause affidavit submitted in the first appearance that had been unsealed. It contained significant information that had never been made public, including that "investigators believe motives for this murder stemmed from the desperate desire of the Adelson family to relocate Wendi and the children to South Florida, along with the pending court hearing that might have impacted their access to their grandchildren."

Indeed, the probable cause affidavit revealed the unthinkable: Wendi's mother, Donna, and her brother, Charlie, were named as unindicted co-conspirators, meaning that law enforcement alleged they had been involved in planning the murder and named them in an indictment but had not personally indicted them for the crime. The news was shattering.

Furthermore, the probable cause affidavit revealed the identities of two other suspected co-conspirators: Garcia's childhood best friend, Luis Rivera, and Katherine "Katie" Magbanua, the mother of Garcia's two children who was also, prior to and around the time of the murder, dating Charlie Adelson.

The *Tallahassee Democrat* released an article on June 4, 2016, predicting the arrest of Rivera, known by gang members as King Tato. At this time, Rivera was already serving time in the Coleman Federal Correctional Institute after pleading guilty to a federal investigation targeting twenty-three members of the Latin Kings gang.

There were no details as to why the document was unsealed. Georgia Cappleman, the assistant state attorney, said she believed the judge unsealed the document "on his own motion."[4]

This unsealed document validated allegations that Garcia did not work alone. Rivera was allegedly his accomplice on that terrible day. These articles stated that investigators had video surveillance and cell phone tracking supporting that Garcia and Rivera were in the area on the day of Dan's murder. The two men traveled from Miami in a rented 2008 Prius just days before the killing and stayed in a nearby hotel.

The media began to release videos of the two men driving in the Prius, which quickly spread over the internet. The *Tallahassee Democrat* posted many videos throughout June and July, showing this vehicle through bus cameras and building surveillance. The videos showed that the Prius had followed Dan through his morning route when he left his home, dropped his children off at daycare, and then went to the gym. The two men waited in the Prius in the gym parking lot until Dan finished before following him back to his home where the shooting occurred.

The alleged connection to Magbanua was different. While she had never traveled to Tallahassee during that time, she was personally involved with both Garcia and Rivera and with the Adelson family. As noted, Magbanua had two children with her common-law husband, Garcia, and was dating Charlie Adelson prior to and around the time of the murder. Investigators also showed that Magbanua had started

---

4 Sean Rossman, "Document drop reveals split between TPD, state attorney," *Tallahassee Democrat*, June 2, 2016, http://www.tallahassee.com/story/news/2016/06/02/confusion-over-unsealed-documents-markel-case/85291512/.

receiving checks from the Adelson family business just after the murder, all of them signed by Donna herself.

It was a lot to process, to say the least. And, while this was happening, there were media requests for our family to participate. We were invited to share our reaction on the arrest, but we stayed silent to the media. In our private life, our family and friends all had questions. Most of them were unfamiliar with crime and the justice system, and our limited knowledge made us their advisors.

The period of arrests was fast-paced and eventful, so much so that one time we attended a Toronto grandparent event for an hour and when we finished there had been a whole new development. Lots of texts, Google announcements, and continuous internet searches were part of this time period. It had certainly changed from the waiting, slow pace of the last two years. Now, we were on a treadmill with an incline. There wasn't a private moment without criminal news and continuous updates of information. Once the arrests were made, our experience in the justice system was suddenly transformed.

A Second Indictment & Big Changes in Our Lives as Victims

The next major event occurred on June 17, when Rivera was officially charged with first-degree murder. This marked the second arrest in the course of a few weeks, amplifying our emotions at the same time as attention to the case continued to build around the world.

After these arrests, Craig and Sara Latorre, our victim support advocate with TPD, informed the family that we would now be working with the State Attorney's Office. Our journey as victims was changed permanently as we became accountable to the victims' program at the State Attorney's Office.

We were introduced to Helene Potlock, our new victim support liaison, and Georgia Cappleman, the prosecutor assigned to work on the criminal case, trials, and convictions. Cappleman worked under State Attorney Willie Meggs, who was elected to the role in 1985 and had served ever since. We would later be introduced to his successor, Jack Campbell, who was elected in the fall of 2016 and assumed the office in January 2017.

In our first call with Cappleman, we established a line of communication. We expressed our gratitude and learned more about the process going forward from the prosecutor's office.

During this introductory period, we had to organize our calls very strategically. Here was our plan for that 3 p.m. call:

- Shelly opened the call and said that we appreciate the efforts and information of the TPD and appreciate the same from the State Attorney's Office.
- Shelly then introduced Orin Snyder and Matthew Benjamin. She explained that Ruth and Phil were not lawyers, they were grieving, and they found it especially useful to have had some help navigating these unfamiliar and emotionally charged issues. She then explained that Orin and Matthew have been involved from the beginning, providing legal advice to the family.

Through these interactions, our criminal vocabulary expanded to include new words such as the defendant, hearings, judgments, witnesses, trials, jury selection, death penalty, conviction, appeals, court process and procedures, opening statements, closing arguments, deliberations, and verdicts. These words became our "soup du jour." For us, these words are not from a dictionary; they are very meaningful and can be painful, such as verdicts. We also learned that our case was complicated by different criteria standards for evidence for state, federal, and conspiracy crimes.

My adrenaline surge was high as I learned all the details we discussed with the TPD and Cappleman. More was coming. I was sure that Phil and Shelly were not feeling disconnected but were also running fast, as we had a lot to do as next of kin. In our hearts, our main interest was really to understand the boys' current well-being, logistics, the criminal process, the prosecution, the investigation, and communications.

As these events of early June evolved, my family became increasingly worried about the children. While we were in a river of information during the arrest period, my worries were in the sewers. Our communication was dormant with the boys, and my concerns were mounting: *Are they secure? Are they hurt? What do they hear?*

A few days after the original TPD conference on May 26, I got permission from Craig to write to Wendi, and I sent her a brief email on June 6 through our advocate, Sara Latorre.

Dear Sara,

Thank you again for all your support. I am asking you to pass this message to Wendi with Craig's approval.

Please forward to Wendi from your office. We will connect directly later to Wendi with Craig's support.

Please share this email with Craig Isom.

Thanks,

Ruth

Dear Wendi,

It has taken me a few days to get on my feet. We are concerned!

How are Benjamin and Lincoln?

How are you?

Please keep us posted!

Ruth

Despite efforts to communicate with the boys and Wendi, we had no contact—she never replied, and I yearned for news of their well-being. It was very hard to feel any peace.

* * *

June 24, 2016, was Garcia's first bond hearing for bail.

June continued to progress, and more information surfaced about the suspects in Dan's murder, but there was little time to stop and reflect. Worse, there were dynamics at play that contributed to our family's concern about what would happen next.

State Attorney Meggs had approved the charges against Garcia and Rivera but stated publicly that he did not believe there was enough evidence for further arrests. Many considered this to be highly unusual behavior for a tenured prosecutor and saw it as Meggs undermining the investigation or worse—potentially crippling the case against Magbanua or members of the Adelson family. Internet sleuths puzzled over it, coming up with all kinds of theories. But for our family, the trauma of uncertainty continued.

Months passed. Little did we know, a lot was happening in the silence.

An Accomplice Cooperates & a Third Arrest

While incarcerated for other charges, Rivera decided to cooperate with authorities. On October 1, 2016, Rivera gave an unrecorded proffer—or offer to cooperate—to law enforcement, testifying to his role in the murder and providing corroboration for the allegation that Katherine "Katie" Magbanua had facilitated his and Garcia's hire. On October 4, Rivera provided another proffer, this time recorded, laying out everything he knew. He pled guilty to second-degree murder. In exchange for his cooperation, he was offered an abbreviated sentence that he would serve in part concurrently with his current sentence.

This plea received numerous criticisms from the law community because his plea allowed him to serve his sentence for the murder concurrently with what he was already serving. In other words, it would add only seven years onto his existing prison term—for a second-degree murder charge. With the plea deal, he would now serve a total of nineteen years for both crimes. Despite some people suggesting that Rivera's deal was too generous, his role was significant in securing the arrest of Magbanua. To me, the deal made with Rivera was worthwhile.

Once Rivera decided to cooperate, he admitted to driving the Prius and to traveling not just once, but twice, to Tallahassee to carry out the murder. There was serious evidence stacked against him as he was identified by cell phone data and ATM records and videos. Rivera also told the police the details of how Garcia and Magbanua allegedly split the $100,000 payment for the hit and gave him a cut for his role. The police report also includes statements about Rivera and Garcia buying cars and motorcycles with the money.

When Rivera pled guilty, he turned state's evidence against Magbanua. At the time of Garcia's and Rivera's arrests, Magbanua was working in a real estate office. She had remained friendly with Charlie Adelson since the murder, although the two had stopped dating. Garcia and Magbanua both pled not guilty. Garcia would face the death penalty.

Rivera's account of what had happened aligned with what authorities already knew. Rivera outlined the route that was taken before the shooting, which matched what police had on record. Rivera described how the three had divided up the $100,000 payment and how in the days and months after the murder, Garcia purchased a new car and a motorcycle—all things that official records confirmed. Rivera also was able to attest to Magbanua's actions on and around the day of Danny's murder, such as a phone call he alleged overhearing between her and Garcia on the drive back to Miami. This, too, was affirmed by investigative records.

The paychecks to Magbanua began immediately following Dan's murder in even increments written on sequential checks, all signed by Donna Adelson from the Adelson Institute for Aesthetics & Implant Dentistry, their family's business, commonly referred to as the "Adelson Institute." This was a huge revelation and disturbing to say the least. Investigators found no specific evidence that Magbanua was doing any official work for the family's business or for Charlie himself, despite receiving regular paychecks, which contributed toward the total amount Rivera admitted the three were paid for the murder.

On Saturday, October 1, 2016, police arrested Magbanua and charged her in connection with Dan's murder. This information did not truly start to circulate in the press until Monday, October 3. Many articles had already speculated on her involvement and predicted this development, as she was named throughout the probable cause affidavits released relating to Garcia's and Rivera's arrests.

The family and our lawyers at Gibson Dunn were updated on the arrest of Magbanua through law enforcement and the State Attorney's Office. At the time, our communications with the State Attorney's Office had become more frequent, relevant and timely. Previously, our communications, information, and support came support came solely from the TPD.

The media continued to stay on top of Dan's case, and just after Magbanua was arrested, the news of Rivera pleading guilty appeared. Many news sites concurred that without Rivera's plea, Magbanua would not have been arrested.

Conflict continued to arise between the TPD, the FBI, and the State Attorney's Office. The police and the Feds thought they had enough evidence to arrest members of the Adelson family, but once again, Meggs disagreed. We were frustrated that these various entities were not joining forces to find out what happened to Dan and were instead waiting to see what unfolded with the suspects. Meggs held his position of not supporting further arrests at that time, despite his impending retirement. It was a terrible conflict to witness. We were experiencing the equivalent of growing pains, living the drama that one would only expect to see in TV depictions of court life. As Canadians, we were not accustomed to a justice system that included various elected positions or the dynamics that this brought to the decision-making process. For us, this was a paradigm shift, now known as a "sea change." We accommodated quickly.

Social media flourished with comments on the guilt of Rivera and the arrest of Magbanua. We all followed the media's surge with great interest and hope that justice would prevail.

My last communication with Wendi was October 13, 2016. We tried to reach her after that point, to no avail. That was Lincoln's birthday and I had a gratifying video chat with the children that day.

As there were no further arrests at that time, the drama that had been unfolding quieted down. We spent those days anticipating hearings for case management and trial dates.

Now began another journey of waiting. After the fast-paced experience of the arrests, the progression of the case felt like it came to a halt and we entered a period of disappointment. We were waiting again with more uncertainty. It was at this time I began to describe my life as living on a roller coaster.

* * *

Despite few developments released during this time, the *Tallahassee Democrat* and *Above the Law* continued to cover the case more than other sources. CBC and the *Toronto Star* also seemed to keep up to date on the case. Many articles highlighted who Dan was as a person before going onto a brief summary of the events that had taken place and the ever-changing trial dates.

We were in a continuous state of disbelief, anxiety, and frustration, as our life was in limbo once again.

Rivera never reached trial because he pled guilty, as mentioned above. Magbanua was set to go to trial on February 27, 2017. However, this trial date got postponed to "give both sides more time to prepare their cases and deal with new evidence," as reported by David Lat in *Above the Law* on October 27, 2016.[5] Her trial was then postponed to January 2018, and according to media coverage, would be held at a later date.

Garcia was able to extend his trial date to January 22, 2018, and then a second time to July 2018. At this point, Judge James C. Hankinson noted that he had delayed the trial twice and didn't intend to do so again.

Garcia faced the death penalty. Many academics called and wrote to the prosecutor about Dan's strong disagreement with the death penalty, but this sentence remained on the table throughout Garcia's trial.

We were living on a tightrope, with no predictions from the justice system. Life was never normal for us. In this kind of a situation, the ups and downs of all the changes mean you can't even plan a summer or winter break because the schedule keeps changing.

At first, the state prosecutor decided to try each person involved in the crime separately. This decision was good for the trial and evidence gathering, but, because of its inevitably drawn-out results, it was tough for my own life sentence.

The public defenders for Magbanua and Garcia bowed out due to a possible connection with Dan, but the defendants were able to find private lawyers to take their cases. This led to rampant and enduring speculation about who was paying for their services.

Cappleman then moved to combine the trial of Magbanua and Garcia. We were still waiting and experiencing all the agony of the delays in the justice system from 2017 to 2019. The defense attorneys didn't want their clients to be tried together, but Judge Hankinson allowed the trials to be combined. The joint trial finally occurred in September 2019. "Homicide trials are things that you can work on your entire life

---

5 David Lat, "The Dan Markel Case: More Evidence in Newly Released Documents," *Above the Law* (blog), October 17, 2016, https://abovethelaw.com/2016/10/the-dan-markel-case-more-evidence-in-newly-released-documents/.

and still find more work to do," Cappleman says. "But eventually you need to draw the line in the sand and get some closure for the family."[6]

Flashback: The Sting

Just when I thought I could not be shocked by anything, our family learned a bit more from investigators about what had led to the three arrests, and how dedicated investigators had been to uncovering evidence of who paid these three to carry out such an act.

We learned about the use of extensive wiretapping of Katherine Magbanua and Charlie Adelson, and what detectives learned from listening in—particularly following the use of a "sting" orchestrated by the FBI. This tactic, described in greater detail below, is commonly used by law enforcement to spark conversation between suspected members of a conspiracy.

The investigators needed more incriminating information to document the conspiracies involved in carrying out Dan's murder. But nearly two years had passed since. It was unlikely that any of the parties involved would be casually talking about the murder at this point, and without provoking them to do so, authorities would have spent countless hours listening in on conversations about dental patients, social dinners, and as it turns out, a number of other criminal but unrelated activities, such things as drugs and illegal steroids.

To get Donna, her family members, and Magbanua talking, the FBI had an undercover agent approach Donna on the street near her condo in Miami. This type of law enforcement tactic is commonly referred to as a "bump" or a "sting." The undercover officer handed Donna a printout of an article about Dan's murder, with a demand for $5,000 written on it, saying he was aware of how the family was helping "Katie and Tuto [Sigfredo]" and that they needed to do the same for his "brother" [Tato – Rivera] who had also helped Donna's family with their "problem up north."

The FBI officer was essentially suggesting that the Adelson family was properly paying Magbanua and Garcia for the murder, but that the third participant, Rivera, was not adequately compensated, and he

---

6 David Lat, "The Dan Markel Case: The Wheels Of Justice Turn Slowly," *Above the Law* (blog), June 23, 2017, https://abovethelaw.com/2017/06/the-dan-markel-case-the-wheels-of-justice-turn-slowly/.

needed to be. At the time this "Sting" happened, Rivera was incarcerated on unrelated federal charges, and Garcia and Magbanua had yet to be arrested. Therefore, the communication from the undercover agent was received with alarm by Donna, who at that time may have believed all the drama relating to Dan's murder had quieted down.

The exchange with the undercover agent scared Donna, and she called Charlie immediately after the encounter, but she chose her words carefully in that call.

She told Charlie that someone approached her, and that it had something to do with "the two of us" and "an ex-girlfriend." Charlie didn't ask which ex-girlfriend his mother was talking about, even though he has dated extensively. Donna never said Katie's name. She never even explicitly referenced the murder.

After talking with Donna a few times, Charlie made one specific call—to Magbanua. She was the only ex-girlfriend he would call about this issue. He told Magbanua that his mother had been approached by someone looking for money, and that this person had referenced Katie's name. Again, this is interesting, because while the undercover agent did say Katie's name, Donna had not said her name to Charlie. Charlie and Magbanua made plans to meet to discuss the problem the next day at the Dolce Vita restaurant at a strip mall in Sunny Isles. There, Charlie and Magbanua were observed on a planted FBI camera. They were seen sitting at a table with Charlie showing Magbanua the "paperwork" his mother had been given, which was the flyer handed to her by the undercover agent. The audio from this recording proved difficult to transcribe because the two of them were seated in a noisy restaurant at a distance from the recorder, but experts have attested to some of the things that were said between them—including Charlie telling Magbanua that she had to take care of the problem. At the time of this writing, the audio recording from this encounter is being "enhanced" by audio forensic experts and may in fact prove instrumental in the direction of the case against Katherine and Charlie.

Both at that restaurant and captured on subsequent wiretap recordings, Charlie and Magbanua discussed at length the possibility that the "bump" was "one of two things"—assumed to be either law enforcement trying to get them to admit guilt, or a third party who was attempting to blackmail them. Charlie and Magbanua both stated on numerous occasions the concern that if they were to pay the $5,000, the blackmailer might keep coming back for more, creating a lifelong burden that would never go away.

The FBI surveillance of Donna, Charlie, Magbanua, and Garcia occurred in person and by telephone. The four of them talked in separate conversations about different aspects of the incident, much of it in coded language. Charlie would talk to Donna, and then Charlie would talk to Magbanua. Then Magbanua and Garcia would talk to one another before Magbanua and Charlie would speak again.

We also discovered that while Rivera and Garcia were paid in cash for Dan's murder, Magbanua allegedly received part of her own payment in cash bank deposits, a succession of luxury gifts and trips, and a breast enhancement performed by a Miami plastic surgeon known as "Dr. Boobner." We also learned more about Charlie, who others described as having made connections with some less-than-savory gym pals.

While we were impressed with all of the information that law enforcement was able to collect, our family was also traumatized thinking about the environment that Benjamin and Lincoln were being raised in. We worried about the influences they were being exposed to and about the character and morals of the closest people in their lives. Once arrests were made, there was a lot of public displeasure and concern about Benjamin and Lincoln living in that environment.

Wendi's Interview Released

With so much uncovered by veteran investigator Craig Isom, we wanted things to happen quickly. But law enforcement still moved cautiously in a search for indisputable witnesses and evidence to lock up all the murderers for good. As the arrests, the sting operation, and the audio tapes of conversations between Charlie, Donna, Magbanua, and Garcia were made public, the media became even more intrigued with the case. The reports focused on the complex story lines and the unlikely characters involved.

The media was outraged that only three people sat in jail accused of this murder. Local news was all over the story, and national TV media jumped on board, including shows such as NBC's *Dateline* and ABC's *20/20*. Each produced an episode about the murder, and *People*

Magazine put an active reporter on the case. So, while we received a lot of interview requests, my family and I participated only to talk about the grandchildren and how we missed them. That was our top priority and the only focus we felt comfortable talking about. Questions by reporters would veer to the subject of murder, but we would do our best to bring it back to our grandchildren and our deep desire to reconnect with them.

It was through this media coverage that my family came to see some of the content that we had previously only heard about. In some ways, this was welcome. It gave us context for understanding much of what had happened in the days following Dan's murder when we were in early, consuming grief. Some reporters have a strong investigatory spirit and were able to access and digest evidence that was available to the public but not broadcast widely at that point. We were kept up to date by law enforcement. Many times, the media would elaborate on evidence or records posted to the court docket, making it more real. Yet some of it was challenging, if not nauseating, to encounter.

Things became much darker when the police released Wendi's five-hour interview with detectives on the day of Dan's murder. Some clips of this interview had circulated through media coverage, and much of it landed on YouTube for the scrutiny of anyone who wanted to watch.

In the footage, Wendi demonstrated a range of emotions, including disbelief and sadness, while still somewhat composed and alleging ignorance of why it could have happened.

We always had known that Wendi had several alibis, and we never thought she herself had pulled the trigger. But we didn't realize that following the murder she had gotten so close to the scene. Let me explain. Early that morning, Wendi was at home with the TV repairman who had been called to look at her "broken" flat-screen TV. We learned that Wendi had also been communicating with friends about lunch plans, and ultimately, she did go to lunch a short distance from her home. But on the way there, Wendi drove many miles out of her way to purchase Bulleit brand whiskey, pronounced "bullet," from a liquor store a block from Dan's home, but this would have been easily available closer to her home or lunch destination.

This raises eyebrows to the present day: Why would Wendi choose a liquor store so far away from where she lived and where she was going to next? And even so, why choose to drive there on a route that put her on Danny's street, a small winding residential road, rather than driving on the main road to get there? Wendi had told Craig that she chose that route because it helped her come to terms with the divorce. Regardless of her intent that day, Wendi encountered police tape once on Trescott Drive—after all, the murder had happened just over an hour prior, and the scene was teeming with authorities. Despite the emergency vehicles she must have witnessed on a street her children lived on too, did Wendi call to check on Dan or the boys?

Furthermore, some of Wendi's statements strike many people as odd. One statement in particular stood out most chillingly: she said about Charlie, "He knew that Danny treated me badly, and it was always joked, he said, *'I looked into hiring a hitman, but it was cheaper to get you this TV.'*" She had told this same exact story to the TV repairman who had been at her home that very morning—not the kind of thing that is funny, or normal, in any such exchange.

Wendi's interview made people wonder whether she was sincere or acting. Many commenters on the internet observed that her performance came off as inauthentic. Beyond her affect, however, some internet "sleuths" began to question whether there was more to this whole "broken TV" story than met the eye. Some questioned whether it was a coincidence that the very TV she had been given by Charlie as a "divorce present" because it was "cheaper than hiring a hitman" was being repaired the same day Dan was killed.

Another interesting thing is that throughout her interview, Wendi asked Craig multiple times, "Who would do this?" suggesting that she was uninvolved. She even seemed to insulate herself from scrutiny by disclosing her brother's "joke" about having looked into hiring a hitman. She also implied that perhaps someone had done this to Danny thinking it would be "good" for her. Wendi's tears can be interpreted in many ways—as sadness, yes, or even as relief.

At that time, Wendi herself had not been named as a suspect, as her mother and brother allegedly were in 2016. And, even in their case, authorities are still looking for something more concrete in order to bring charges. The police and the FBI have reluctantly held off on taking any of them into custody.

Losing a loved one to murder is terrible, but other consequences endured in the aftermath of the crime can be nearly as heartbreaking and very disappointing.

As the evidence unfolded and we moved forward in our quest for justice, I gained invaluable insights. On a very personal level, Craig shared with me that Garcia's arrest was postponed to protect me and my time with the boys. Three weeks before his arrest, I was in Miami with Benjamin and Lincoln. My last visit was April 30, just a few days after the "bump" had occurred unbeknownst to me, and the arrest was May 25, 2016. I always appreciated Craig's gesture and cherish memories of that visit.

As I had been working closely with Craig and Pat Sanford with the FBI, I became introduced to even more criminal language, such as autopsies, bullets, evidence, charges, warrants, bumps, and stings. These would become yet more unfortunate pieces of my new vocabulary.

Estrangement & More Loss

After the arrests, I started to have more upsetting thoughts about the possibility that the boys could be in danger or could end up exposed to further unnecessary trauma. It was bad enough that Benjamin and Lincoln were spending unlimited time with their Adelson grandparents and uncle Charlie day to day. But during this time, when further arrests were being forecast by authorities, our minds worried even more about how this could unfold for the children: *What if they are at a park, school, or the beach, and the police swoop in? Could the boys be taken by Florida's Department of Children & Families and put in foster care before anyone has contact with us?*

I reached out to Jewish Adoption and Family Care Options (JAFCO), located in South Florida, and inquired about a potential emergency backup plan to avoid any foster care and maintain continuity with family members for the boys.

Regrettably, my email to the State Attorney's Office relaying my communications with JAFCO were accidentally released for discovery, and it became available in the media, with crushing consequences. Wendi falsely inferred that I was trying to take the boys away from her, and she forbid me and my family from seeing the children or having any more contact with them. It was the end of our communication with the boys, a turn of events almost as terrible as losing Dan. As previously mentioned, it wasn't as though Wendi was receptive to our communications during this period of arrests anyway, and the timing of her cutting us off could easily have happened anyway, without the JAFCO message. That said, the email did give Wendi something she could point to as a reason for cutting off contact, and it was a decision that caused us enormous and ongoing pain.

We tried, behind the scenes, through our lawyers and Wendi's lawyer, to explain the email, repair the relationship, and find common ground. It was not successful. Even Sarah Franco from JAFCO provided a public statement to clarify our intentions. Here is what she wrote:

STATEMENT OF SARAH FRANCO,
EXECUTIVE DIRECTOR OF JAFCO

> Ruth Markel called JAFCO to inquire about a backup emergency safety plan for her grandsons. Ruth wanted to ensure that her grandsons would not be placed in State foster care should members of the Adelson family be arrested at a time the children were present. At no time did Ruth suggest seeking temporary or permanent custody, or doing anything to remove the children from their mother.
>
> We are saddened to learn that Ruth's inquiry to JAFCO has resulted in a decision to deny the children any relationship with their paternal family. We are deeply concerned that the abrupt disruption of visitation with their paternal grandparents has caused further harm to the children. JAFCO remains committed to providing any needed services to the Markel children and their families.

Besides sharing my experience and knowledge for interested audiences, as well as fellow victims' families, another reason for writing this book is to highlight the issues and problems surrounding the legal rights of grandparents in Florida, as well as in other states. As previously mentioned, following the arrests, Phil and I were unceremoniously blocked from seeing Dan's children, our grandchildren, while Wendi's family enjoyed unlimited access to them.

Parental rights laws in Florida are strongly predisposed toward birth parents, and most grandparents do not even have the liberty to file a lawsuit to ask for visitation rights with their grandchildren, let alone pursue such litigation. There are only two conditions in current Florida law that would allow grandparents to petition a court for visitation, and neither yet applied to me and Phil. In Florida, either both parents must be deceased or the living parent must have been convicted of a felony. The gravity of this reality shook us once again.

Creating a break between grandparents and grandchildren seems brazenly unfair in a legal sense but can also have a calamitous emotional effect. According to Alienated Grandparents Anonymous, children who are blocked from having an emotionally close bond with their grandparents are at a higher risk of mental health problems. In addition, the boys have been kept away from their aunt, uncle, and cousins, another loss for them and their overall well-being. Alienation from close family members in the aftermath of a tragedy can compound a child's sense of grief and instability—something that we hoped so desperately to avoid for Dan's two boys. The reality of not seeing the grandchildren has caused me tremendous pain and anger. Not only am I crushed about the estrangement from Dan's children, but the entire family is destroyed.

How can I tell this to Dan? Here is where I have to lift the veil to personal suffering. I have frequent visits to Dan's grave, but I am consumed with fear to share with Dan that I am not able to see his children. I feel I let him down. *If his mother can't come through for his children, who can?*

We tried to contact Wendi's lawyer through our lawyers, but there was no progress toward resolution, and the silent treatment continued.

I felt punched again and ready to fall to the bottom of the rabbit hole. This situation did have physical repercussions. I became diagnosed with atrial fibrillation and was introduced to the world of cardiac rehabilitation and heart medications. Fortunately, I attended a cardiac rehabilitation program—a great program where I was able to receive all kinds of support and address my dilemma of losing contact with my grandchildren. I also sought out outside consultation on children's issues related to trauma.

As always, I climbed out of the rabbit hole—this time, more dependent on support. I had been introduced to the idea of writing a bill on grandparents' rights by Matthew Benjamin, one of our lawyers from Gibson Dunn. Sarah Franco from JAFCO became a guiding light and mentioned that we needed to get lobbyists. These suggestions were heard, deeply—though it was not yet the time to pursue those things. Instead, the seeds were planted, and it would be three years before they resurfaced.

While we were devastated from the lack of time with our grandchildren, we had to face the challenges of the trial life.

More Unfolds & the Media Dials In

There was so much new information that I had to learn from the period of waiting and uncertainty. We were plunged into the investigation outcome and a "murder-for-hire" reality.

We learned about victim rights that included the right to participate and be informed in the process, as well as the availability of victim support and victim communications.

We received a flurry of support from Dan's friends, such as Ethan Leib, Eric Abrahamsen, Tor Friedman, Stephen Webster, Steve Frank, and others on a variety of issues. We were provided links to victims' rights information, specific information on wrongful death suits, claims against the Consolidated Dispatch Agency (CDA), and family law consultation. One source about the rights of victims in Florida is found on the Florida Attorney General's website.[7]

Our lawyers from Gibson Dunn, Matthew and Orin, were right on top of the situation and prepared us for the next steps. We then contacted Helene Potlock, our victim liaison support person from the State Attorney's Office. She advised us that "our role as next of kin is to have the right to participate (the right to be informed, the right to be heard, and the right to speak, etc.)." We also learned that Georgia Cappleman intended to be our prosecutor and kept our case.

Our media relationship needed to be managed. We needed media statements and developed a protocol for inquiries and interviews. Here is an example of the family statement: "Dan's parents and sister remain grateful to the authorities for their commitment to solving and bringing justice to those allegedly responsible for Dan's tragic murder. They will have no further comments at this time and we ask that you please respect their privacy."

---

7 http://myfloridalegal.com/pages.nsf/main/a15edbdd3d1c2e1f85256cc6004b3ea4!opendocument

And here is our response in the event of a press contact: "We are not speaking to the media at this time. Feel free to contact our representatives, Orin Snyder and Matthew Benjamin at Gibson Dunn."

Many of the expert reporters knew how to get critical information early by checking the public records office. For example, the arrest on May 25, 2016, was recorded at the public records office at midnight that day. The media was able to access the release of records after midnight. This gave them a jump on the news then, and we knew it would happen this way again.

Our protocol going forward was to put all questions from the media to Gibson Dunn: "Any inquiries from law enforcement, the state prosecutor's office, or the media should be directed to the cell phone number listed below."

We informed our estate lawyer, Sarah Butters, and Eric Abrahamsen that the TPD was expected to make a statement. We provided them with the guidance that "if anyone calls you (or your firm) asking for any statements or information please do not provide any comments but send them to Gibson Dunn—Matthew Benjamin or Orin Snyder."

Craig continued to play a significant role, along with Pat Sanford from the FBI, in helping us understand the next steps of the criminal process. We also had lots of media updates and frenzies joining us in this journey. Below is a list of some of the media headlines that appeared during the arrest period of Dan's case:

- *Canadian Jewish News*, "Man Charged for Murder of Toronto Law Professor Dan Markel"
- *Forward*, "Police Arrest Alleged Hitman for Cold-Blooded Murder of Law Professor"
- Fox News, "Arrest Leaves Unanswered Questions in Killing of Popular FSU Professor"
- *The Star*, "Florida Man Arrested in Killing of Toronto-Born Professor—But Questions Still Remain"
- *Tallahassee Democrat*, "Friends, Colleagues Find Hope in Arrest, Eager for Details"
- *Tallahassee Democrat*, "Garcia Neighbors in Disbelief Over Murder Charge"

- *Tallahassee Democrat*, "Markel Suspect: 'This Is Not My First Rodeo'"
- *Tallahassee Democrat*, "Markel's Ex-Wife Lauds Investigators, Arrest"
- *Tallahassee Democrat*, "Witness: Police Swarmed Garcia During Arrest in Markel Case"
- *Times of Israel*, "Man Charged for Murder of Jewish Law Professor Dan Markel"
- WCTV, "Neighbors, Colleagues of FSU Professor React to Murder Arrest"
- WFSU, "Slain FSU Professor Markel's Ex-Wife Hopes For Closure After Suspect Arrested"

On a more informal and local level, we also learned that there were lots of politics of the case and heard that "all of Tallahassee was lawyering up." We were facing adversity and an unimaginable set of legal circumstances.

The month of June 2016 had an extremely high criminal learning curve. We kept up the pace as our lawyers steered us with agendas, strategy, and structures for communications. I thrived on this support because I am very proactive by nature.

I originally wanted to prepare scripts for use with the media in advance of arrests but was told that this would be premature in May and June 2016. We benefitted from our advisors managing the process, which I wrote to them about on June 4, 2016, as follows:

> *Finally, I want to thank you for your patience, legal knowledge and organizational skills. I like strategy and action plans. I will not ask for "timelines" (joking).*
>
> *I do like options such as preparing scripts for an arrest which was vetoed as premature. Hindsight that is humorous.*
>
> *Your personal support and sensitivity are special. You have both the "art of law" and legal capability.*

Our life in those days was full of drama, challenging discussions, behind-the-scenes research, legal opinions, writing, receiving memos, and legal communications. Our sentiments were totally tied to the children's well-being. We only hoped that there would be no more disruptions in their lives.

Lessons Learned: Arrests

Support: Many of Dan's closest friends rallied around us at this time with legal advice and interpretations. We were blessed with their input on the criminal matters and possible civil actions. Most importantly, they all offered continuous friendship. Our family and personal friends also provided ongoing emotional support. Some even started following every detail of the criminal processing, giving us advanced alerts. The support would later expand to lobbyists and learning about advocacy, including how to develop legislation.

Politics and Conflict: Conflict about further actions was highly explosive, and the major players were not on the same page. There appeared to be friction between law enforcement (TPD and the FBI) and the State Attorney's Office on the timing of the release of documents. As I was handling the law enforcement relationships, it became obvious to me that I needed to keep separate contact with all the agencies. Even after the arrests, this proved to be very fruitful for my own understanding of the courts and the criminal system.

Family Meetings and Updates: It became clear that we all had to be in sync and headed in the same direction with regard to media, lawyers, and law enforcement. We started to schedule family conferences for the exchange of information to make sure that our direction was coordinated with all the parties involved.

Communications: As in my leadership job (my previous life), a key ingredient was timely communication and planning. My preferred personal style is very strategic, and I decided we needed to start having family calls with the State Attorney's Office and our lawyers at Gibson Dunn. We also began having regular family conferences with prosecutor Georgia Cappleman and Helene Potlock. Our lawyers from Gibson Dunn developed very timely family statements that we would share with media as needed.

Criminal Terms: In moving forward from the period of arrests, learning terms such as murder-for-hire, sting, and bump became important—also, what it means when the defendant pleads not guilty to the murder charge, such as Garcia did. One should familiarize oneself with the defendants' lawyers and legal expenses. Also, we had many questions relating to who was paying the defendants' legal fees.

Consultation with Victims: Victims have a right to be heard. In the Florida victims' rights statutes, victims are given specific rights and privileges. It is very important to find out when and where victims have rights in the criminal process.

Media: We quickly learned to follow a strict drill of "no comment." When we went public, it was deliberate and well timed. We requested that the media respect our privacy. The following example is a family statement that had a purposeful timing:

Statement on Behalf of Ruth, Phil, and Shelly Markel.

> Although it does not diminish their immense pain, Ruth, Phil and Shelly are grateful to local, state, and federal authorities for their tireless work resulting in today's arrest. They are also thankful to Dan's friends and local community for their love and support since Dan's tragic murder. They will have no further comment at this time and ask that you respect their privacy.
>
> Orin Snyder, Attorney for Ruth, Phil, and Shelly Markel.

Press Conferences: Press conferences, such as those held by law enforcement agencies, are important at major events, such as arrests, and should always be followed. Many times, the updates from law enforcement have new information that is unfamiliar to the victims and their family members.

Evidence: Evidence becomes the mantra of a new belief system. *Is there enough evidence? Does it meet the standard for criminal evidence? What is the credibility of the witness? Is this the right evidence for this crime?*

Uncertainty: Waiting becomes your life work. Unlike TV shows, a crime is not solved in one hour. The justice system is very complex and unnerving. Even after arrests had been made, we were waiting again for trials and appeals.

Advocacy: We chose the road map to find justice with legislation and writing new bills, as will be shared in depth in the chapters to come.

CHAPTER 5

Pretrial Life

Developing Victim Impact Statements

Although the actual trial started in 2019, due to the volume of pre-trial hearings that had transpired already, our victim impact statements were prepared well in advance.

Victims of crime experience an unexpected and significant loss, causing unthinkable harm to their lives and the lives of their loved ones. Not only are victims forced to deal with sudden victimization, they often experience confusion and frustration when encountering the criminal justice system. Most victims have limited knowledge of the law, which can make court proceedings all the more concerning. This complex system of confusing rules and procedures often contributes to the victims' burden instead of providing ease and direction in a time of sorrow.

I have described the scene of going with my family to my son's gravesite for the unveiling of his tombstone, an event that took place April 2015. I had been to the cemetery numerous times between 2015 and 2019 and participated in the annual Yahrzeit memorial of my son's death. However, in 2019, the preparation of the victim impact statements reopened every pain and wound from the murder. Although this is often a legal requirement prior to trial, it is a tremendous burden on the victim.

These statements give the victims the opportunity to inform the court of their emotional damage and to demonstrate their suffering. The impact statement also gave our family the opportunity to tell the jury how special Dan was. This preparation brought out the pain of old wounds, and the depths of my grief made me unsettled again. It was a very emotional experience because it brought me back to my intense heartbroken feelings over the loss of Dan.

Shelly, Phil, and I were each asked to write two "victim impact statements" to read in front of the court, one for the main trial and one for the death penalty phase, should Garcia be found guilty. Composing these documents was a traumatic undertaking; I had to bring the more excruciating memories to the surface to ensure the jury understood our loss. "I had been forced to experience the unthinkable and to live a life filled with unimaginable pain and heartbreak that no mother should ever have to endure," I wrote.

The victim impact statement dealt with the shooting and the murder, the defendant, the courts, and the trial process. This experience only added to the unwanted and unfamiliar ways of trial life.

Although this was a new and unpleasant experience, we were well supported with information from Helene Potlock. On April 30, 2019, she wrote:

> *Let's focus first on writing your victim impact statements. As we discussed on the phone, there are 2 types of victim impact statements. In our Victim's Rights Statutes under FS 921, every victim (or next of kin) of crime has the right to be heard before the imposition of sentencing. I have attached that statute for you as well as an informational handout with a sample letter to help you get started. The parameters are very pretty broad here about what you may include in these statements. You should prepare one statement for Garcia's sentencing and one for Magbanua's sentencing. Other family, friends, and colleagues of Dan may also submit written statements to me prior to May 30. I would then make copies for the State and the Defense and submit a packet of the originals to Judge Hankinson on May 31 so that he has time to review them before sentencing. At the sentencing hearing, your family can either read your statement to the judge yourself, ask me to read it for you or submit it in writing. But we try to*

limit the number of statements read aloud to immediate family and sometimes close friends.

I have also attached some information about writing a victim impact statement in a death penalty case. This would only apply to Garcia's case. You will see the difference in the language for a victim impact statement that is presented to a jury during the penalty phase of the trial. The statute I attached talks about how your statement must be limited to Dan's uniqueness in the community and the resulting loss to the community as a result of his death. This statement must be written and submitted to me by the first week in June. I will then have our General Counsel Eddie Evans review it before it is presented to the jury.

We are limited in the number of statements we present during the death penalty phase so I would like you to work on one or two statements from your family and one or two from close friends or co-workers of Dan.

Then we can talk about whether you will read it to the jury or if you would like me to do so.

Feel free to let me know if you have any other questions. My first phone meeting with you will be on Monday, May 6 so we can talk more then too.

We received further preparation from Helene on understanding the penalty phase as follows:

Understanding the Penalty Phase in Death Penalty Case

After the Guilt Phase of the trial has been completed and the Jury of 12 has unanimously voted to convict the Defendant of the crime of First-Degree Murder, then the court will usually take a short recess of one-half day to one full day before starting the Penalty Phase of the trial.

During the Penalty Phase, the jury first hears Opening Statements from both the State and the Defense. The State's presentation of evidence must focus on the Aggravating factors in the case. Florida Statutes define a limited number of Aggravating factors that must exist before the State may seek the death penalty. Aggravating Factors include that the homicide was committed in a cold, calculating and premediated way; or that the homicide was heinous, atrocious or cruel; or that the homicide was committed for Pecuniary (monetary) gain to name a few. The State may call witnesses to testify to prove each Aggravating Factor that exists in the case and/or rely on testimony presented during the trial.

The State may also introduce Victim Impact evidence to the Jury regarding the victim's uniqueness and the resulting loss to the community. This is done by family or friends (or the victim advocate) reading a prepared statement to the jury from the witness stand.

The Defense is then allowed to argue and present evidence about any Mitigating factors that exist. They are not limited by statute and may argue anything they believe is relevant, which may include a Defendant's family history, substance abuse history, and mental health history among other things.

The attorneys will then give their closing arguments to the jury, and the jury will retire to deliberate a second time. The Jury must be unanimous in deciding what if any Aggravating Factors the State has proven beyond a reasonable doubt. They must then be unanimous in their recommendation for the Death Penalty. If all 12 jurors do not agree to recommend the Death Penalty, then their recommendation must be life in prison.

Once they deliver their recommendation, the jurors are excused from service. The case is then scheduled for a Spencer Hearing in roughly 30 days. At the Spencer Hearing, the Defense may submit any additional argument or documents in mitigation for the judge to take into consideration before imposing the sentence. The court will then schedule a Sentencing hearing Date 2-4 weeks after the Spencer Hearing.

At the sentencing hearing, Victim Impact Statements may be presented before the judge imposes sentence. The Victim Impact Statement is presented to the Judge, not to the defendant. The statement can include the victim's feelings regarding sentencing in addition to the impact on their lives. The impact can be discussed on more personal terms. Unlike the Penalty Phase statement presented to the jury which focuses on the loss to the community, this statement can focus on your loss and how your life has changed since your loved one's death.

After the judge imposes the sentence, the defendant will automatically file an appeal within 30 days of the sentencing.

April to early May of 2019 was a very tense period as there were numerous attempts by defense lawyers to postpone the trial. On May 6, 2019, our lawyers from Gibson Dunn wrote Cappleman as follows:

GIBSON DUNN

Gibson, Dunn & Crutcher LLP

200 Park Avenue
New York, NY 10166-0193
Tel 212.351.4000
www.gibsondunn.com

Orin Snyder
Direct: +1 212.351.2400
Fax: +1 212.351.6335
OSnyder@gibsondunn.com

Client: 62527-00001

May 6, 2019

<u>VIA E-MAIL</u>

Georgia Cappleman
Assistant State Attorney
Office of the State Attorney
Second Judicial Circuit
301 S. Monroe Street
Tallahassee, FL 32301

Re: *State of Florida v. Sigfredo Garcia*, No. 16-CF-1581

Dear Assistant State Attorney Cappleman:

I represent the family of Dan Markel—his mother Ruth, his father Phil, and his sister Shelly. On behalf of the Markel Family, I write to respectfully oppose any further continuances in this matter.

It has been nearly five years since Dan Markel was brutally murdered outside of his home. After years of repeated delays and adjournments, trial is now scheduled to begin on June 3, 2019. On April 30, defense counsel Mr. Zangeneh filed his latest motion for a continuance, on the grounds that he is required to care for his pregnant girlfriend. While the Markel Family appreciates that Mr. Zangeneh is expecting the birth of a child in July—an event he has presumably been aware of since late 2018, yet conspicuously has never mentioned in connection with prior requests for a continuance—we are compelled to respectfully oppose any further adjournments.

At this late date, nearly five years after Dan's murder and more than two and a half years since indictment, further delay would cause the Markel Family significant additional pain and anguish, and would not be in the interests of justice. *See Martel v. Clair*, 565 U.S. 648, 662 (2012) ("Protecting against abusive delay is an interest of justice."). The Markels have suffered unfathomable grief and loss. They continue to suffer, some in declining health, each and every passing day. Of course, no trial or verdict could ever heal the profound wounds caused by Dan's brutal murder. Maintaining the current trial schedule would begin to provide, however, the closure and justice that the Markels deserve. As your Office and the Court well knows, justice delayed is justice denied. The interests of both the Markel Family, as victims of this heinous crime, and the public compel the denial of any further requests for continuance.

Beijing • Brussels • Century City • Dallas • Denver • Dubai • Frankfurt • Hong Kong • Houston • London • Los Angeles • Munich
New York • Orange County • Palo Alto • Paris • San Francisco • São Paulo • Singapore • Washington, D.C.

GIBSON DUNN

Georgia Cappleman
May 6, 2019
Page 2

We believe it is important that the Court hear the family's concerns before ruling on the pending defense motion, and therefore respectfully ask that you provide a copy of this letter to the Court.

Sincerely,

Orin Snyder

Our task became more complicated because we had to write the victim impact statement for Magbanua and Garcia's joint trial. We were told we would have to wait for their sentencing and then enter another, separate, hearing for the death penalty phase.

The victim impact statement should talk about and emphasize the victim's uniqueness, and Dan was surely unique. Nevertheless, I strongly disliked this process and still felt very vulnerable, even with all the support.

Our plan was to work with our lawyers to review our statements. Simultaneously, to our personal writing, Gibson Dunn embarked on a major endeavour with our family. We provided numerous names of Dan's family, friends, and colleagues from around the world who were all invited to submit a victim impact statement.

The summer of 2019 was very busy, as July 19 was the fifth anniversary of Dan's murder. By July 10, we started writing drafts of family statements and had them finalized with Gibson Dunn for the release on July 19 as follows:

> Dan Markel was a light in the world. Five years ago, Dan was murdered in cold blood outside his home—only hours after saying goodbye to his two young boys for what would be the last time. Five

years later, his friends and family are still waiting for all of his killers to be brought to justice.

The Markels used to travel to Tallahassee to visit Dan and the boys at home—to visit their preschool, to play in the park, to attend music programs. Now, as they prepare to return to Tallahassee for the trial of some of Dan's alleged killers, they will be forced to re-live the nightmare of Dan's murder all over again. The Markels continue to be grateful for the support of the Tallahassee community and the efforts of law enforcement, and they are counting down the days until justice is done. More than anything, the Markel's want to reunite with their beloved grandsons—Dan's young boys—whom they have not been allowed to see in more than three years.

By midsummer of 2019, I submitted my final draft and pushed to get it approved before the September trials. I wanted to have this task out of the way, so I could focus my energy solely on the trials.

There were two victim impact statements required for the trials in 2019. One is intended for a death penalty eligible conviction:

Dear Judge Hankinson:

My name is Ruth Markel. I am Dan Markel's mother. Parents are not supposed to outlive their children; a mother should never have to bury her own child—perhaps this is why there are words to describe someone who loses a spouse or their parents (widow/orphan), but there is no word in the English language for someone who loses a child. And yet because of the terrible, heinous acts of a few, my son Daniel's life was cut very short, and I have been forced to experience the unthinkable and to live a life filled with unimaginable pain and heartbreak that no mother should ever have to endure.

As the letters that this Court has received from Dan's family, friends, colleagues, mentors, and others reflect, Dan was a loving, caring, uplifting, and inspiring person to everyone around him. Dan was a devoted son and family member, cherishing family celebrations and always making time for lengthy phone calls with me and other family members in Canada, United States, and Israel. As my son, everything about Dan and everything he did made me proud—from his love of music, dance, sports, and travel to his dedication to and hard work in school, culminating in his acceptance into Harvard University, where he studied politics and philosophy as an undergraduate, the Hebrew University of Jerusalem, and Emmanuel College in Cambridge, where he earned a master's degree in political theory, and finally Harvard Law School, where he received his J.D. and began his impressive legal career. After graduating law school, Dan served as a law clerk for a deferral circuit court judge and then worked as an associate at a prestigious law firm in Washington, D.C. Dan then began what proved to be a successful career in academia, becoming a professor of law and landing a coveted teaching position at a top U.S. law school right here in Florida—FSU College of Law.

Of all of my son's accomplishments, however, I am most proud of the father Dan was to his two beautiful boys, Lincoln and Ben. It is hard to capture in words the joy and excitement I felt when Dan became a father and I became a grandmother. I derived even more joy and happiness watching Dan raise his two sons. Dan was a present, devoted, loving, supportive, and selfless father, and he always acted with his sons' best interests in mind. Dan regularly attended the boys' daycare, leading holiday programs for all the children. Dan's office and home were covered with the boys' drawings and the family's living room was always full of the boys' toys. Regardless of the situation, Dan always put his children's safety and well-being ahead of his own. Lincoln and Ben loved their father; he was their hero.

Dan offered the world his love, his wisdom and opinion, his energy, his friendship, and his warmth. Since the day he was born, Dan was alert and energetic. He did not waste this energy—he used it to live life to the fullest. For example, even in his short life, he pursued his passion for travel, and lived in many cities, including Montreal, Toronto, Boston, New York, London, Jerusalem, Washington, D.C., Phoenix, San Francisco, Miami, and Tallahassee. He made meaningful connections with people wherever he went. He made friends all over the world and continued to stay in touch with everyone he befriended. When Dan moved to Tallahassee, he quickly became an integral part of the community. Dan made many close friends at FSU and in the broader Tallahassee community. He regularly attended community events and frequently hosted others at his home. Dan was on the board of the Shomrei Torah synagogue and frequently attended services, holiday and children's programs. He was also involved with the Chabad community.

Dan's murder has not only deprived his large network and community of a dedicated and caring family member and friend, but it has also deprived the world of a brilliant attorney, teacher, and legal academic. Dan was a prolific scholar in the areas of criminal law and punishment and published a book on the intersection between criminal justice and family, numerous articles in the nation's leading law reviews, and opinion pieces for The New York Times, Slate, and the Atlantic, among other publications. Dan's scholarship on retribution in criminal law and sentencing was highly influential and is still widely read and cited today. Dan also co-founded a blog, PrawfsBlawg, which focuses on a variety of topics related to law and life. Due to Dan's amazing dedication and tireless work, PrawfsBlawg continues to grow and inspire legal scholars and students around the world. In addition to his scholarship, Dan was a devoted professor who was deeply involved in the FSU community. Dan was passionate about teaching and his students adored him—after his death over 200 students from FSU attended his memorial service. Dan served on the law school's recruiting committee and worked to recruit high-level academics to FSU, including by personally hosting many of the recruits and new faculty members. Dan's energy, drive, and sociability enhanced both the student body and faculty of the FSU College of Law.

As the Court knows, Dan's life was brought to a sudden, abrupt, and tragic end when he was murdered in July 2014. The losses sustained and the damage caused by this crime cannot be overstated. In one fell swoop, my son, a brother, and the father of two young boys were all killed. My life was shattered. Dan's pain has caused me a deep pain that is both disruptive and permanent. After the death of a loved one, you are supposed to face the loss, the void, experience the grief, and maybe get closure if you are lucky. But when you lose a child, life's progression comes to a complete stop and the grief and pain of a mother who loses her child never ends. For me, closure and normalcy are only words in a dictionary, not a reality that I will ever experience again. I have waited more than five years for those involved in Dan's murder to be brought to justice, which has only exacerbated my pain, grief, anxiety, and health. It is very cumbersome to navigate and participate in the legal processes encountered in the days, weeks and years following the murder. From the day I learned about Dan's death I experienced a Life Sentence. But I know that even after justice occurs, Dan's murder will continue to torment me for the rest of my life.

Our lives were destroyed as well. The lives of Dan's two sons, my grandchildren, were forever turned upside down as a result of this crime. Benjamin was three years old, and Lincoln was only two years old when their father was murdered. Benjamin and Lincoln have been forever deprived of a relationship with their father. These boys have also been robbed of their childhoods as they were forced to confront and try to understand the heinous and unthinkable crime of murder at such a young age.

My life as a grandmother was yanked away from me. My relationship with my grandsons has been put in serious jeopardy—despite my requests and unrelenting efforts to maintain a relationship with them, I have been denied any and all visits with Lincoln and Ben for the past three plus years, and direct lines of communication between me and them have been blocked. In fact, Lincoln and Ben have been completely cut off from their father's entire family. This situation has only added to the pain and suffering my family and I have gone through since the day of Dan's death. My daughter, Shelly, and her husband, Ian, have also been traumatized by Dan's tragic death and the simultaneous loss of any contact with their nephews. Dan's nieces and nephews, ranging from ages eight to thirteen, were forced to confront murder at a young age. Dan's older relatives could not comprehend this tragedy. My maternal 97-year-old uncle had a special bond with Dan and suffered greatly from Dan's murder. He gave up and died only three months after Dan was murdered. Of course, there are many more individuals not named here whose lives were devastated as a result of this crime.

Respectfully,
Ruth Markel

The second victim impact statement is written for what is called a non–death penalty eligible conviction:

Dear Judge Hankinson:

My name is Ruth Markel. I am Dan Markel's mother. Parents are not supposed to outlive their children; a mother should never have to bury her own child—perhaps this is why there are words to describe someone who loses a spouse or their parents (widow/orphan), but there is no word in the English language for someone who loses a child. And yet because of the terrible, heinous acts of a few, including the Defendants in this case, my son Daniel's life was cut very short, and I have been forced to experience the unthinkable and to live a life filled with unimaginable pain and heartbreak that no mother should ever have to endure. I would not wish such pain and heartbreak on Ms. Magbanua or Mr. Garcia, or anyone else who may have had a hand in my son's murder.

This was a particularly heinous and senseless crime—murder is the worst, most serious crime a person can commit. The crime in this case was all the more tragic because an innocent, good person was murdered in cold blood. The murder was not revenge for or related to some other crime, nor was it a sad but predictable event that could happen to someone living a life of crime. Dan was never involved in any criminal activity and did not put himself in dangerous situations or live recklessly. Dan was instead an upright, thoughtful citizen and a devoted father and loving son, who lived a law-abiding and productive life dedicated to teaching and helping others.

As the letters that this Court has received from Dan's family, friends, colleagues, mentors, and others reflect, Dan was a loving, caring, uplifting, and inspiring person to everyone around him. Dan was a devoted son and family member, cherishing family celebrations and always making time for lengthy phone calls with me and other family members in Canada, United States, and Israel. As my son, everything about Dan and everything he did made me proud—from his love of music, dance, sports, and travel to his dedication to and hard work in school, culminating in his acceptances into Harvard University, where he studied politics and philosophy as an undergraduate, the Hebrew University of Jerusalem, and Emmanuel College in Cambridge, where he earned a master's degree in political theory, and finally Harvard Law School, where he received his J.D. and began his impressive legal career. After graduating law school, Dan served as a law clerk for a federal circuit court judge and then worked as an associate at a prestigious law firm in Washington, D.C. Dan then began what proved to be a successful career in academia, becoming a professor of law and landing a coveted teaching position at a top U.S. law school right here in Florida—FSU College of Law.

Of all of my son's accomplishments, however, I am most proud of the father Dan was to his two beautiful boys, Lincoln and Ben. It is hard to capture in words the joy and excitement I felt when Dan, our son, became a father and I became a grandmother. I derived even more joy and happiness watching Dan raise his two sons. Dan was a present, devoted, loving, supportive, selfless father, and he always acted with his sons' best interests in mind. Dan regularly attended the boys' daycare, leading holiday programs for all the children. Dan's office and home were covered with the boys' drawings and the family's living room was always full of the boys' toys. Regardless of the situation, Dan always put his children's safety and well-being ahead of his own. Lincoln and Ben loved their father; he was their hero.

Dan offered the world his love, his wisdom and opinion, his energy, his friendship, and his warmth. Since the day he was born, Dan was alert and energetic. He did not waste this energy—he used it to live life to the fullest. For example, even in his short life, he pursued his passion for travel, and lived in many cities, including Montreal, Toronto, Boston, New York, London, Jerusalem, Washington, D.C., Phoenix, San Francisco, Miami, and Tallahassee. He made meaningful connections with people wherever he went. He made friends all over the world and continued to stay in touch with everyone he befriended. When Dan moved to Tallahassee, he quickly became an integral part of the community. Dan made many close friends at FSU and in the broader Tallahassee community. He regularly attended community events and frequently hosted others at his home. Dan was on the board of the Shomrei Torah synagogue and regularly attended services and holiday and children's programs. He was also involved with the Chabad community.

Dan's murder has not only deprived his large network and community of a dedicated and caring family member and friend, it has also deprived the world of a brilliant attorney, teacher, and legal academic. Dan was a prolific scholar in the areas of criminal law and punishment and published a book on the intersection between criminal justice and family, numerous articles in the nation's leading law reviews, and opinion pieces for The New York Times, Slate, *and the* Atlantic, *among other publications. Dan's scholarship on retribution in criminal law and sentencing was highly influential and is still widely read and cited today. Dan also co-founded a blog, PrawfsBlawg, which focuses on a variety of topics related to law and life. Due to Dan's amazing dedication and tireless work, PrawfsBlawg continues to grow and inspire legal scholars and students around the world. In addition to his scholarship, Dan was a devoted professor who was deeply involved in the FSU community. Dan was passionate about teaching and his students adored him—after his death over 200 students from FSU attended his memorial service. Dan served on the law school's recruiting committee and worked to recruit high-level academics to FSU, including by personally hosting many of the recruits and new faculty members. Dan's energy, drive, and sociability enhanced both the student body and faculty of the FSU College of Law.*

As the Court knows, Dan's life was brought to a sudden, abrupt, and tragic end when he was murdered in July 2014. The losses sustained and the damage caused by this crime cannot be overstated. In one fell swoop, my son, a brother, and the father of two young boys were all killed. My life was shattered. Dan's murder has caused me a deep pain that is both disruptive and permanent. After the death of a loved one, you are supposed to face the loss, the void, experience the grief, and maybe get closure if you are lucky. But when you lose a child, life's progression comes to a complete stop, and the grief and pain of a mother who loses her child never ends. For me, closure and normalcy are only words in a dictionary, not a reality that I will ever experience again. I have waited more than five years for those involved in Dan's murder to be brought to justice, which has only exacerbated my pain, grief, anxiety, and health. It is very cumbersome to navigate and participate in the legal processes encountered in the days, weeks and years following the murder. From the day I learned about Dan's death I experienced a Life Sentence. But I know that even after justice occurs, Dan's murder will continue to torment me for the rest of my life.

Other lives were destroyed as well. The lives of Dan's two sons, my grandchildren, were forever turned upside down as a result of this crime. Benjamin was three years old, and Lincoln was only two years old when their father was murdered. Benjamin and Lincoln have been forever deprived of a relationship with their father and will grow up and go through life without a father. These boys have also been robbed of their childhoods as they were forced to confront and try to understand the heinous and unthinkable crime of murder at such a young age.

My life as a grandmother was yanked away from me. My relationship with my grandsons has been put in serious jeopardy—despite my requests and unrelenting efforts to maintain a relationship with them, I have been denied any and all visits with Lincoln and Ben for the past three-plus years, and direct lines of communication between me and them have been blocked. In fact, Lincoln and Ben have been completely cut off from their father's entire family. This situation has only added to the pain and suffering my family and I have gone through since the day of Dan's death. My daughter, Shelly, and her husband,, Ian, have also been traumatized by Dan's tragic death and the simultaneous loss of any contact with their nephews. Dan's nieces and nephews, ranging from ages eight to thirteen, were forced to confront murder at a young age. Dan's older relatives could not comprehend this tragedy. My maternal 97-year-old uncle had a special bond with Dan and suffered greatly from Dan's murder. He gave up and died only three months after Dan was murdered. Of course, there are many more individuals not named here whose lives were devastated as a result of this crime.

While still processing and reeling from the catastrophic effects of this devastating loss, my family and I nevertheless appreciated the importance of and made it a priority to respect and to fully cooperate with and provide any assistance we could to the law enforcement officers and the prosecutors handling this case. We patiently waited as this case wound its way through the criminal justice system. While no trial or verdict can ever heal the profound wounds caused by Dan's brutal murder, the time has finally come for the Court to impose sentences on and to bring to a close the cases against Mr. Garcia and Ms. Magbanua. Based on the seriousness of the crime, Defendants' lack of cooperation throughout the case, and Defendants' limited remorse, we believe that justice requires and that the Court should therefore impose a significant sentence on each Defendant.

Respectfully,
Ruth Markel

Our lawyers at Gibson Dunn were very successful in organizing numerous victim impact statements from our extended family and Dan's friends and colleagues, which were all prepared and submitted on October 10, 2019.

Introduction to the Trials

We headed into our period of waiting after the marathon of the arrests.

We endured this arduous waiting period from the arrests until the settings of trial dates. After Garcia's Arthur Hearing in Florida, which is a bond hearing for very serious felony offenses, the outcome relied on the decision of the judge. For Garcia, the decision was for him to be held without bond in Leon County Jail. Garcia's lawyer at the time, Jim Lewis, said, "It looks like a weak case." The judge clearly disagreed, because Garcia was not offered bond. He was still charged and would face a life sentence and the death penalty if convicted.

Evidence presented in this Arthur Hearing again relayed what we had learned about the State's evidence against Garcia: details about the Toyota Prius in the garage where Dan was shot, the same car that followed Dan to his sons' daycare and the gym, and later went to a motel in Tallahassee. The shooting was not seen as a random act, and investigators established that the car was rented from a North Miami rental car agency, Hybrid Auto Rental Center, and driven to Tallahassee. There was a record from the SunPass electronic toll collection and security camera footage from surrounding buildings and city buses to prove where Garcia had been. The cell phone location was also a key finding included in the evidence for the trial.

Dan was well known for holding an anti–death penalty position in his scholarly writing and on *PrawfsBlawg*, the blog that Dan cofounded in 2005, which had an international network. At the FSU memorial, one of his previous students commented, "What would Prof. Markel say now?" referring to the death penalty.

In late 2014, this was a hypothetical question for our family. In 2016, it became very real.

The Adelson family denied involvement in the murder by any family member. According to a statement issued by their lawyers, "none of the Adelsons—Wendi, her brother Charlie, or their parents Donna and Harvey—had anything to do with Dan's murder."[8] Through their lawyers, they called any insinuation of their family's involvement to be "fanciful fiction."

The media had their first big TV production on September 16, 2016, when ABC News aired "In-Laws and Outlaws," a *20/20* episode based on the murder investigation. The story of my son, the murdered attorney and legal academic, was all over international television news coverage, print media, and social media.

The 2018 developments were even more disappointing. After the previously mentioned delays, the trial of Garcia and Magbanua was scheduled for October 2018. In September 2018, only a month before the trial, there was another delay until 2019.

Waiting for the wheels of justice to grind is wearing. During this period, the defendant's pictures and fingerprints are taken, and their experience of accountability begins. For the victims, this stage has a quite different feel and look. The victims are lost.

To begin, I will describe my experience during the waiting period. I had a full array of players in my world, such as law enforcement officials, who provided support with significant escort protection and criminal information.

---

8 Curt Anderson, "Ex-Wife of Slain Florida Law Professor Denies Role in Death," Associated Press, August 3, 2016, https://apnews.com/article/146781db9a3c49a3b48ba4f372972f3b.

This is what it is like to live a life sentence. Waiting is the biggest part of that profile, filled with uncertainty, angst, powerlessness, suffering, and trauma.

As mentioned previously, I was concerned that Benjamin and Lincoln could be at risk should the police arrive to take members of their maternal family into custody. Certainly, the regrettable release of my JAFCO memo to the defense attorney further complicated matters.

During the post-arrest period, along with the numerous preparations and dates for hearings, I visited the Fort Lauderdale area for my winter break, as I always had. The strain of being in Florida and not seeing my grandchildren, who were only miles away, was horrible.

Luckily, I was able to visit JAFCO and their amazing grounds and programs while there. For their emergency services, they had several children's beds adjunct to a daycare facility. The staff, specifically Sarah Franco, the executive director, and Wendy Jenkins, the clinical director, were very compassionate and attentive. It was a relief to know that my concerns for Benjamin and Lincoln landed on very responsible leadership in this desperate situation.

* * *

It was during this time that I resolved I would not allow myself to become accustomed to not seeing my grandchildren in Florida. The situation was unacceptable, and I refused to accept it as a fact of life. The pursuit of visitation with my grandsons propelled me at the same time as my quest for justice for Dan's murder.

This journey is self-motivated but is also driven by a feeling of responsibility to Dan, to ensure we tried everything possible to ensure Dan's family remained connected to Benjamin and Lincoln since his murder and did not just accept it when Wendi cut off contact. This quest for justice will be a continuous mission in my life.

We had regularly sent presents and cards for the boys' birthdays and Hanukkah. We also send Valentines and Halloween cards to the boys, but we are not sure if they are received.

I recall an earlier visit with Benjamin and Lincoln, prior to the arrests, when I brought them some of Dan's childhood treasures, specifically two of his freshly washed toddler blankets. I asked Wendi,

"How do you want me to handle the blankets?" She responded with, "Give them to the boys yourself." I did. Wendi stayed in the kitchen as I brought Benjamin Dan's blanket. He clung to it—it was very meaningful for me and brought tears to my eyes. Benjamin had not had a chance to express how deep his grief was, it seemed, as his response was profound and intense. Lincoln's response was appreciative. He placed the blanket on the bed with his stuffed animals and gave me a big hug.

To my disappointment, on my next visit a few weeks later, the blankets were gone—and I never saw them again on my later visits.

This disheartening situation left a permanent fear in me that our grandchildren might feel that we abandoned them. We had no idea what they were told by their mother or her parents, if anything at all. There would be no concrete evidence or memories about how we continuously tried to contact them. I was determined to make sure that could never be so.

There are several TV shows today that highlight dramatic reunions of families. We are ready for our reunion and will be prepared with records of our attempts through TV appearances, media interviews, legislative advocacy, and of course, this book.

My mantra to never give up and my determination always propel me to continue to the next steps.

Florida grandparent visitation laws feel like the Dark Ages compared to other American states and Canada. Much explanation is needed for people to comprehend the limited opportunity for grandparent visits in the state of Florida. Most people, including Dan's legal friends, find these laws draconian.

Nevertheless, there is strong opposition to making changes to the status quo, and powerful lobby groups work to block challenges to the strong natural parental rights of autonomy and privacy.

As my life story unfolds—a life story I now call "trauma and gifts"—I am continuously grateful to all our legal friends, Matt Benjamin from Gibson Dunn, and his wife, who suggested I consider initiating legislation to challenge the law. Other American friends have also suggested that lobbyists are the way to go.

Even before we embarked formally on these efforts, Dan's friend Jason Solomon started a Facebook page, Justice for Dan, which at that time was still in its embryotic phase and has grown significantly over the years. Jason boldly started an online petition and encouraged/invited people to sign, imploring Wendi to provide us with the opportunity to visit our grandchildren in Florida. There were more than a thousand signatures and a beautiful response that included many Canadian family members as well as friends and followers around the globe.

Nevertheless, Wendi continued to refuse us access to the boys.

Justice for Dan, this action-oriented platform, continued to monitor and share numerous other case developments. Websleuths and other social media platforms have kept comments flowing on the absence of our ability to see our grandchildren. We continue to receive many supportive comments to this day. People are stunned and appalled by this situation, as shown by words like these:

> "Thinking of you, Ruth Markel. Praying that justice is served and you are reunited with your grandchildren."
>
> "I was in college with Dan and think of your family often. I hope you will be able to be reunited with your grandchildren soon and that justice will be served."

Previously, my family had chosen a low profile on traditional media. We certainly broke our silence when the visitation restrictions to Benjamin and Lincoln were imposed upon us.

Transition to the Trials

During the pretrial waiting period, I thought often about the various "costs" of murder. For one, there were the financial costs as a result of Dan's murder, detailing the types of expenses that the families of crime victims face. Attorneys, therapists, travel, and time away from work all add up. Then there is the emotional toll, which is even harder than the tangible financial costs and affects family members in varied and challenging ways.

For example, Shelly, who is as focused on Dan's case as I am, feels that she has to take care of my needs as well—and conversely, I worry that no one is taking care of her. There is also the cost of good health—as mentioned, I developed atrial fibrillation after I learned that I could no longer see my grandsons. And there's the cost of lost time, not only the time you can never recover to spend with your loved ones, but also time with family members and friends, enjoying the normal connections of your social and emotional life.

When you are immersed in a case, sometimes it's hard to concentrate on other parts of life that seem extraneous, but then you miss what passes you by. You "get a life," as in you get to go on with living in the difficult times. These expressions, such as "move on," "leave it behind you," and "close the door on the situation," do not apply. It is incredibly stressful during the pretrial waiting with continuous postponements. The long delays are not just measured in months, but years.

Before the trial began, we were involved in a variety of hearings, subpoenas, and motions. We welcomed the activity after waiting for so long to get started, but the delays were not over; before the jury had been empaneled, the trial date would once again be changed. Then it was set again, and again. It was nerve wracking to wait and learn who had been assigned as the judge presiding over the murder trial and even more stressful to wait for the selection of the jury that would be making critical evaluations of the case.

The judge assigned to the trials, James C. Hankinson, was a tough jurist who had presided over many difficult criminal cases during his time on the bench in Tallahassee. The prosecutors and the defense attorneys had great respect for Judge Hankinson, having argued a variety of cases before him over the years. It was comforting to learn that he had a reputation for being fair and had put away his share of murderers.

While we were waiting, we sent information that we thought would be helpful to the TPD and the FBI. We managed the press, and as much as possible, we were polite.

During the pretrial discovery, many more truths came to light. Magbanua was a top phone contact on Charlie Adelson's phone, and she had been driving around Miami in Harvey Adelson's Lexus.

Wendi contacted me right before the trial of 2019, which did not feel like a coincidence given that she was scheduled to appear as a witness in September. During our conversation, I suggested she call Sarah Franco from JAFCO who could further affirm what my communications with their organization had been about. The following is an email I sent Wendi on July 25, 2019:

Hi Wendi,

I am glad we had a chance to talk.

Below is an automatic reply from Sara Franco.

I will also write her tonight with your phone number.

Thanks,

Ruth

We knew that Wendi was a witness at the scheduled September trial and then in August 2019, and sure enough, Wendi made contact with me via email. One of the most successful English TV shows is called *Keeping Up Appearances*, which is an apt description of Wendi's sudden interest in communicating with our family. She hinted that there could be more opportunity for us to create contact.

Hopeful for a breakthrough, I ventured into a pretrial phone call with her. Wendi told me she had a scripted message, which she read to me on the phone. We did receive a picture of Benjamin and Lincoln going to school in August. I was happy to see how they were growing up, as May 2016 was the last time I had seen them.

Wendi behaved as though she wanted to make amends with us by offering to send videos of the boys, but only if we told Dan's friends and strangers to stop harassing her and making her life difficult. This was in reference to friends and their allies creating an uproar because, while keeping her own children alienated from their father's family, Wendi had been working for an organization involved in humanitarian causes, including advocacy to stop separating undocumented children from their families at the border. Some of Dan's friends and strangers questioned why someone who wouldn't let her children see their grandparents should be considered credible to help other families reunite. Wendi emailed us stating that we were hurting her professionally and personally, which she said also affected the boys' lives.

Wendi's invitation to be in contact, however, was not an offer for real contact. She suggested that we could exchange recorded messages and videos. There was no opportunity for direct contact by Skype or FaceTime. In other words, Wendi did not suggest that we have actual, real-time communication with the boys, which meant that her offer gave us zero assurance that the boys would hear or see our messages at all. And this restricted offer was only words anyway, as she rescinded it immediately after she appeared as a witness in the September 2019 trial for Garcia and Magbanua.

Our assumption was validated that Wendi just wanted to be able to tell the jury and the public at large that she was in contact with us and making an effort to reconnect but had no actual intention to do so.

In fact, it got worse. Previously, Wendi had acknowledged the arrival of gifts we sent for the boys for their birthdays and Hanukkah. Amazon would deliver the gifts, and I'd ask Wendi by email if the gifts arrived. She would answer "yes." On October 13, 2019, Lincoln's birthday (one day after mine), the trial had ended, and there was nothing further from Wendi.

It would be well over two years before we had any responses from or contact with her. During that time, we did not receive any notes of thanks for birthday and Hanukkah gifts, and so more time went by without communication with our grandsons.

CHAPTER 6

Trial Life in Tallahassee

Courtroom Life

Initially, some questioned whether the trial would need to be held outside of Tallahassee because of how many people knew about the case locally. Luckily, the jury selection wasn't as difficult as expected. Considering the amount of press there was about the case, there had been some concern it would be hard to find jurors who were not already deeply familiar with the case, or to find individuals without prior relationships with Dan, Wendi, or any of the lawyers involved. As it turns out, Tallahassee may be a bit larger than its reputation suggests, and finding impartial jurors went smoothly.

Cappleman asked potential jurors about their ability to evaluate evidence and their attitude toward its collection. "In the course of this trial you may learn there are other folks who aren't these two who have some culpability. Is there anything unfair about law enforcement conducting an undercover operation?" Cappleman asked.

The judge told the potential jurors that the case should last about four weeks and that they would not be sequestered. I watched Judge Hankinson's communications with the attorneys, witnesses, and jury, along with relevant sidebars, rulings on evidence, and verdicts on contempt of court, with interest.

The opening argument and early trial days were attended by Matt Benjamin and Sarah Kushner from Gibson Dunn. This was a blessing for us because they provided further explanations and a map of what was yet to come.

We were given the roster of witnesses by Helene Potlock, who as a victim advocate was particularly sensitive to my desire to avoid being exposed to some of the more terrible images of Danny's murder. Because of this, I chose not to attend the first afternoon, which dealt with the police and medical murder scene. I stayed in the hotel to avoid the horrid details of the first hours after the murder. But Phil and Shelly attended.

Every gesture, comment, and facial expression you make as the family of the victim in court is scrutinized. You learn to avoid mistakes and to use the attention to your best advantage. Abe Anhang, my "murder coach," gave us the following advice:

> *By the way, you may not think it is important for you to sit in the front row of the visitor's gallery—not a waste of time! You have to be there since the members of the jury expect you there, and indeed want to see that you care as much as they do—remember, they are making less than minimum wage to sit there!*
>
> *Abe*

I was experiencing the day-to-day proceedings in Tallahassee's Leon County courthouse. At this point, I was fully immersed in the trial life and was learning to play by its rules and apply the newfound skills I acquired. With the help of Abe, our ever-growing network of advisors, and our victim support advocate, I picked up further valuable tips. We were advised to sit close to the front of the room but could only be in the fourth row behind the prosecutors' table, as the media took up the first three rows. We told several reporters that we would speak with them once the trial was over, so they were not chasing us during the trial.

We also came to understand how and when to react to evidence presented in court, because the jury wanted to see how the trial was affecting us. We were very fortunate to have the support of our friends Ricky Belman and Bailey Daniels. Phil's visitors included Max Haupt, Aaron Glassman, and Bruce MacDougall. Sometimes, they sat beside us; sometimes, they positioned themselves so that they could see the jury. They debriefed us with their opinions at the end of the day. Our experience was augmented by the friends who visited—we were not alone in this stressful period.

We discovered what not to say at the trial, even just in passing. We learned this lesson the hard way when one reporter asked Shelly her opinion about attending court during the High Holy Days, and she answered that it was hard to be there on Yom Kippur and that she wished the trial could have been suspended for that day, as the judge had been previously announced that it would be. This simple remark led to several stories on the local news, reporting that comment. We remembered to bring blankets in order to stay warm in the overly air-conditioned courtroom, and we knew to avoid eating from vending machines, as nutritious meals would give us strength for the hard days—days in which we had to face the accused killers of our son as well as a number of hostile witnesses who appeared to bolster their defense. This was our new normal. It was a surreal experience to see Garcia dressed in a suit and Magbanua wearing a professional-looking outfit with glasses.

As the testimony in court took several unexpected twists, I had more questions than answers. I could not believe that so many answers from certain witnesses were incomplete and untrue.

On prior occasions, Magbanua had been offered an immunity deal in exchange for information. But she'd turned it down. This surprised many, as Magbanua and Garcia had young children, and it was assumed that she would not want to risk a jail term. This added to our suspicions about who was paying for Magbanua's legal fees. Another bizarre strand of inquiry arose from an earlier finding that Katherine's sister-in-law, Samantha Magbanua, embezzled money from her job at an accounting firm, parking more than $600,000 with a Miami spiritual healer. In some of Samantha's court documents, Dan's murder case was mentioned, including reference to how Samantha said she had been aiding Katherine with legal fees.

Shelly, Phil, and I were ready to read our victim impact statements aloud, but at the last minute we were told that the judge only wanted to hear one of our statements, which I delivered. I was disappointed that our hard work had been put aside for the sake of expediency.

The case came to a conclusion after two weeks of testimony—two weeks filled with suspense, high tension, and much rapid learning. We longed to take a breath outside the building while the jury was out, but we had to stay close, as the court was reconvened for every question the jury asked. During the process of jury deliberations, jurors can ask for a meeting with the judge to clarify some of their issues. The jury asked repeated questions about the judge's instructions, especially his explanation of Magbanua's role, and whether she should be defined as a principal of the crime or a participant in the crime. As the jury sent out its requests, there were signs that the deliberations might be contentious, and it appeared that they were having trouble coming together in their opinions about her.

In the end, the jury found Sigfredo Garcia guilty of murder, but a mistrial was declared in the case of Katherine Magbanua. Polled after the verdict, it appeared that two of the jurors were confused by the judge's instructions and thought they couldn't convict Magbanua under the guidance they were given. Ten out of the twelve-person panel voted to convict her. Garcia looked grim as the sentences were read, and Magbanua started to cry. It seemed that she thought her testimony would exonerate her. Magbanua and her lawyer, Tara Kawass, were both in tears after the verdict.

Of course, the media had made informal requests to us at the trial and formal requests to Matt at Gibson Dunn for interviews. We just wanted to "hang in there" and wait until after the trial for the sentencing of Garcia and Magbanua. Updates on the ongoing trial and conclusion were shared simultaneously by Karl Etters and Jada E. Williams on Twitter. Websleuths and other media platforms were full of comments as well. There was no loss for words. The trial had garnered opinions from all over the world. For Dan Markel trial updates on Twitter, refer to the following links:

https://twitter.com/KarlEtters
https://twitter.com/JadaEWilliams

The period from May 2016 to September 2019 was a long haul, with many delays until justice was on the horizon. We wrestled with the prosecutor's decision to seek the death penalty for Dan's killers even though our son vehemently opposed the practice.

On the advice of Gibson Dunn attorneys, who wanted to seek the harshest possible punishment as a negotiating tool, the prosecutor had pressed for the death penalty for the killers. We felt the irony of this considering Dan's opposition to such sentencing. However, I was relieved that all three of us were invited to read our respective statements during the death penalty phase of the trial. When the jury handed Garcia a sentence of life in prison, not the death penalty, I was secretly comforted. It is what Dan would have wanted.

Garcia went to prison to begin serving his life sentence, and Rivera went back to federal prison. Our newest and most unexpected dilemma was the mistrial of Magbanua.

This mistrial was a major setback and left us at a standstill. With this situation, the justice outcome felt frozen in time. The stakes were high, and more waiting began. The trial of Magbanua and Garcia ended on Friday, October 11, 2019. The media was sitting in front of us, and we had said we would reserve comments until the trial finished. They were very respectful of our promise to comment. After the trial, they waited outside the courtroom, and Cappleman went out first to make her comments. When we came out of the courtroom, I kept my promise and addressed the reporters: "We respect the process. There is a lot more work to be done, and we are looking forward and hoping it will be done soon. We want to thank all of the law enforcement and the State Attorney's Office."

The outcome of the trial was as follows: the judge, James C. Hankinson, imposed a life sentence on Garcia and another thirty years for conspiracy to commit murder. Garcia's lawyer, Saam Zangeneh, said Garcia was "still numb from the conviction," and talked about the appeal process. "In a death penalty case, when you get a guilty on first degree murder, that's it. Your life is over," Zangeneh said. "You're either going to die of natural causes in a maximum-security prison, or you're going to die on death row as a result of lethal injection." He also mentioned that Garcia did not take the stand because "he didn't want to hurt Katie.... He was very concerned about his testimony hurting or implicating Katie."

But that's not all that Zangeneh said. After the trial, as well as in media interviews down the road, Zangeneh alluded to members of the Adelson family, saying that at least "three" others should be "quaking in their boots." When asked about this later, he affirmed that the three he was referring to were Donna, Charlie, and Wendi. Zangeneh made it clear that Garcia was opting not to cooperate based on what he believed was best for Magbanua—a generous act considering that her defense was complicit in the attack on Garcia for being guilty. In other words, Katherine's lawyers were clear during the trial, telling the jury that they believed Garcia had committed the murder, somehow having communicated directly with Charlie Adelson to do so. The dynamics between co-defendants are often complicated, and we learned that this is even more the case when the co-defendants have romantic connections and children together.

We had prepared post-trial family statements for convictions and for acquittals, but we had not prepared for a mistrial. We had to regroup as a family to see the retrial go forward, but the setback was hard to cope with and created tension within the family. Shelly, Phil, and I were quite exhausted from the trial, and we had to come up with another family statement. Thankfully, Shelly's husband, Ian, was there, and he made suggestions to keep us focused and complete the task in a timely manner.

Social media coverage of the verdicts blew up, as did the online commentary on sites such as YouTube and Court TV. We participated in a series of media interviews, still carefully keeping the focus solely on our forced separation from our grandchildren. The jury participated in post-trial interviews as well—and members revealed more about the split vote for Magbanua. It gave us hope that, with some clarification, there was a good possibility that a retrial would bring a better outcome for us. The main question still stood: *When will there be more arrests?*

* * *

October 12, 2019, my birthday, occurred in Tallahassee. My thoughts were already on the reality that I was in Florida and my American grandchildren, Benjamin and Lincoln, lived in that state. We were still cut off from seeing the grandchildren, even after we clarified with a statement from JAFCO that we had no intention of taking the children away from Wendi—only wanted to be assured that a plan was in place for what would happen to them if other family members were arrested.

This was a day after the verdicts but two days before sentencing. Garcia's death penalty trial would occur on Monday.

That weekend was used by our family for some reflecting and rebounding. It was a special weekend for me because Saturday was my seventy-fifth birthday.

I flashed back then to my birthday celebration just a few weeks prior to the trial in Toronto when I made a very meaningful birthday brunch. I knew that after the trial I would not have the strength or interest for a social event. I planned my birthday celebration with the purpose of thanking my friends and family for their support. I prepared two cakes—one with "Happy Birthday Ruth" and one with "Thank You" for all my guests. My talented Canadian grandchildren provided all the entertainment along with a digital photo display of different periods in my life. Shelly created a beautiful scrapbook in which the guests could contribute greetings and photos. I will always treasure this memory. I wanted a celebration to take place so I could share my gratitude for this special group. In essence, my life has been filled with trauma and gifts. These people were all my gifts.

Shelly and Ian had also had a big joint birthday celebration on Saturday, before my Sunday brunch. Even though the anxiety-producing trials were only a week away, we enjoyed a fabulous celebratory weekend.

At the time of my pre-birthday celebration, we all knew major stress and uncertainty were around the corner. This flashback was on my mind on my actual birthday, that Saturday in Tallahassee. It turned out to be a day I'd never forget.

An Unexpected Meeting

I often say that I am a hairdresser junkie, because wherever I travel, I find beauty salons in each city. The Tallahassee hairdresser scene was known to me as I had frequently visited Dan. So that was my birthday plan for October 12, 2019. As I walked into the hairdresser, Fuel Salon, there was a young woman who jumped out of her seat and asked, "Can I give you a hug?"

She introduced herself as Dan's acquaintance and member of Tallahassee's small Jewish community and recognized me from the trial coverage that had been ongoing the weeks prior.

"Can we meet for coffee?" she asked.

I said, "Sure, I am free, and I have no specific obligations this morning."

It turned out that Karen Halperin Cyphers would be one of the best gifts of my life, and not just my seventy-fifth birthday gift. Let me explain. She told me about how she and a group of friends had an intense interest in Dan's murder, the investigation, and the trial. Apparently, their involvement never waned, and they have been continuously on top of the investigation.

We ended up meeting for sandwiches at a deli in the same plaza as the hairdresser, and she asked me, "What can I do for you?"

I blurted out, "Grandparent alienation."

She said, "Done."

I had been sitting on a planted seed in my mind that I never nurtured. Previously, the notion of getting a bill written and the need for lobbyists was introduced to me on several occasions. I was always too preoccupied with my rights and experiences as a homicide victim, as there was a lot to learn about the American criminal justice system, let alone the stress of searching for justice. Advancing a bill just seemed impossible. Deep down in my heart, however, I knew I had to embark on this advocacy journey to see our grandchildren.

It turned out that Karen was ready to roll. She had been working in Florida's political process for seventeen years at that point—as staff in Florida's Senate and House, as staff in the governor's office, as a contributor to Florida's eminent political blog, and in private consulting as a partner in a public relations and public affairs firm. Armed with a doctoral degree in public policy, relationships in Tallahassee, and a passion for justice in this case, Karen began mobilizing her networks to find a path forward.

Karen kept her word about initiating a new bill to change Florida visitation laws. I jumped on the bandwagon of her energy, motivation, and leadership to move forward.

By the start of 2020, Karen had organized all the moving parts. Following a deep dive on the history of grandparent rights in Florida and other states, she and her allies had connected with Senator Jeff Brandes, who agreed to sponsor and introduce a narrowly worded bill. Karen also joined forces with Jason Solomon, founder of Justice for Dan, in order to mobilize not only the political process but also the public's engagement with the issue. In 2020, the "grandparent bill" by Sen. Brandes was heard in one committee and passed unanimously. I prepared a video and family statement for the hearing: "Following the horrible murder of our son Dan Markel, our goal has been to embrace his children, our grandchildren, and preserve the loving relationship they have had with us and the rest of their father's family."

Dan's close friend, Jeremy Cohen, was there as a friend and as the family representative. He did a wonderful photo presentation of Dan and his family and also came through with a great speech. Jeremy would continue to show up, hearing after hearing, in the coming years, never wavering in his commitment to see Phil and me reconnect with Dan's sons.

Despite significant obstacles in terms of Florida's constitutional limits, and as mentioned, the lobbying efforts of one section of the Florida Bar against us, our efforts didn't end there. Karen helped line us up with exceptional lobbyists Jeff Johnston and Amanda Stewart, who agreed to take on our advocacy efforts free of charge. In 2021, even during the height of COVID-19, this team was able to secure a bill workshop in the Senate, led by committee chair, Senator Lauren Book, where multiple lawmakers expressed their commitment to finding a path forward. Karen met with staff in the governor's office, who also expressed their willingness to support our efforts. And at the time of this writing, we are in the midst of Florida's 2022 legislative session, blessed with the support of Florida House Speaker Chris Sprowls, as well as bill sponsors Representative Jackie Toledo, Senator Keith Perry, who are advancing legislation to expand access to courts for grandparents such as us. These efforts resulted in refined and improved bill language over the years, a process that could not have been achieved without the collaboration and energy of so many.

Karen's support to develop legislation for grandparents to visit will help children subjected to experiences related to violent crime. Legislation such as this will ensure their best interests are protected, and in the process, could help grandparents such as me and Phil who wish deeply to be in their lives. See what can happen from a hairdresser appointment and coffee with a stranger?

Karen's spirit continues to propel me as I piggyback on all her initiatives. We have developed a tremendous personal relationship as we go through challenges together. All hurdles aside, we are still continuing on this journey.

Instead of letting these traumas overwhelm us, we are trying to make positive changes. Phil, Shelly, and I are grateful that Florida lawmakers have introduced a bill advocating for grandparents following violent crimes to have a court hearing to see their grandchildren. Its success began as a long shot, and changing the tide in Florida as well as in other states with similar draconian laws will be a difficult battle. However, we miss Lincoln and Benjamin terribly, and we will never give up on them. Dan would have wanted us to fight on.

Back to the Saturday night.

Shelly and Ian treated Phil and me to a great dinner in Tallahassee. Sunday was a quiet day around the pool. Monday was Garcia's death penalty trial. In preparation for the death penalty argument, Georgia Cappleman told the jurors that Dan's murder was "reckless" and "callous." Cappleman told jurors that Garcia and Rivera had a chance to walk away from a murder, but they didn't, and Dan Markel didn't get a choice in any of this. Instead, she said, "his death was the product of a cold, calculated act driven out of pure greed."

Garcia's Death Penalty

The jurors, family, media, witnesses, and general public returned to the Leon County courthouse on Monday, October 14, 2019.

The closing arguments were set for the next day, and the jurors would make the decision on whether Garcia should be put to death. A unanimous decision by the jury would be needed.

Garcia's legal team organized for a psychologist, Dr. Julie Harper, to be a witness to talk about his childhood mental health. Dr. Greg Prichard was the expert for the State who argued in his rebuttal that Garcia's criminal behavior of twenty arrests could not be dismissed.

The jury of ten women and two men deliberated just over forty minutes and returned with their decision against the death penalty for Garcia. After Garcia's sentencing, Cappleman said, "We will be going forward with Magbanua's case. The State will retry Ms. Magbanua."

At the end of the death penalty sentencing, the lawyers discussed what would be the next steps for defending Magbanua and for appealing Garcia's life sentence.

When the trial was officially concluded, we released to the media the following family statement:

> "Danny was brutally murdered in cold blood. After waiting five long years, we are relieved that at least one of the people responsible for Danny's murder was convicted today and are grateful for the tireless efforts of law enforcement and the State Attorney's Office. Yet justice was only partially served today. In light of the mountain of evidence presented by the State Attorney's Office, we are confident Katherine Magbanua will be re-tried and convicted.
>
> As all who followed this trial know, there is more work to be done to ensure that everyone responsible for Danny's murder is held accountable. Until that day comes, we will continue to fight for complete justice and to be reunited with our grandchildren, Danny's two young boys, whom we love and miss dearly."

While we were satisfied with Garcia's verdict, my family and I were dismayed by the fact that Magbanua would get a second chance in court. A new trial date for her case was scheduled for April 2020, and I wondered how many more times I would have to recount the story of Dan's murder and what it meant for us as a family. It was clear that the court cases had become a carousel that would spin and spin, and I would have to find the strength to again sit through the evidence and another group of witnesses.

Our final thoughts, shared by others, were gratitude for everyone's support and that the ordeal was far from over. We held on to the hope that ultimately, everyone who was responsible for Dan's killing would be brought to justice.

Roster of Witnesses—Personal Notes

The witnesses play a major role in providing evidence to the judge and jury. We were not disappointed, as most of the State's witnesses provided complex and informative evidence, although it was challenging to refrain from reacting to the testimony of witnesses who were clearly providing deceptive responses. Below is the roster of witnesses.

Helene Potlock had provided us with the names of witnesses as they appeared each day. I knew few by name, and others I learned more about in real time. For the most part, I did not come into the trial with any preconceived notions about the witnesses who would testify.

After the opening argument, the trial had a planned schedule. The early witnesses were selected to establish the medical and criminal evidence that linked the hospital reports and criminal scene to the same time period as the shooting. The evidence, such as the injuries, cause of death, and time of death, was very disturbing. Vivid visuals were a part of the presentation, which was too descriptive for me. As I mentioned, I chose not to stay, and I went back to the hotel. Phil and Shelly remained at the trial.

James Geiger

One of the most important witnesses in the investigation and trial was James Geiger, Dan's next-door neighbor. The role he played was major, as he heard the shots and saw what appeared to be a light-colored Prius leaving Dan's driveway.

James expressed major frustration with the EMS, who came nineteen minutes later, after his first call. James had discovered Dan in a pool of blood and was distraught about how long it took for the ambulance to arrive. His recorded 911 call was frequently played by the media, and in it he emphasized to the dispatcher, "You need to send an ambulance in a hurry. He is still alive. He is moving."

When I returned to Tallahassee in September 2014 for the FSU memorial, I knocked on James's door to thank him, but he was not home. After that visit, I wrote him a thank-you letter but did not hear back from him until the trial.

On occasion, there is a chance to leave the courtroom between witnesses at the trial. At the 2019 trial, I left the courtroom for a brief moment, and James was in the hallway and recognized me. He acknowledged receiving the letter, and I thanked him again. He turned out to be the main lead to the car and the critical evidence for the investigation. I will never forget his bravery in going over to Dan during a shooting.

As I mentioned, we later sued the Consolidated Dispatch Agency and reached a settlement after a lengthy delay. Our settlement was with the insurance company for $40,000, based on the delays in their response to the 911 calls when Dan was shot.

Stewart Schlazer

We knew that Dan was alive after the shooting, and this was confirmed by David Sims from the Tallahassee Police Department (TPD), as well as James.

As mentioned in the earlier chapters, I was on the phone with Dan before the shooting but was spared the last few minutes because Dan wanted to make a call to Stewart Schlazer. How fortunate I was not to be the person on the other end of the phone when Dan was murdered does not escape me. Many times, I think about this unimaginable situation, as I could have been the person to hear the shooting.

Dan was looking for information about a charter school, which Wendi was advocating for Benjamin. The witness, Stewart, was on the phone with Dan when Dan said that there was someone at his home he did not recognize. Right after hearing Dan say this, Stewart heard a loud noise and shallow breathing. He hung up and called 911.

I can't thank Stewart enough for calling 911. Life has so many paradoxes—an unknown contact was now mixed up in the middle of this murder case. This is a real example of being in the wrong place at the wrong time, a situation that has now impacted Stewart's life. He has been a crucial witness in the investigation and Dan's trial.

Craig Isom

Craig Isom, from the TPD, was not only the chief investigator in the murder but also the lead contact with our family. As I saw him outside the courtroom where the witnesses congregated, I recalled many complex and fond memories. The most troubling memory would be our first encounter with Craig.

On the Sunday morning after our arrival in Tallahassee, two days after Dan had been shot, we had our first meeting with law enforcement, specifically Craig. He gave us the details of the murder, including the murder scene. On that same day, Craig drove us to Dan's house to search for financial documents and other important personal evidence. Looking back, I do appreciate Craig's time and engagement with my family, particularly with me. The investigation and communication with law enforcement were part of what I thought of as my "portfolio" in our family's division of labor. Craig maintained phone follow-ups with me on an interim basis. He also helped us navigate the criminal system as victims. This became especially apparent when there were arrests, and Dan's case became active with the State Attorney's Office. We had grown accustomed to Craig's caring and thoughtful communications with us, and we appreciated how he helped our family transition to our new victim liaison with the State Attorney's Office.

On that same first day, July 18, 2014, Craig had a lengthy interview with Wendi, which became highly publicized and elicited many opinions. The interview raised eyebrows, and people's opinions and impressions varied as to how much drama or truth was revealed by her.

Now I am back at the long-awaited trial, five years later, watching Craig take the witness stand.

Craig and the TPD obtained video of the Prius's route from the gym to Dan's residence. The TPD collected major evidence along with Patrick Sanford from the FBI. The evidence started with the type of car and moved to the information on the SunPass toll-paying device, car rental, and pawn shop tickets. Craig was also a crucial player for all the arrests. Craig and Patrick planned the timing and organized the arrests with other major criminal agencies and local police stations in the Miami area. At the time of the trial, Craig had already retired from the TPD.

In his testimony, Craig was clear and credible. We will be forever grateful for his commitment.

Patrick Sanford

FBI Special Agent Patrick Sanford was called on another day in the trial. He was active with Craig in identifying witnesses and critical evidence.

Due to the work of Patrick and the FBI, there were many discoveries relating to the geographic capability of the investigation within Florida and other states. The local police department's range of influence in an investigation is more limited than the FBI's. The FBI has better forensic and technological equipment as well as available manpower and an international network. At the trial, Patrick testified about the wiretapping and evidence gathered from the cooperating witnesses. We have not heard the end of what was uncovered during the wiretapping. Despite much being public record at this point, few have heard the extent of communications between all of the conspirators. Patrick's efforts were extensive and thorough. Patrick, Craig, and their colleague, TPD investigator Sherrie Bennett interviewed huge numbers of people who provided evidence and many surprising discoveries.

On a personal note, Patrick also shared communications with our family, which helped guide us through the criminal maze from the FBI's perspective.

Luis Rivera

Rivera was in prison serving a twelve-year sentence for a racketeering charge. As noted, Rivera had already pled guilty to his role in the murder. His appearance in the trial was therefore as a State witness, testifying about his knowledge of both Garcia and Magbanua and their respective roles in the murder. Anticipating how his testimony would go was a great source of tension for me.

Rivera provided important details on the murder and major information on Garcia and Magbanua as co-conspirators. Rivera's cooperation was significant for Cappleman. He identified all three defendants: he was the driver; Garcia was the shooter; and Magbanua passed along the payment from those who had hired them.

Despite all the criticism of his plea-bargain deal, Rivera provided key details to the jury and those in attendance at the Tallahassee courthouse. At the trial, Rivera again stated that he was the driver on July 18. It was confirmed by Daren Schwartz that Rivera rented a green Prius in Miami from his company, Hybrid Auto Rental Center.

Rivera also said that they dumped the gun in a lake that was alongside the highway on their drive back to Miami, and then he made an effort to aid authorities in recovering the gun from various bodies of water that were located around the route they took.

During the trial, Rivera confirmed that the first trip to Tallahassee was on June 4 or 5, 2014, when he received a speeding ticket. This trip was not successful, because they lost contact with Dan, so they drove back to Miami.

Despite his criminal history and gang affiliations, Rivera's testimony was seen as forthcoming and honest. He was respectful and seemed comfortable providing every detail that was asked for. Many of these details were corroborated by physical evidence, such as which motel the two stayed at, the people they encountered during their time in Tallahassee, and the timing of phone calls to and from Garcia and Katie.

He testified that Garcia said they were hired by "the lady" who "wants her kids back."

I was drained from hearing Rivera's testimony. It was essential to the case that he needed to be credible. Fortunately, it turned out that his testimony was effective.

Christopher Corbitt

Sergeant Christopher Corbitt testified as an expert in cell phone forensics. He investigated the phones of various people in the case, including Garcia, Magbanua, Wendi, and others.

The cell phone evidence was both fascinating and convincing. The cell phone records showed the calls throughout the day of July 18, 2014, between Garcia, Magbanua, Wendi, Charlie, and others, and were some of the most compelling evidence and significant revelations.

Cell tower dumps were used to determine where certain cell phones were located and at what time. Christopher testified that Wendi was on Trescott Drive where Dan's home was located, shortly after the murder, and Rivera's phone was in a tower dump server near the Premier Gym in Tallahassee. The tower data does not provide the exact location; however, the video of the car following Dan from the gym coincided with the cell phone location and was again consistent with videos collected from city buses.

Christopher came back at another time in the trial to confirm that he taped the phone calls between Charlie and Magbanua.

The cell phone evidence exposed the reality that this information is so easily available with the proper expertise, material, and equipment. My thoughts lingered on the slogan "Big Brother is watching you," from George Orwell's novel *1984* dealing with surveillance and security cameras in a totalitarian society.

Jeffrey Lacasse

I was very curious to hear the testimony of Jeffrey Lacasse on day three of the trial. His testimony turned out to be more than intriguing and brought out major contradictions with Wendi's testimony, which had been earlier in the trial.

Jeffrey is a social work professor at FSU. He dated Wendi until just before Dan's death, or just after it—as the two had not officially broken up at that time. We were very familiar with that situation, as Jeffrey had been resolute in his contact with the TPD, and multiple interviews with him had been taped.

According to Jeffrey, Wendi told him that her brother, Charlie, had talked openly about killing Dan well before the murder, using the same story, or "joke" as she put it, that Wendi had shared with the TV repairman and Isom himself.

In 2016, law enforcement could have interpreted Jeffrey's comments and information as a disgruntled boyfriend, as we learned that Wendi initiated taking a break from the relationship just days before the murder. Fortunately, this was not the case, and Jeffrey's comments and information were credible and candid. Unfortunately for Jeffrey, though, his testimony suggested that he may have been used by Wendi as some sort of foil or patsy in the murder. Jeff reported that Wendi may have done things to make him look suspicious.

Ironically, however, it was through Jeffrey's testimony that Wendi started to look more suspicious herself. At the Leon County courthouse, Jeffrey said he met Wendi's family while they were dating and that he saw Charlie's car collection. Garcia's attorney, Saam Zangeneh, asked, "So she knew what a Ferrari was?" Wendi had claimed during her testimony that she was unaware of the type of car that her brother drove, claiming, "I drive a minivan." Jeffrey's testimony opened many questions about how forthright Wendi had been about details even as small and trivial as that one. Jeffrey's testimony suggested it was hard to believe Wendi wouldn't know what types of cars her brother drove and talked about continually.

There were many other contradictions between Wendi's testimony and Jeffrey's. For example, Jeffrey testified to how deeply Wendi wanted to move to South Florida and how upset she had been when the court ruled against her—directly contradicting Wendi's statement at trial that she had been "relieved" when forced to stay in Tallahassee.

As noted, one of the most important parts of Jeffrey's testimony was what he claims Wendi had told him on July 13, 2014: "She said that Charlie had explored all options to take care of the problem and looked into having Professor Markel killed."

I felt that Jeffrey's contribution provided significant evidence and was very meaningful.

Wendi Adelson

My life of hardship is intertwined with Wendi Adelson, Dan's ex-wife, who was called by prosecutors under a "limited immunity deal" as a key witness for setting the context of the case for the jury. Ultimately, the court offered Wendi a limited immunity deal in which she would testify and could not be prosecuted for any truthful things she said on the stand.

The prosecutor and State Attorney's Office needed to show the background for the murder-for-hire and the significance of Wendi's desire to relocate with her children from Tallahassee to Miami. The murder-for-hire was seen as resulting from the divorce and the custody battle between Dan and Wendi, most notably her inability to relocate to South Florida. She had attempted to get the court to allow her to relocate multiple times, but the court sided with Danny about keeping the boys nearby. In fact, the court ruled on this "with prejudice," meaning that Wendi was barred from bringing it back up. This was extremely upsetting to Wendi and her family. Yet when asked about it on the stand, Wendi said that she had been "relieved" when the court ruled against her. This was a surprising statement, as she was vocal with numerous people about her anger with the outcome in the relocation fight. Within days of Dan's murder, Wendi relocated to Miami just as she had clearly desired to all along.

Public opinion was significant and aroused in response to Wendi's claim of being "relieved" when the court ruled she couldn't move away from Tallahassee, and even a few of her old friends no longer trusted her after this testimony.

Wendi's testimony impacted many people's opinions of what she knew and when. These inconsistencies added up and called into question the veracity of the more consequential things Wendi had attested to.

Seeing Wendi in court brought back the devastation we felt when she changed the names of Benjamin and Lincoln from Markel to Adelson. At the trial, I was seated on the inside of the aisle and never made eye contact with Wendi.

Katherine ("Katie") Magbanua

Katherine Magbanua has been in jail since October 1, 2016, and was arrested based on information from Rivera that corroborated other physical and financial evidence collected by authorities.

Magbanua and Garcia are intertwined through common law marriage and have two children together. Magbanua's defense lawyers, Christopher DeCoste and Tara Kawass, maintain her innocence.

In a move that surprised many, Magbanua appeared on the witness stand on October 9, 2019, and denied any involvement in the murder. One of the more interesting statements she made was when she was asked if she believed that Charlie was involved in the murder—she answered affirmatively, based on everything she had seen and heard at the trial.

Her lawyers continued to claim her innocence and showed little inclination for plea bargaining. It turns out that her testimony was on Dan's birthday and the Jewish holiday of Yom Kippur.

Other Witnesses

Other witnesses provided further insight into the background of Katherine Magbanua.

Her longtime friend, Yindra Velazquez Mascaro, described Magbanua's work history as ranging from dental and dermatological offices to nightclubs and real estate. She also testified that in July 2014, around the time of the murder, Magbanua requested that she watch her children.

The opportunity for Magbanua to earn cash from her night club employment was used by the defense team as a reason why she could compile so much cash. Their argument was that the cash did not come from the payment for the murder-for-hire scenario.

Money was very relevant in this case, and on day six there was a serious review of the "follow the money" story. Mary Hull presented very explicit information on the bank records, resulting from her investigation into white-collar crime and financial crime expertise. Her testimony provided a glimpse into the money trail and connection. Hull's review included Magbanua, Rivera, Garcia, the Adelson Institute, Charlie Adelson, Harvey and Donna Adelson, and Charlie's independent "traveling" dental practice.

Other witnesses, particularly Charlie's previous girlfriend, June Umchinda, provided insight into how Charlie accumulated cash and stapled his cash—an uncommon practice to be sure, and yet "stapled money" is how Rivera claims he was paid. Umchinda had offered this information about Charlie's safe full of stapled cash to the FBI in an interview prior to the trial, during a period when she had been particularly upset with Charlie because of how he had cheated on her with other women. On the stand, Umchinda appeared more hesitant to divulge these details and admitted to the jury that she and Charlie had been talking again, as recently as the night right before her testimony began. Umchinda also shared how Charlie had been unusually upset and distracted around the time of the "Bump."

Oscar Jiménez was an FBI agent who took part in the sting operation and confirmed some of the findings. Jiménez went undercover as a member of the Latin Kings and had approached Donna Adelson with the flyer about the Dan Markel murder. A telephone number and the amount of $5,000 were written on the flyer. Their conversation was recorded and later published.

Suddenly, we were at the close of all the witness testimony for the trial. In this challenging and tense environment, the sentencing period was approaching. It soon became time for our victim impact statements.

Our family was already in pain, and I was traumatized by the murder. Facing law enforcement, the judge, the prosecutor, and Magbanua's team at the trial, and now the jury, was unthinkable. The trial came after years of waiting. My turn at the witness stand gave me a chance to voice my pain and struggle since Dan's murder. The fight for justice is very hard and lengthy, and it needs perseverance. I'm still struck that as a victim you have few opportunities to alter the slow pace of the court system. With all the delays and challenges, justice does not come fast.

We had been in court since late September, and the family finally had a chance to talk about Dan's life and legacy. On the Monday of Garcia's sentencing, which is the same day as the death penalty was deliberated, I read my victim impact statement facing the court, my family, the jury, and the media.

In essence, I summed up my own experience of a "life sentence" and heartbreak. Some people on social media made comments saying that I was queuing the jury to choose a life sentence for Garcia rather than the death penalty, but I was not.

After the trial and the death penalty sentencing ended, Shelly and Phil were able to catch a flight on Tuesday, October 15, 2019, and return to Toronto.

I needed more time and left the next day. The intense experience and punch from the trial was real, and I sensed my body and mind needed more time there.

There was too much unfinished business, and I needed to remain sturdy to see the job through.

CHAPTER 7

Post-Trial in Toronto

Our Return Home

Our return home from our three-week stay in Tallahassee was so welcome. We had a moment to regain our composure and to prepare for the retrial of Magbanua in 2020.

Our foray into the public arena included ABC, *Dateline NBC*, and *Inside Edition*. I had appeared on TV and in print for my previous book tours and work; however, I was a novice to the new world of podcasts. We were invited to be interviewed and participated on a podcast by Matt Shaer called *Over My Dead Body* by Wondery. It was greeted by an enthusiastic audience and downloaded millions of times. We learned that the podcasters were planning a sequel timed for right after the retrial. We received professional support from Gibson Dunn. Teneo Communications, specifically Jim Asci and Daniel Strauss, were very instrumental in making the arrangements for preparing us and keeping us on script.

I felt during this time a strong drive to still seek justice and not allow the traumas of the murder of my son to interfere with this path. I was, and still am, determined to overcome the obstacles faced in visiting my grandchildren. I would not allow the brutal storm to tug at my energy. Our family was then, and is still, committed to persevere. We pulled together, and we will pull through going forward.

On May 26, 2020, I received this encouraging email from Abe Anhang:

Hello Ruth—

Has a new trial date been set yet? It took them five years to complete mine too. Problem is, the defense lawyers have figured out that if they delay, in a small percentage of cases they will win because witnesses forget, they pass away, they get intimidated, etc. After I finished law school, I too worked in criminal law for a couple of years and saw the terrible abuses. It was those abuses which chased me away to business law.

When the law's delays get you down a little, remember, that for a lawyer this is just another case, while for the person affected (you), it becomes the world, since (to paraphrase Pirkei Avot): when a life is taken, is it as if a world has been destroyed! Cannot be said better than that!

Soon after our tragedy, I realized that the onus to bring the accused to justice was on me, just as it is now on you. You are not required to take the law into your own hands, only to ensure that justice is done.

All the best as we celebrate Shavuot, the day when the Torah Law was given to the Hebrews.

Abe

As expected, the media coverage of the trial heightened in the post-trial period. On October 1, 2020, *Dateline NBC* produced a two-hour post-trial update. Along with Court TV episodes and other TV news reports, social media exploded and paralleled traditional media with comments, petitions for the next arrest, and even interviews of jurors. The debate on the issues, the trial outcomes, and the future was highly charged, and social media became the public square. Early 2020 came around with some hope of moving forward with the grandparent bill.

Our experience told us that something would surely come along and postpone our next court date. Who knew this would in fact be nothing less than a global pandemic? We hoped that the case would resume before July, because our judge announced that he would be retiring at the end of June 2020, which meant we would have to restart with a completely new judge without the institutional knowledge of the entire process. I did not relish this thought.

The pandemic now took over our lives and the justice system. We entered 2021 with no date for the retrial of Magbanua.

It was during this time that Magbanua's lawyers once again attempted to secure bail or pretrial release for their client. Although the court had been clear on numerous occasions that the evidence was strong enough to warrant her continued incarceration, there was a new judge—and it was also clear that her defense would try whatever chances they had.

Our lawyers from Gibson Dunn wrote directly to the new judge for the first time (exhibits on following pages):

GIBSON DUNN

Gibson, Dunn & Crutcher LLP

200 Park Avenue
New York, NY 10166-0193
Tel 212.351.4000
www.gibsondunn.com

Orin Snyder
Direct: +1 212.351.2400
Fax: +1 212.351.6335
OSnyder@gibsondunn.com

October 1, 2020

VIA U.S. MAIL

The Honorable Robert R. Wheeler
Second Judicial Circuit Court Judge
Leon County Courthouse
301 S. Monroe Street, Room 365-K
Tallahassee, FL 32301

Re: *State of Florida v. Katherine D. Magbanua*, No. 16-CF-3036

Dear Judge Wheeler:

We represent the family of Dan Markel—his mother Ruth, his father Phil, and his sister Shelly. On behalf of the Markel family, we respectfully submit this letter to oppose Katherine Magbanua's motion for pretrial release.

More than six long years after Dan Markel was brutally murdered outside his home, justice has only partially been served. His boys are growing up without their father, and his parents are spending their elder years in searing pain, mourning the death of their son and the loss of their beloved grandchildren. There is still far more work to be done to ensure that every person responsible for Dan's brutal murder is held accountable. The upcoming retrial of Ms. Magbanua is an important step on the path to justice for Dan, his family, the countless friends, colleagues, and loved ones who continue to mourn him around the world, and the public.

During Ms. Magbanua's trial last fall, the State presented a mountain of evidence proving that Ms. Magbanua played an integral role in the conspiracy to murder Dan. Ms. Magbanua's co-conspirator Sigfredo Garcia was convicted of first degree murder and conspiracy to commit murder, and we are confident that Ms. Magbanua will be convicted at the retrial. If Ms. Magbanua were released pending retrial, there is a significant risk that she would flee, attempt to influence witness testimony or otherwise tamper with trial evidence, and/or conspire with or be influenced by members of the Adelson family. These are many of the same reasons Judge Hankinson already twice ruled that Ms. Magbanua was not entitled to bond or pretrial release—including after the first trial—and the First District Court of Appeal denied Ms. Magbanua's petition for habeas corpus challenging her pretrial detention.

Beijing • Brussels • Century City • Dallas • Denver • Dubai • Frankfurt • Hong Kong • Houston • London • Los Angeles • Munich
New York • Orange County • Palo Alto • Paris • San Francisco • São Paulo • Singapore • Washington, D.C.

GIBSON DUNN

Circuit Judge Robert R. Wheeler
October 1, 2020
Page 2

See Magbanua v. McNeil, 230 So. 3d 832 (Fla. 1st Dist. Ct. App. 2017). Those reasons are even more compelling today.

Flight Risk. Ms. Magbanua is a quintessential flight risk. She faces charges of first degree murder, conspiracy to commit murder, and solicitation to murder, and the real prospect of decades in prison isolated from her family. The evidence against Ms. Magbanua at her first trial was overwhelming, as was the jurors' reported vote in favor of conviction. Ms. Magbanua has also been able to finance (whether alone or with the support of unknown others) representation by two private Miami-based defense attorneys for four years, and therefore has the financial means to flee.

Witness and Evidence Tampering. There is a substantial risk that Ms. Magbanua would attempt to influence trial testimony or otherwise tamper with trial evidence. Facing the prospect of an effective life sentence and a near-certain conviction, Ms. Magbanua has every incentive to intimidate or otherwise influence witnesses who will testify at her retrial. Ms. Magbanua has a personal relationship with certain witnesses—for example, Yindra Velazquez Mascaro, who has been Ms. Magbanua's friend since childhood and testified as the State's witness at trial. And recorded telephone calls played at Ms. Magbanua's first trial, as well as the other evidence of Ms. Magbanua's central role in Dan's murder, demonstrate that she is capable of heinous violence toward others.

The Adelson Family. There is a substantial risk that Ms. Magbanua would conspire with and/or be influenced by members of the Adelson family. In our opinion, at the first trial the State presented overwhelming evidence that Ms. Magbanua was the critical connection between the men who gunned down Dan in his own garage (Mr. Garcia and Luis Rivera) and the members of the Adelson family who allegedly commissioned Dan's murder. Ms. Magbanua was Charlie Adelson's former girlfriend, and the evidence linking Ms. Magbanua to Charlie and Donna Adelson in connection with Dan's murder is, in our view, overwhelming. For example, in the days and weeks before the murder, Ms. Magbanua and Charlie Adelson were in frequent contact with each other. Ms. Magbanua often communicated with Mr. Garcia, and Charlie Adelson with Donna Adelson, in close proximity to those calls. In the 90 minutes immediately after Dan's murder, again, Ms. Magbanua communicated with both Charlie Adelson and Mr. Garcia; Mr. Adelson and Donna Adelson also spoke during that same time period. And in the weeks and months after Dan's murder, Ms. Magbanua received thousands of dollars from the Adelsons, including "paychecks" for a no-show job and a car. And of course, no plausible explanation has ever been offered as to why Mr. Garcia and Mr. Rivera—two gangsters from South Florida who had no connection to Dan whatsoever—would have killed Dan, other than the obvious one:

GIBSON DUNN

Circuit Judge Robert R. Wheeler
October 1, 2020
Page 3

that they were hired by members of the Adelson family through Ms. Magbanua, the only known connection between each side of the murder-for-hire conspiracy.

In our opinion, the State has presented overwhelming evidence demonstrating that members of the Adelson family orchestrated Dan's murder. Releasing Ms. Magbanua now would present a significant risk that she would conspire with, or otherwise be influenced by, members of the Adelson family. There is a substantial risk that Ms. Magbanua and members of the Adelson family would strategize, coordinate defenses, script testimony, or work together to influence other witnesses. Alternatively, members of the Adelson family could harm, threaten, bribe, or otherwise attempt to influence Ms. Magbanua and/or members of her family. Indeed, during the first trial, Ms. Magbanua admitted on the stand that she too believed Charlie Adelson was involved in Dan's murder. Her release now would place her at obvious risk of physical and/or financial harm. Any of these scenarios would threaten the integrity of both Ms. Magbanua's retrial as well as any ongoing criminal investigations of members of Adelson family and other potential unindicted co-conspirators.

In sum, all of these factors—the weight of the evidence against Ms. Magbanua, the serious felony offenses with which she is charged, the lengthy prison sentence she faces, the risk that she would flee, the risk that she would influence trial testimony, and the risk that she would conspire with or be influenced by members of the Adelson family—compel the denial of Ms. Magbanua's motion for pretrial release. *See, e.g., Dollar v. State*, 909 So. 2d 399, 401 (Fla. Dist. Ct. App. 5th Dist. 2005) (holding that trial court properly denied motion for bond because "the weight of evidence against the [defendants] is substantial," their "offenses are serious," "there was evidence to conclude that they are a flight risk," and "there is a probability of . . . intimidation of [witnesses]").

In the more than six years since Dan was brutally murdered, the Markel family has endured unfathomable grief and loss. Their only son was stolen from them, and members of the Adelson family have not allowed them to see their grandchildren—Dan's two young boys—in more than four years. Throughout this horror, the Markels continue to fight for complete justice for their son and to be reunited with their grandsons. The interests of the public and of the Markel family, as victims of this heinous crime, compel the denial of Ms. Magbanua's motion for pretrial release.

We believe it is imperative that the Court has an opportunity to hear the Markel family's concerns before ruling on Ms. Magbanua's motion for pretrial release and would respectfully request the opportunity to address the Court directly at any hearing. *See* Fla. Const. Art. I, § 16(b)(6)(b) (victims have "the right to be heard in any public proceeding involving pretrial or other release from any form of legal constraint, plea, sentencing, adjudication, or parole, and any proceeding during which a right of the victim is implicated"); *Baugh v. State*, 253

GIBSON DUNN

Circuit Judge Robert R. Wheeler
October 1, 2020
Page 4

So. 3d 761, 764 (Fla. Dist. Ct. App. 1st Dist. 2018) ("Our state constitution establishes that a victim's rights include the rights to be present 'and to be heard when relevant' during 'all crucial stages of criminal proceedings'" (quoting Fla. Const. Art. I, §16(b)).

We thank the Court for its kind consideration.

Respectfully submitted,

Orin Snyder

Matthew Benjamin

On October 16, 2020, Judge Robert R. Wheeler submitted his "order denying the defendant second motion for pre-trial release following mistrial." The highlights of his comments follow:

- On January 22, 2020, Defendant filed a motion for Bond and/or a Reasonable Form of Pretrial Release Following Mistrial. By that motion, Defendant summarized their version of the facts presented at trial, and again argued that the State failed to meet its burden that the proof is evident, or the presumption is great that Defendant is guilty of first-degree murder.
- The argument portion of Defendant's motion presents two grounds for granting Defendant's pre-trial release: (1) that the facts and testimony adduced at trial, coupled with the declared mistrial, compels a finding that the proof is not evident, and presumption is not great' and (2) that Defendant's continued detainment in the Leon County Detention Facility poses a great danger to her health in light of the COVID-19 pandemic.

- Whether the facts and testimony adduced at trial, coupled with the declared mistrial, compels a finding that the proof is not evident, and presumption is not great has previously been considered and ruled upon by this Court. In its January 31, 2020, Order Denying Defendant's Motion for Bond and/or Reasonable Form of Pretrial Release, this Court held that based on the information and testimony presented during trial, and with consideration of the mistrial for failure to reach a unanimous verdict, "[t]he Court is still of the view that proof of [D]efendant's guilt is evidence or the presumption is great." Consistent with this prior ruing, Defendant's motion for pre-trial release on this ground is again denied.
- Whether Defendant's continued detainment in the Leon County Detention Facility poses a great danger to her health in light of the COVID-19 pandemic is irrelevant to this Court's proof is evident or presumption is great analysis for bond consideration or pretrial release. Nonetheless, this Court finds that the Leon County Sheriff's Office Pandemic Standard Operating Procedures and the COVID-19 Preparation and Prevention Strategies in place at the Leon County Detention Facility are sufficient to address any danger to Defendant's health. The Leon County Sheriff is providing adequate constitutionally required care to its inmates, including Defendant. Defendant's motion for pretrial release on this ground is denied.

The *Tallahassee Democrat* and WTXL Tallahassee informed the public of the judge's decision to deny the pre-release.

The process of getting to the murder trial is always complicated. The COVID-19 pandemic slowed the wheels of justice further, with most trials suspended. Magbanua was now scheduled to face retrial in the spring of 2021 at the earliest. The judge on the case, Hankinson, had retired as planned at the end of June 2020, expressing disappointment and frustration that he wouldn't oversee the end of this important case. Judge Robert Wheeler would now preside.

The new trial of Magbanua was eventually set for October 4, 2021. While waiting for her retrial, there were several requests for her to have bail to avoid the pandemic and for her to be released. All the requests were refused.

In the sixth year since the murder, we released a family statement that thanked the police and prosecutors and expressed hope that they would persevere and continue with the investigation.

"We understand that due process takes patience," we wrote. "We pray that this next phase of the legal process moves quickly and that all those responsible for Dan's murder are held accountable. And we pray for the chance to see and know Dan's two boys—our beloved grandsons—again."

The internet and social media are still active with comments on Justice for Dan and on the YouTube channel of local lawyer and internet personality, Mentour Lawyer.

Unless every detail of the case has been resolved, which, in light of our experience, seems unlikely, I find myself, six years after Dan was killed, asking the same question I asked when I heard that he had been shot: *Will we ever see justice?* I describe my plans to continue to pursue the truth for Dan and see those responsible be held to account. This is my mission now, along with my quest to see my grandsons, and to give the boys the Jewish roots I had promised at the memorial. In the writing of this book, I have been driven to share my experience and insights in this sincere wish to provide help and relief to anyone else whose life is touched by this kind of dreadful misfortune. Working on behalf of Dan and his sons has given me a meaningful path forward and the hope for some sort of healing.

The Path to Katherine Magbanua's Retrial

We waited anxiously for the case management meeting on August 25, 2021, to find out about a continuation, meaning a postponement of the trial. Katherine's defense team had requested a delay, saying they wanted to try the case but to do so safely.

Kawass explained that their defendant would not be able to get a fair trial because they would be unable to see each person's face if they had on a mask. Sometimes, they rely on facial expressions when selecting jurors. She explained that they could tell a lot by a person's facial expression when asked a question. She stated that this helps when determining a lie or how someone is feeling. She believed that the jurors should also be able to see her client's face as well. Before the judge was able to respond, DeCoste interjected that him and his partner were both immunocompromised and would like a continuance.

Assistant State Attorney Sarah Dugan, who was brought on to join Cappleman, objected to the motion of continuance, saying that there was no way to know how long we would have to wear masks, and that "we would object to continuing the case. We're ready for trial. We want to try it as soon as possible and would like it to be kept on the docket for October."

While Judge Robert Wheeler denied the verbal request to continue the trial to a later date, he instructed the defense to file a written motion about their concerns. The filing deadline for this was September 17, 2021. When the date came for the next case management hearing, we learned that Katherine Magbanua had had COVID-19 ten days earlier but was in the courtroom because she'd tested negative that morning.

The defense did indeed submit their motions in writing, saying, "Undersigned has zero confidence that the court system can ensure safety during the retrial. On August 25, 2021, the parties were before the Court for the first time since the pandemic began and within seconds Ms. Kawass and Mr. DeCoste were exposed to COVID-19. Prior to the day of Court, Ms. Magbanua tested positive for COVID-19. The morning of the Court the Leon County Sheriff's Office (LCSO) did a rapid test, which are known to be inaccurate. The rapid test came back negative. She was transported to court directly from the area within the unit housing COVID-19 positive inmates without being allowed to shower or change clothes. She was brought into the courtroom and seated at defense counsel table. After Court, LCSO did a molecular test, which is the gold standard. Ms. Magbanua was still COVID-19 positive. For these reasons, undersigned concerningly finds themselves weighing their health against the personal and professional consequences for refusing to try a case under the current conditions. Further evidence and argument will be presented to the Court at hearing on this motion."

There we were on September 20, 2021, ready to leave on October 4, 2021, for the scheduled retrial of Magbanua in Tallahassee. The defense team had gone out on multiple media interviews, including with local lawyer and internet personality Mentour Lawyer, and used every maneuver in the book to postpone the trial.

Much to our disappointment, the October trial would not take place. The case management hearing on September 20, 2021, was intended to be the last big hearing prior to the trial, but instead Magbanua's attorneys had thrown up several motions that got in the way.

After their media campaign, their motions to delay began. They had filed a motion to disqualify the State Attorney's Office from even trying the case, which was a bold move in which they alleged prosecutors had intentionally obscured or withheld evidence and filed a motion to delay the trial again due to COVID-19. Both of Magbanua's attorneys are cancer survivors, and despite the rates of infection in Leon County dropping precipitously during that time, their doctors submitted letters saying that it would not be safe for them to appear in court.

The motion to disqualify read as follows:

WHEREFORE, the Defendant, Katherine D. Magbanua, respectfully requests that this Honorable Court enter an order disqualifying the Office of the State Attorney for the Second Judicial Circuit and for Leon County from continuing to prosecute this case.

The motion to disqualify accused the prosecutors of "intentionally presenting misleading evidence and substantial misconduct." The motion described the trial exhibit issues relating to banking and employment as well as phone records as inaccurate.

Magbanua's lawyers contended:

The actions of the State Attorney's Office here have called the integrity of the entire case into question. A criminal defendant should have, at a minimum, enough confidence in trusting that the prosecution will proceed fairly and honestly. That confidence no longer stands here. The misconduct of the prosecution in this case was discovered by happenstance. Who is to say that more does not exist? As a result, Ms. Magbanua has now inherited the burden of scrutinizing each and every action of the prosecution in fear that misleading and/or false evidence will be presented to the jury. This is precisely the type of prejudice that disqualification is set out to prevent—one which Ms. Magbanua would not otherwise bear if the prosecution was disinclined to obtain a conviction at the expense of a fair trial.

Cappleman's response was quick and clear:

The State categorically denies any misconduct including the allegations made by Defendant in her recent Motion to Disqualify. The State did not intentionally withhold evidence or misrepresent anything to the jury in Defendant's last trial. It should be noted that her co-defendant, Sigfredo Garcia, was convicted in that same trial and his direct appeal does not cite any of the issues raised in this motion to Disqualify. Defendant's Motion further alleges the reason her counsel was not able to competently cross-examine witnesses Hull and Corbitt was because the defense was not given the exhibits in a timely manner. This is false. To the contrary, the State, pursuant to common practice and the Judge's strong preference, made all exhibits available for inspection by the defense prior to trial, but the defense chose not to examine the items. This was possibly done to preserve the strategy of making speaking objections and commentary during trial indicating that the defense had never seen the exhibits before and suggesting to the jury that the State was attempting to ambush the Defendant in some way. The State anticipates this strategy could be employed again in the upcoming trial and therefore moves this Honorable Court to order the defense to examine the exhibits prior to trial; and/or in the alternative to preclude the defense/Defendant from making speaking objections or engaging in any commentary in the presence of the jury regarding alleged discovery violations. The State requests that any such objections be addressed at sidebar outside the presence of the jury.

In other words, none of the issues that Katherine's defense was raising in this motion were included in Garcia's appeal, and had there been merit to them, this would surely have been the case. Further, Cappleman made clear that the defense appeared to be intentionally neglecting to review evidence in order to preserve their strategy of securing more delays, perhaps attempting to make the State appear noncooperative.

There was even a formal rebuttal by the state attorney himself, Jack Campbell, who released the following, according to the *Tallahassee Democrat*:

State Attorney Jack Campbell denied his office misrepresented the case—it's being tried by Assistant State Attorney Georgia Cappleman—and said it would be inappropriate for him to discuss evidence of the case in the media.

"The idea of saying, 'we don't like their evidence so they should be on the other side,' is preposterous. The time and the forum to discuss evidence is at trial. I will definitively say that our office did not, would not, misrepresent the evidence."

Thankfully, Cappleman and Campbell ultimately prevailed when Judge Wheeler dismissed the motion. Regarding the motion, "the judge ruled there are no indications here that it was intentional, and this was not substantial misconduct."

The second claim by Magbanua's lawyers was that it would be "unconstitutional, unfair, and unsafe" for the trial to proceed during the pandemic, and that having witnesses and their client appear in court wearing masks would reduce the ability of the jury to observe them earnestly. This was frustrating, to say the least. Furthermore, masks during trials were now commonplace across the United States, and if there had been a constitutional issue with them, that would apply everywhere, not just in our case.

Not surprisingly, Judge Wheeler ruled against the defense motion to disqualify the State Attorney's Office from trying the case. There was no basis for doing so. However, he did seem to agree that the defense deserved a bit more time to complete depositions of new witnesses who had been listed and to maintain their safety from COVID-19. The case was again delayed, this time to February 14, 2022—Valentine's Day.

My knees buckled when the judge commented that the delay was based on the number of witnesses still to be deposed. The defense team said that the State had added new witnesses to its list in the last few weeks.

"The COVID issues are really moot at this point," Wheeler said in granting the delay. "I am granting this on legal reasons."

We were devastated again and again that Magbanua's trial was delayed during the pandemic.

I am still very anxious about the pandemic in Florida and conflicted about going forward. The unknown is both draining and concerning. Not just due to the pandemic, as I'll continue to follow all safety conventions and be aware of my surroundings.... It's the what-ifs. The thing that there is no control over—the trial. *What if another mistrial is declared? What if she is found not guilty?* The link between Magbanua,

Rivera, and others is not to be underestimated. A conviction could mean the difference in moving forward with others being charged in this murder-for-hire plot.

Trial life has many similarities to COVID-19 confusion.

Just as science, bureaucracy, and individuals provide conflicting messages—about which vaccine shots work best, for example—the constant obstructions attempted by the defense led to confusion and doubt. For the victims, it only creates disappointment. Repeated waiting, slowness, confusion, and uncertainty all torment our daily lives and make us feel powerless.

Throughout our waiting for Magbanua's retrial, there were attempts by the defense to create delays and obstructions. For the victim, it only creates disappointment, sluggishness, and lack of action.

As an adult and victim of crime, my daily life parallels the COVID-19 issues and questions. Should students be in the classroom, and what are the consequences of missed learning? Most school staff, administrators, and students are living a yo-yo lifestyle. My family and others have no established daily routines but live the stop-and-go existence of the criminal system. At least there are some initiatives to improve remote learning and child-centered designs for tech products to make learning more accessible for students.

I must say I am concerned that my life feels more like a playground of seesaws, roller coasters, ping pong, and ups and downs. This doesn't feel like play, but rather hard work and stress.

At this point, our lives as victims are back on the roller coaster. If this was fiction, there would be a narrow road with only twists and turns, but *this life story is real.* The drama between August 25 and September 2021 was so intense and great for storytelling, but we are living the turmoil.

Everyone says, "Ruth, you are strong." Although I have been through many tragedies, I wonder, "Will my strength run out with time and age?" Nevertheless, I cherish the people who are here with me and who help prevent life's events from pulling me down.

At the time of this writing, Magbanua's trial was once again delayed from Valentine's Day 2022—until mid-May 2022.We pray that it will happen, or that she will cooperate and plead before then to expedite the next arrests.

Appeal Process: Garcia

The justice system dictates uncertainty as a way a life. In 2019, we ended the trial for Garcia only to learn that the appeal was planned in the same breath as the conclusion of the trial. Garcia's lawyer, Saam Zangeneh, stated that he would not be doing the appeal.

As Garcia's appeal became a reality, we were introduced to Melissa "Katy" Russell, a victim services program specialist at the Office of the Attorney General. Melissa would become our third victim advocate. She communicates with our family and keeps us informed on everything relating to Garcia's appeal. One such communication occurred on February 25, 2021, when we received an update. We were waiting to talk to Robert "Charlie" Lee, the attorney responsible for the State in the appeal of Garcia.

Garcia's lawyer for the appeal was Baya Harrison, and this was how the appeal was structured:

- *The trial court erred in finding that failure to disclose expert opinion on bullet trajectory and height of shooter was not a willful discovery violation and did not result in procedural prejudice*
- *The trial court erred in its response to jury questions during deliberations*

The answer brief and cross-appeal were handled by Ashley Moody, the attorney general, and Robert "Charlie" Lee, the assistant attorney general. The issues were presented as follows:

- *Issue I: When the State's ballistics expert Robert Yao made new findings about the height of the person who shot Daniel Markel, the State neglected to inform Garcia. Although Garcia became aware of Yao's new finding's [sic] several days before trial, Garcia waited until Yao took the stand to object and ask the trial court to exclude Yao's new findings. Did Garcia wait too long to object, and was Garcia's proposed remedy (exclusion) too extreme?*
- *Issue II: During deliberation, the jurors submitted a cryptic question in writing about the jury instruction on principals. While Garcia proposed his own answer to the jury's question, he ultimately agreed with the trial court's response which asked the jurors*

to clarify their question. When the jurors declined to clarify their question, Garcia took no further action. Did Garcia waive any objection to the trial court's response to the jury's question?

The State's cross-appeal argument was stated as follows:

- *Issue I: The Florida Constitution and Florida Statutes give a homicide victim's next of kin the right to be in the courtroom during the defendant's jury trial—unless their presence would prejudice the defendant's right to a fair trial. Did the trial court abuse its discretion by excluding Daniel Markel's parents and sister from the courtroom when the State only planned to call them for the purpose of authenticating voices on phone recordings?*

We then embarked on another lengthy legal process, along with the pandemic, navigating uncertain times. We had recently learned that Denise Williams, in another famous murder case in Tallahassee, had her life sentence reduced on appeal. In 2018, Denise Williams was convicted of orchestrating the murder of her husband, Mike Williams, in a conspiracy with Williams's best friend at the time—a man who Denise was having an affair with. By 2020, Denise had her first-degree murder charge and life sentence reversed after filing an appeal. A panel of three judges determined that the State failed to prove that Denise abetted Mike's killer, who had admitted committing the crime. While her murder conviction was reversed, the charge for conspiracy to commit murder still remains.[9]

We learned that the family of Mike Williams felt humiliated by Denise Williams's success on her appeal. We shared their sense of grief about that outcome. I had been in touch with Mike's mother, Cheryl, who shared her profound disappointment.

After the trial of 2019, we had hoped to have peace of mind that Garcia's conviction would hold. But since February 26, 2021, when we talked to the lawyer for the State, Robert "Charlie" Lee, there were more steps to take in the appeal of Garcia.

9 "Murder Conviction for Denise Williams Reversed by Appeals Court, Conspiracy Charge Affirmed," WTXL, November 25, 2020, https://www.wtxl.com/news/local-news/murder-conviction-for-denise-williams-reversed-by-appeals-court-conspiracy-charge-affirmed.

On October 25, 2021, we learned that Garcia's appeal was denied, with the court issuing a strongly worded retort. Although Garcia could have appealed to the Supreme Court, it was clear to all that the facts were not in his favor, and he declined to do so.

As Garcia lost the appeal, we can finally take a deep breath. There is one conviction for the gunman—a conviction that took five years to finalize.

New Drama & More Developments

Just as we were hoping to move into the retrial of Magbanua, with the dates ever changing and delayed, we heard news that the defense received letters from another man, Walter Rayborn, a man awaiting a dual homicide trial, who had spent time with Rivera while incarcerated.

The *Tallahassee Democrat* reported that an inmate at the Leon County jail, Walter Rayborn, claimed that Rivera was coerced by Georgia Cappleman to testify and commit perjury.

This event prompted a strong reaction from our family, and we requested a telephone conference with Cappleman and Helene. We had this call on February 23, 2021.

Attorneys for Magbanua asserted that these letters from jail could be key in securing a "not guilty" verdict this time around. Rayborn claimed that Rivera lied in Magbanua's first trial to get a plea deal.

"Mr. Rayborn reached out to me from jail and wrote me the letter that we've provided in discovery," said Katherine Magbanua's attorney Tara Kawass. During Magbanua's first trial, when asked who convinced Garcia to shoot Markel, Rivera replied, "His wife Katie."

In one of the letters sent to Kawass from Rayborn, he claims the prosecution held up color-coded folders while Rivera testified to remind him what to say. The letter also reads, "Rivera told me and other inmates countless times that Katie never truly was involved."

"The evidence actually does support that because of the amount of times that they had met with Luis Rivera and didn't cut a deal with him. Then in September right before Katherine's arrest, all of a sudden, he met, mentioned Katherine's name, and he had figured out at that time that 'if I don't say her name, they're not going to put any deal with me,'" said Kawass.

State Attorney Jack Campbell refuted this, calling Walter Rayborn a threat to society.

"The allegations are preposterous, and they're being made by a multi-murderer, neo-Nazi, convicted felon," said Campbell. "Right now, Mrs. Cappleman is an extremely good prosecutor seeking to have him incarcerated for the rest of his life and perhaps have him put to death. He's trying to disparage the person prosecuting him for murder and seeking the death penalty."

Campbell explained that this wasn't the first time he'd encountered problems with Rayborn. In December 2018, Campbell sent a letter to Sheriff Walt McNeil, asking him to keep Rayborn in confinement until his trial. The letters read in part, "It has come to the attention of my office that this inmate poses special security concerns to your staff and mine, as well as to witnesses in the community."

The changes in the defense strategy for Magbanua included media announcements about Rayborn's letters and participation by her lawyers on TV shows claiming Magbanua's innocence.

Of course, to have more obstructions stirred something in my stomach and brought a groundswell of emotional worry. It became a part of our agenda to get more background on the Rayborn incident from the prosecutors.

We continued to learn that Rivera was writing to the prosecutor in June 2021. My initial worry was that he wanted to change his testimony; luckily for us it was about a second matter related to his safety, as noted in the letter that follows:

Filing # 128935808 E-Filed 06/17/2021 10:06:02 AM

IN THE CIRCUIT COURT OF THE
SECOND JUDICIAL CIRCUIT, IN
AND FOR LEON COUNTY, FLORIDA.

CASE NO. 16CF03036
SPN 247204

STATE OF FLORIDA

vs.

Katherine D. Magbanua,
Defendant.
_______________________________/

AMENDED: ANSWER TO DEMAND FOR DISCOVERY

COMES NOW the State of Florida, by and through the undersigned Assistant State Attorney, and files this Amended Answer to Demand for Discovery. The State's Answer to Demand for Discovery is amended to include the following:

EXHIBIT: Letter from Luis Rivera to Georgia Cappleman, 6/8/21

I HEREBY CERTIFY that a true and correct copy of the foregoing has been furnished to Christopher DeCoste, 40 N.W.3rd St. #1, , Miami, FL 33128, on June 17, 2021 by U.S. Mail/hand delivery or by e-service to cmd@christopherdecoste.com.

JACK CAMPBELL
STATE ATTORNEY
SECOND JUDICIAL CIRCUIT

/s/Georgia Cappleman
Georgia Cappleman
Assistant State Attorney

Luis M. Rivera
United States Penitentiary-Tucson
P.O. Box 24550
Tucson, Arizona 85734

RECEIVED
2021 JUN 14 AM 10: 10
JACK CAMPBELL
STATE ATTORNEY

Georgia Cappleman
State's Attorney
301 South Monroe Street
Tallahassee, Florida 32301

June 8th, 2021

Dear Attorney Cappleman:

I'm writing to you in your capacity as the State's Attorney for the State of Florida. This correspondence is in reference to **State of Florida v. Luis M. Rivera, Case No. 16CF01581.** In that case I pled guilty to the crime of second degree murder. In exchange for my guilty plea I received a sentence of ninteen (19) years to run concurrent with my federal sentence in **United States v. Rivera, Case No. 1560094-CF-COHN.** As part of plea agreement, I agreed to cooperate with your office. My cooperation included my testimony against my co-defendants. It's my understanding that further cooperation in the way of testimony is forthcoming.

I'm currently serving my federal sentence of 151 months. My state sentence, although it was ordered to run concurrent, it exceeds my federal sentence. This essentially means that once my federal sentence expires, that I will then be turned over to the State of Florida, Department of Corrections. In light of that, I have serious concerns for my safety. I was an active gang member in the Latin Kings Gang in the State of Florida. By cooperating with your office, I've become a target. Serving a prison sentence in the State of Florida would place me in grave danger from other Latin Kings who are serving time in the Florida Department of Corrections.

Since my incarceration in the Federal Bureau of prisons, I have been a model prisoner. I've been free of misconduct reports, and I have been actively engaged in rehabilitational programming, including a six month non-residential drug abuse program. My federal sentence will be complete in May of 2026, by then, a large portion of my state sentence will be served. I'm requesting, if at all possible, that your office consider the possibility of modifying my state sentence to time served upon the completion of my federal sentence. This of course would be contingent on my continued good behavior during the course of serving my federal sentence. In the alternative, if sentence modification isn't possible, I would request that your office contact the Florida Department of Corrections to request that my state sentence, (what remains of it upon the completion of my federal sentence), be served in the federal Bureau of Prisons at

(1).

the facility I'm currently incarcerated at. I'm currently safe from any harm in the facility I'm in.

My cooperation resulted in the conviction and life sentence of my co-defendant, that fact alone places me in grave danger, especially in the Florida Department of Coorections.

Thank you in advance for your review of my concerns. Your anticipated reply is appreciated.

Sincerely, Luis M. Rivera

Luis M. Rivera

We are still very concerned about Rayborn's claim, as Rivera was a major witness in our case.

Keep the Fire Burning

Throughout all of our communications with the State Attorney's Office, we expressed our family's strong interest in when the retrial would occur. As early as October 21, 2020, Shelly wrote Helene, "Any word on when jury trial will be starting up again?" The court system, in general, is not as advanced as the schools' reopening. Schools have the guidance from the Centers for Disease Control and Prevention that certain schools should be safe for reopening, provided mitigation measures are in place. Some of these decisions on January 13, 2021, from the Center for Disease Control and Prevention reported results of in-person versus remote learning.

But there are still international worries of community spread of COVID-19 with lockdowns and quarantines impacting the criminal justice system. In our case, both of Magbanua's attorneys are cancer survivors and pushed hard to delay the trial due to the risk of COVID-19. They even had their respective physicians write letters to the court explaining their heightened risk.

We live in Canada, which still has closed borders with the United States other than for essential workers and medical and food delivery services. It may stand in the way of justice.

I also received an email from Abe Anhang expressing his concern and experience with waiting:

Sorry about your having to wait. Such are the trials and tribulations of the criminal justice system as it is practiced in the U.S. Often, despite their obvious guilt, these people demand (and receive) the best legal advice available, FREE OF CHARGE, thanks to the American taxpayer! In fact, even after conviction, they ALWAYS want to appeal, since they are in jail with nothing to do, and besides, it costs them nothing, so why not appeal since they have nothing to lose? That is where we are at right now—going into year 16!

While I understand that the latest delays are pandemic related, if there had been a conviction, this would now be behind you, and for that I feel truly sorry, since these people play every angle to get delays, always with the hope that something may happen to a witness, or the state will lose interest, etc.

So, like us, you have no choice but to wait it out, sort of like having a tiger by the tail, you cannot let go, no matter what. It took us 14 years, chasing her across Europe before she was finally brought back and convicted. Ruth, I am not certain what the odds of getting caught and convicted are in Florida, but I do know that in Puerto Rico, they have an 80% chance of never being convicted. Knowing this statistic (and the murderers do know it), people are prepared to risk murdering for profit. You see, these people know that the court system only too well and know that it is over loaded to begin with! To our embarrassment, they also happen to believe that with the help of a good lawyer, they will get away with it, they really do! JUSTICE HAS VERY LITTLE TO DO WITH IT.... That is why, in my opinion, it is so important to get to know the prosecutors and communicate with them often, since with the volume of cases they carry, it is only too easy for your case to get overlooked in the shuffle!

Happy New Year!

Abe

Dan's friends remained concerned that momentum on Dan's case was slowing and that the delays in the legal system due to the pandemic might mean prosecutors wouldn't take the next step and investigate the question of who paid for the killing.

"As time passes, we worry that people will forget that there were leaders in the plot and that the people who are most responsible for this murder, specifically the Adelson family, won't be held accountable. There will be people who will say, 'We've gotten some justice and we have to move on,'" said Dan's friend Jason Solomon.

We do have the support of many friends and platforms, particularly the social media site Justice for Dan, operated now by Jason and Karen. In addition to founding Justice for Dan, Jason wrote an op-ed in the *Tallahassee Democrat* that noted a concern: "It's quite possible that they decided on going after the lower people on the totem pole on a criminal enterprise first, with the hope that they will flip and cooperate and testify against the people who are at the top of the criminal enterprise."

Because the three defendants who are currently incarcerated are people of color or Latino, while other named co-conspirators have not been arrested yet, it has raised the issue of systematic racism in the criminal justice system.

We never were sitting idle and worked hard on promoting reforms to Florida law to allow visitation to our grandchildren. As previously discussed, a bill inspired by our family was introduced in the Florida legislature in early 2020 to provide grandparents with greater access to courts to petition for visitation with grandchildren in extraordinary cases like ours. After being filed by Senator Jeff Brandes, it was approved unanimously by Senator Lauren Book's Children, Families, and Elder Affairs Committee. Book continued to pledge her support for this ongoing initiative. We are blessed with the leadership of Karen Halperin Cyphers and our lobbyists, Jeff Johnston and Amanda Stewart, who continue their work to pass this legislation into law.

In the very next Florida legislative session, on March 30, 2021, there was a special workshop in the Senate. Senator Book scheduled the workshop to discuss grandparent visitation laws in Florida and to work on the proper language needed to draft this new bill. The workshop discussed options for increasing access to courts and protecting the emotional welfare of children in extraordinary cases, specifically those involving ongoing criminal investigations. Testimony in support of the bill was provided by multiple stakeholders, including legal experts and psychologists, as well as members of our family. Advocacy efforts have also been led by Justice for Dan, the Facebook group started by Dan's friends. These friends even helped produce a video explaining the grandparent visitation problems in Florida law, which was presented to the Senate committee and offered a primer about the challenges families like ours face. I provided a video testimony to contribute to this, which remains viewable with the following link: https://www.youtube.com/watch?v=EiHit7Beas0&t=71s

A piece of Dan's writing has gained new, tragic relevance for his own life: "Keep the fire burning." Dan wrote this message to a friend prior to his death. We have listened and learned to "keep the fire burning" despite the obstacles of the pandemic.

We cannot sugarcoat the agony of waiting.

My life is filled with trauma, hurdles, surprises, and strain. Maybe because I am a Libra—I am very uninformed about astrology, but I am led to believe that I continuously seek balance. Although my disappointments are very surreal and serious, I am lifted by all the supports and gifts just described. If I was not optimistic, I'd still be in the rabbit hole.

These circumstances do create anxiety for us as a family—we were extremely sad that on July 19, 2021, we acknowledged the anniversary of Dan's murder with many unresolved questions.

Life in Toronto had continued, and it was complex. The pandemic came to a slowdown, and we opened up for restaurants, travel, and indoor gyms. Our family would take advantage of the "new season," but there were limits to our gravitation to the good vibe.

We had worked hard to prepare the family statements for July 19, 2021 (the seventh annual day of Dan's death). The Jewish Yahrzeit for Dan was on July 1, 2021, and I had just gone to the cemetery on June 25, 2021. I still keep my cemetery visits because these are the most private movements when I can still share with Dan my devastation and my feelings about the current reality. Even though I am heartbroken, I hold onto my hope and my mantra: never give up.

Our hearts were consumed approaching the seventh anniversary of Dan's murder. This was not a quiet period; there was no shortage of suffering and contradictions. Einstein wrote that "men cannot be healthy without meaning." We passed the seventh anniversary of Dan's murder on July 2021.

Our drafted statement alluded to the challenges of waiting and our confidence that the justice system was working toward resolution:

Family Statement

Seven years ago, our beloved Dan Markel was taken from us in an act of terrible, calculated violence.

Danny was a beautiful spirit, a passionate thinker, a devoted brother and son, and a dedicated, joyful father. He brought people together and celebrated the passages of life with all of his heart. Our family mourns his loss today, as always, with profound gratitude for the community of law enforcement, prosecutors, friends, and strangers who continue to seek justice in Dan's memory.

Seven years is a long time, but waiting is made tolerable by the belief that justice will come, and that we will have a chance to see and know Dan's two sons again. We pray that in the long course of our grief and sorrow for Dan, this seventh year brings renewed energy and progress—both in honoring his life and in finding accountability for all of those who are responsible for taking it.

All of our communities have suffered a horrific year of loss and isolation. Throughout, we thank all who remain engaged in our, and Dan's story. Our hearts are together as we move forward in the pursuit of peace and justice.

On this special 7th year anniversary, we produced a video (see below), which you can also find on the Facebook page "Justice for Dan."

This link will lead you to a YouTube video:

7th Anniversary of Dan Markel's Murder–A Message from his Family

https://www.youtube.com/watch?v=wwmJiypSbWs

Justice For Dan
July 2, 2021 ·

This week marks the 7th Yahrzeit, or anniversary, of Dan Markel's death on the Jewish calendar.

In observation of this, the Markel family shares: "Seven is an important, meaningful number in our Jewish faith. Each seventh day of the week is set aside for rest and reverence; and each seventh year marks the beginning of a new cycle of restoration and freedom. We pray that in the timeline of our grief for Danny, this seventh year brings renewed energy and progress - both in ho... **See more**

Our network of family and friends remembers Dan's anniversary each year with their support and comfort. Here are some of their wise words:

Danny remains in our hearts forever! We pray for Justice with renewed energy. May you always have the strength and support to never give up the quest to bring those responsible to pay for their despicable unthinkable crime. One day we hope you can reunite with your beautiful grandsons.

Our thoughts are with you on this sad Anniversary when Danny's vibrant life was taken,

Pearl for Larry too

Thank you for sharing this, Ruth. What a touching reminder of the man that Dan was and the fight you have waged all of these years. Wishing you health and comfort and justice in the year to come.
Love,
Rusty Silverstein

We continue to remember Dan every day, and more publicly every year on July 19.

At the same time, I have been blessed by the people who have helped me along the way in dealing with Dan's death. I have shared their contributions in the book to show that having this important network has been a blessing. My group of friends, legal advisors, outsiders, and well-wishers, including my own "murder coach" (a person who experienced a similar tragedy and generously shared his legal, media, and emotional strategies with me) has been an unexpected gift in the midst of so much loss.

October came slowly, with anticipation of the season's gravity and meaning. Our family observes a number of special birthdays this month, not to mention it often coincides with the High Holidays in our faith.

Justice for Dan didn't want Danny's forty-ninth birthday to pass by unobserved, especially because it would have fallen in the middle of the trial, which was no longer happening at that time. Karen Cyphers, Jason Solomon, Jeremy Cohen, and Tamara Demko arranged virtual and in-person celebrations to honor his memory. They created a toy drive, in which friends could donate toys or money to Toys for Tots Tallahassee. Those who lived in town brought these toys to Winthrop Park—located just a block from where Dan had lived and where he had loved to bring the boys to play. The park has a bench with a plaque in his memory. Karen and Tamara decorated the bench with flowers and donated toys, which had been sent from friends around the world. News coverage of the event led to others contributing gifts. It was a joy to know that children would receive these gifts in Dan's honor at a time when our family was missing him and his boys so deeply.

While we continued to honor Dan in the ways only a family and friends can, our lawyers remained steadfast and focused on the case. On December 9, 2021, they issued a letter to Georgia Cappleman, imploring the State to fight hard against any further continuances.

And then, the waiting continued.

GIBSON DUNN

Gibson, Dunn & Crutcher LLP
200 Park Avenue
New York, NY 10166-0193
Tel 212.351.4000
www.gibsondunn.com

Matthew J. Benjamin
Direct: +1 212.351.4079
Fax: +1 212.351.6279
MBenjamin@gibsondunn.com

Client: 62527-00001

December 9, 2021

VIA E-MAIL

Georgia Cappleman
Assistant State Attorney
Office of the State Attorney
Second Judicial Circuit
301 S. Monroe Street
Tallahassee, FL 32301

Re: *State of Florida v. Katherine D. Magbanua*, No. 2016 CF 3036A

Dear Assistant State Attorney Cappleman:

We represent the family of Dan Markel—his mother Ruth, his father Phil, and his sister Shelly. On behalf of the Markel Family, I write to respectfully oppose any further continuance in this matter.

It has been more than seven years since Dan Markel was brutally murdered outside of his home. After years of repeated delays and a hung jury, on September 12, 2021 defense counsel for Katherine Magbanua again filed a motion for continuance. The Markel Family understands and respects the Court's decision to grant the requested continuance, and appreciates the challenges presented by the current public health circumstances. At the same time, we believe it is important that the trial proceed on the current schedule (to begin on February 14, 2022) and would therefore respectfully oppose any further adjournments.

At this late date, more than seven years after Dan's murder, nearly five years since Ms. Magbanua's arrest, and two years after Ms. Magbanua's first trial, further delay would cause the Markel Family significant further pain and anguish, and would not be in the interests of justice. *See Martel v. Clair*, 565 U.S. 648, 662 (2012) ("Protecting against abusive delay is an interest of justice."). The Markels have suffered unfathomable grief and loss. They continue to suffer, some in declining health in their elder years, each and every passing day. Of course, no trial or verdict could ever heal the trauma and loss the Markel Family continues to suffer every day. Maintaining the current trial schedule would begin to provide, however, some of the healing and justice that the Markels deserve. As your Office and the Court well knows, justice delayed is justice denied. The interests of both the Markel Family, as victims of this heinous crime, and the public compel this trial to proceed on the current

Beijing • Brussels • Century City • Dallas • Denver • Dubai • Frankfurt • Hong Kong • Houston • London • Los Angeles • Munich
New York • Orange County • Palo Alto • Paris • San Francisco • São Paulo • Singapore • Washington, D.C.

GIBSON DUNN

Georgia Cappleman
December 9, 2021
Page 2

schedule. We would therefore respectfully ask the Court to deny any requests for further continuance that might be made.

Respectfully submitted,

/s/ Matthew Benjamin
Matthew Benjamin

Part III

REFLECTIONS AND LOOKING FORWARD

CHAPTER 8

Seeking Justice in the Pandemic

The COVID-19 pandemic poses risks for people who work in the courts system, and it has halted the capacity of the justice system to stay open and run trials.

We have seen limited collaboration on global levels and great suffering from death and loss of personal livelihoods.

Amid the pandemic, many countries have reported an increase in domestic violence and sexual exploitation. This increase, along with acts of suicide and violent and criminal incidents, puts further demands on the justice system. As the backlog of case hearings occurs, many victims feel trapped due to an absence of investigations, charges, and convictions. Violence has exacerbated amid shutdowns, economic hardships, and isolation from COVID-19.

Under normal circumstances, hearings and trials proceed routinely without consideration for the victims. It is important to articulate your concerns as a victim, not just at the beginning but throughout the process.

Keep an open mind during the investigation and stay engaged and active. Continue to ask for support and information because it will become useful as your case progresses.

The repercussions of the pandemic affected the preparedness of the criminal justice system and still pose current and future challenges. For example, "the right to proceedings free from unreasonable delay, and to a prompt and final conclusion of the case and any related post-judgment proceedings" has been impacted by the pandemic.

The loss of presence and visibility for victims of crime during these unprecedented times further damaged their participation.

Previous high-profile criminal trials are on pause and no longer in the limelight due to the new medical, economic, and social issues of the current pandemic reality.

The justice and court system around the globe faces new challenges. Even forensic activity is compromised as people work from their homes and don't have access to the necessary equipment.

We cannot let our quest for justice diminish, even in this crisis as other issues of the pandemic become the priority. Continuous investigation and legal documentation are critical as evidence and witnesses' memories are time sensitive. It is well known that the accuracy of witnesses' testimonies change as time moves on.

Access to jury selection, trials, and convictions has become limited during the pandemic. In our experience, travel bans between Canada and the United States have greatly impacted our victim participation. Even within the Florida state criminal justice system, interviewing witnesses, visiting inmates, and carrying on investigations have decreased.

Victims are seeing their cases postponed, even beyond temporary measures. In our case, for example, the health of the defense team was compromised, and the judge granted an extension to October 2021 after the court was ready to start the retrial in July 2021.

We continue to keep our cause for the support of homicide victims alive and to seek justice, even after the long delay of two years from the trial of 2019 to the new retrial in 2021.

We have become experts in waiting and uncertainty. We experienced a major setback with the mistrial of Magbanua. I have experienced some of the events and knowledge of the trial life, such as my introduction to new language—murder-for-hire, witnesses, sentencing, and the death penalty. This language has given me some understanding to participate in the court system.

As we were well into the trial process and finally gaining some momentum, nobody could have anticipated the setbacks caused by the COVID-19 pandemic.

But in a moment, everything changed. Life in the general population and our private lives are now full of virtual experiences—Zoom is an everyday activity like brushing your teeth. We all search for normalcy and routine in a world turned upside down.

We were hopeful to move forward in our search for justice but now faced extraordinary challenges.

Can we still remain steadfast? Can we still expect a better outcome? Will the court system reinvent itself to operate in a safe environment? Will there be a live trial or remote trial? Will the building be wiped down due to COVID-19?

Our family is not alone in the disruption; murders, shootings, hate crimes, and losses have been experienced by other families since Dan's death in 2014. The pandemic has brought so much grief and uncertainty to families and nursing home residents.

When the pandemic first started, Canada's outbreak mimicked other countries in nursing homes, which caused catastrophic health and safety issues, and high numbers of death.

Together, the world navigated through all the difficulties to get personal protective equipment (PPE) and enough vaccines. And millions confronted the inequities in Black, Brown, and Indigenous communities of the determinants of health, such as poverty, poor housing, and discrimination.

With aggressive approaches to vaccine "hot spots" with "pop-up clinics," we were hoping to see the light at the end of the tunnel. Suddenly, in May and June 2021, the Canadian COVID-19 experience became even more grim. It was revealed that 215 indigenous children's remains were found near a residential school.

Here are some examples of terrible tragedies where the path to justice was disrupted by the pandemic:

Parkland School Shooting Trial Still in Limbo
February 14, 2018

Three years ago, on February 14, 2018, a gunman, Nikolas Cruz, burst into a Florida high school, killing seventeen people and wounding seventeen others. The trial of the twenty-two-year-old has been postponed due to the COVID-19 pandemic. Cruz's lawyers have stated that he would plead guilty in exchange for a life sentence, but prosecutors are planning to seek the death penalty at trial. So far, a trial date has not been set.[1]

In June of 2020, Alyssa's Law, which requires all Florida public schools to have a mobile panic alarm system to reduce law enforcement response time, was signed by Governor Ron DeSantis. Alyssa's Law was named in honor of fourteen-year-old Alyssa Alhadeff, who lost her life in the Parkland shooting. After years of advocating for increased safety measures in the public school system, Raptor Technologies, a school safety software, was selected by seven Florida counties as the mobile panic provider to meet the Alyssa's Law requirement for the 2021–2022 school year.[2]

Toronto Danforth Shooting
July 22, 2018

Around 8:30 p.m. on July 22, 2018, Faisal Hussain went on a deadly shooting rampage in Toronto's Danforth neighborhood, killing two people and injuring thirteen others. Shortly after the shooting, Hussain was found dead of a self-inflicted gunshot wound to the head. About a year after the shooting, no clear explanation or motive has emerged.[3]

Pittsburgh Synagogue Tree of Life Shooting
October 27, 2018

On October 27, 2018, gunman Robert Bowers, forty-six, opened fire at a Pittsburgh synagogue where Sabbath services were being held. The shooting killed eleven people and wounded several police officers before Bowers was taken into custody. Bowers was charged with twenty-nine federal counts, which included eleven counts of use of a firearm to commit murder. Before opening fire in the

1 Curt Anderson, "3 Years Later, Parkland School Shooting Trial Still in Limbo," Associated Press, February 11, 2021, https://apnews.com/article/shootings-trials-florida-coronavirus-pandemic-school-shootings-ece0803d42d5d4c11ebadcf96d9d4399.

2 Raptor Technologies, "Florida School Districts Select Raptor Technologies as their Panic Alert Solution for Alyssa's Law Requirement," Cision, June 24, 2021, https://www.prnewswire.com/news-releases/florida-school-districts-select-raptor-technologies-as-their-panic-alert-solution-for-alyssas-law-requirement-301318906.html.

3 "Faisal Hussain, Gunman in Danforth Shooting Rampage, Killed Himself: Police Source," CBC News, July 26, 2018, https://www.cbc.ca/news/canada/toronto/danforth-gunman-suicide-1.4761775.

synagogue, Bowers allegedly said, "All Jews must die." The shooting was prosecuted as a hate crime.[4]

Ethiopian Airlines Crash, Flight 302
March 10, 2019

An Ethiopian Airlines flight from Addis Ababa crashed shortly after takeoff on Sunday morning, March 10, 2019, killing all 157 people onboard. Six minutes after taking off, the plane, en route to Nairobi, Kenya, lost contact at 8:44 a.m. After takeoff, the pilot reported technical difficulties and was given clearance from air traffic controllers to return to Addis Ababa. After thorough investigations, it was deemed that this crash occurred due to a fatal flaw with the plane.[5]

Various attorneys have been monitoring the investigations and are representing surviving family members whose pain and anxieties are exacerbated by the uncertainty surrounding the crash.[6]

Ukraine International Airlines, Flight 752
January 8, 2020

On January 8, 2020, after taking off from Tehran, Iran, Ukraine International Airlines Flight 752 was shot down by an Iranian air missile. All 176 people on board were killed, including fifty-five Canadians and thirty permanent residents. On March 17, 2021, Iran released an accident investigation report into the crash; however, there remains a lack of convincing evidence and information.[7]

Families of the Canadian victims called on the Canadian government to conduct an investigation into the causes of this tragedy. Canada has been committed to working with its allies to ensure a thorough and credible investigation to determine liability. In June 2021, the government of Canada released a report confirming that

---

4 Kalhan Rosenblatt, Tom Winter, and Jonathan Dienst, "11 Dead in Shooting at Pittsburgh Synagogue, Suspect in Custody," NBC News, October 27, 2018, https://www.nbcnews.com/news/us-news/active-shooter-reported-near-pittsburgh-synagogue-n925211.

5 "Ethiopian Airlines: 'No Survivors' on Crashed Boeing 737," BBC News, March 10, 2019, https://www.bbc.com/news/world-africa-47513508.

6 "Ethiopian Airlines Flight 302," Podhurst Orseck, accessed June 25, 2021, https://ethiopianflight302.com/.

7 Christopher Reynolds, "Ottawa Rejects Iran Report That Blames Shootdown of Flight 752 on 'Human Error,'" CTV News, March 17, 2021, https://www.ctvnews.ca/canada/ottawa-rejects-iran-report-that-blames-shootdown-of-flight-752-on-human-error-1.5350716.

Iranian authorities, through their decisions and actions, are fully responsible for the crash of Flight 752.[8]

George Floyd
May 25, 2020

On May 25, 2020, a forty-six-year-old Black man, George Floyd, was killed in Minneapolis while being arrested for allegedly using a counterfeit bill. After Floyd was handcuffed and lying face down, a white police officer with the Minneapolis Police Department, Derek Chauvin, knelt on Floyd's neck for eight to nine minutes. During this arrest, Floyd expressed being unable to breath and his fear of dying. Several minutes after, Floyd stopped speaking and was pronounced dead. The next day, videos of the event were released by witnesses. Autopsies found Floyd's death to be a homicide. Officer Chauvin was charged with second-degree manslaughter, second-degree unintentional murder, and third-degree murder. Floyd's death has sparked worldwide protests against police brutality, specifically the mistreatment of Black people by police.[9]

The Capitol Insurrection
January 6, 2021

On January 6, 2021, the U.S. Capitol was stormed by Trump supporters declaring that they would go to violent lengths to keep Trump, the former president, in power. The Capitol went into lock-down while rioters vandalized the building for several hours. This violent invasion, which left five people dead, has been deemed the "White Riot." Many have commented about the racial dimensions of the insurrection, stating that if the mob had been Black, the Capitol would have been "painted" red with their blood.[10]

---

8 "Canadian Report Blames Iranian Recklessness for Shoot-Down of Ukraine International Airlines Flight 752," Prime Minister of Canada, accessed June 25, 2021, https://pm.gc.ca/en/news/statements/2021/06/24/canadian-report-blames-iranian-recklessness-shoot-down-ukraine.

9 Helier Cheung, "George Floyd Death: Why US Protests Are So Powerful This Time," BBC News, June 8, 2020, https://www.bbc.com/news/world-us-canada-52969905.

10 Mallory Simon and Sara Sidner, "Decoding the Extremist Symbols and Groups at the Capitol Hill Insurrection," CNN, January 11, 2021.

In May 2021, the U.S. House of Representatives voted to create an independent commission to investigate the attack on the Capitol. However, this bill failed in the Senate in a 54–35 vote.[11]

Pandemic Death Lawsuits in US Against Nursing Homes
February 25, 2021

Throughout the pandemic, nursing homes across the United States have been hit hard by the COVID-19 virus. This included spreading the virus at alarming rates and running short on essential resources to protect against the virus. Not enough attention was being paid to those who live in nursing homes, a high-risk population.[12]

Lawsuits against nursing homes have been filed by grieving family members across the country. For example, families are suing a home in Kentucky for not educating the staff about the importance of wearing protective equipment. In New Jersey, fifteen families are suing a home that made national headlines when twenty bodies were found piled in a morgue built to handle only a few. Lawsuits against homes are increasing as reports of shocking conditions continue to emerge.[13]

Atlanta Spa Shooting Massacre
March 16, 2021

On Tuesday evening, a gunman killed six Asian women and two others in spas across the metropolitan Atlanta area. This massacre shocked the entire country, because it deals with a surge in violence against people of Asian descent. Three hours after the shooting, Robert Aaron Long, twenty-one, was arrested after being intercepted by police on Interstate 75 in Crisp County. The motive behind Long's rampage is still undetermined. Authorities are continuing to investigate.[14]

---

11 Peter Stevenson, Adrián Blanco, and Daniela Santamariña, "Which Senators Supported a Jan. 6 Capitol Riot Commission," *The Washington Post*, May 28, 2021, https://www.washingtonpost.com/politics/interactive/2021/january6-commission-senators-vote/.

12 Ritu Prasad, "Coronavirus: How Bad Is the Crisis in US Care Homes?," BBC News, July 13, 2020, https://www.bbc.com/news/world-us-canada-53172302.

13 Ritu Prasad, 2020.

14 Intelligencer Staff, "What We Know About the Atlanta-Area Spa Attacks," Intelligencer, March 21, 2021, https://nymag.com/intelligencer/2021/03/7-dead-after-shootings-at-multiple-spas-in-atlanta-updates.html.

In May 2021, President Joe Biden signed legislation that tracks and responds to hate crimes, with a focus on stopping anti-Asian violence. Given the long history of silencing Asians in America, this law aims to elevate their experiences and amplify their voices by making hate crime reporting more accessible.[15]

Derek Chauvin Trial
April 20, 2021

On April 20, 2021, a jury found Derek Chauvin, former Minneapolis police officer, guilty of second-degree murder, third-degree murder, and second-degree manslaughter, stemming from the killing of George Floyd on May 25, 2020. The jury reached the verdict on only their second day of deliberations. This case has become a milestone in American history for the accountability of law enforcement.[16]

Many of these families are amid investigations, hearings, and trials, which have been delayed by COVID-19. We join the mourners seeking justice during the pandemic.

While many trials were delayed, the Derek Chauvin trial took place in April 2021, which attracted lots of publicity and high interest across America during the pandemic. The trial culminated in a period of condemning police brutality and searched for fairness and justice among Black and Brown communities.

The twelve jurors unanimously agreed that Chauvin caused Floyd's death. There was pride and relief across America when the verdict was announced.

Remains of 215 Indigenous Children
May 30, 2021

In the city of Kamloops in southern British Columbia, the remains of 215 Indigenous children were found. All of the children had been students at the Kamloops Indian Residential School, which was the largest school in Canada's residential school system. Unfortunately,

15 "Will a New Law to Tackle Hate Crimes Make Asians in America Safer? | Pro/Con," *The Philadelphia Inquirer*, June 7, 2021, https://www.inquirer.com/opinion/commentary/asians-hate-crime-law-prevention-20210603.html.

16 Tucker Higgins, "Former Police Officer Derek Chauvin Found Guilty of Murder, Manslaughter in the Death of George Floyd," CNBC, April 21, 2021, https://www.cnbc.com/2021/04/20/derek-chauvin-trial-verdict.html.

many more children are unaccounted for; thousands of children died in these schools, and their bodies were never returned home and left in unmarked and neglected graves. These findings created mass outrage and anger across Canada, with many people building temporary memorials throughout the country.[17]

This discovery has also called upon communities to further investigate the number of missing and murdered Indigenous children. For example, a Saskatchewan First Nation was preparing to locate bodies using a ground-penetrating radar. On June 24, 2021, they announced the discovery of 751 unmarked graves near the former Marieval Indian Residential School.[18]

The Canadian and American Catholic community hopes for an apology from the pope.

Then suddenly, on June 6, as we anticipated some relief from vaccine initiatives, we were faced with a crime against Muslims in London, Ontario.

Muslim Family Killing in London, Ontario
June 6, 2021

On June 6, 2021, a Muslim Canadian family was murdered by a speeding truck in a hit-and-run during their evening stroll. This unthinkable tragedy was not an accident; this family was targeted and attacked because of their Muslim faith. The only survivor of this terror attack was a nine-year-old boy, who was hospitalized with serious injuries. His father, mother, grandmother, and fifteen-year-old sister were all killed.[19]

While many Canadians are shocked by this mass murder, the warning signs of white nationalist violence have been growing. Between 2012 and 2015, hate crimes against Muslim communities

---

17 Tom Yun, Creeson Agecoutay, and Alexandra Mae Jones, "Tiny Shoes and Lowered Flags: Memorials Spread for 215 First Nations Children Found Buried in Mass Grave in B.C.," CTV News, May 30, 2021, https://www.ctvnews.ca/canada/tiny-shoes-and-lowered-flags-memorials-spread-for-215-first-nations-children-found-buried-in-mass-grave-in-b-c-1.5448699.

18 Bryan Eneas, "Sask. First Nation Announces Discovery of 751 Unmarked Graves Near Former Residential School," CBC News, June 24, 2021, https://www.cbc.ca/news/canada/saskatchewan/cowessess-marieval-indian-residential-school-news-1.6078375.

19 Jasmin Zine, "Muslim Family Killed in Terror Attack in London, Ontario: Islamophobic Violence Surfaces Once Again in Canada," The Conversation, June 8, 2021, https://theconversation.com/muslim-family-killed-in-terror-attack-in-london-ontario-islamophobic-violence-surfaces-once-again-in-canada-162400.

in Canada increased by 253 percent. Many officials, including Prime Minister Justin Trudeau, have promised Canadian Muslims action against Islamophobia.[20]

A new wave of victims was confronted with grief. Our expectations for a summer of relief were thwarted. This pandemic year also had other complications, as adults, artists, athletes, and professionals battle the challenges of depression, anxiety, addictions, and suicide; messages abound that say, "Look after yourself and talk about it."

Mental Health and Addictions; COVID-19 Pandemic
March 2020 to June 2021

The COVID-19 pandemic has negatively affected the lives of all people everywhere. In Canada, the ongoing economic recession, the changes to our daily lives and routines, and the separation from family and loved ones, among other stressors, have been linked to an increase in substance use and to the worsening of mental health among many Canadians. As the pandemic entered its second year, an ongoing survey of Canadians' mental health and substance use indicated that depressive symptoms, loneliness, levels of anxiety, and binge drinking remained as high as they were in late May 2020.[21]

Florida Condo Building Collapse
June 24, 2021

On Thursday, June 24, 2021, there was a partial building collapse in Surfside, Florida. To date, ninety-eight people have been confirmed dead, and all 242 are accounted for. Search and rescue teams worked around the clock to find the missing. City officials said that the cause of the collapse was unknown, but new details have emerged about the structural integrity of the building. A 2018 engineering report highlighted the building's need for repairs due to significant breaks and cracks in the concrete.[22]

---

20 Jasmin Zine, 2021.

21 "Mental Health and Substance Use During COVID-19," Canadian Centre on Substance Use and Addiction, accessed June 17, 2021, https://www.ccsa.ca/mental-health-and-substance-use-during-covid-19.

22 Maureen Chowdhury and Melissa Macaya, "Key Things to Know about the Condo Collapse Investigation So Far," CNN, June 28, 2021, https://www.cnn.com/us/live-news/miami-florida-building-collapse-06-28-21-intl/h_1a983d6cacc981d9376cb19080700719.

Families of the missing gathered around the building collapse, hoping that someone could be alive somewhere under the broken rubble.[23]

Other health conditions have also had serious and long-lasting tolls, as regular medical and dental visits have declined.

Keeping your family and those around you safe, with vaccinations, hygiene, social distancing, and wearing masks.

We could only hope that our vulnerability would be reduced as we welcomed the innovations of the pandemic and provided health care to where people are, such as in their homes through telemedicine. We hoped that this past fall and winter would turn the tide and allow for some normalcy.

A long year of hardship revealed inequities and resentment.

For some people, faith and courage have helped to manage expectations and despair. We are all searching for a sense of peace and connection. There is screen fatigue, and people are remembering the physicality of sharing space in transportation and even grocery shopping. Life is different for now, and people have struggled in isolation to avoid staying apart by creating little communities, getting pets, and staying sober. We are all waiting for the day to be together again.

The theme of COVID-19 isolation came full circle for our family as we prepared a statement for the 2021 grandparent bill hearing in the Florida Senate. We acknowledged to the committee that "millions of people around the world were estranged from their families due to the deadly disease, but for our family, this distance would not be overcome through vaccines or a cure alone. For us, the distance from our grandchildren was caused by a different evil, one that we would need the help of lawmakers to fix. We are on that path today."

---

23 Associated Press, "Families of the Missing Visit Site of Florida Condo Collapse," Politico, June 27, 2021, https://www.politico.com/news/2021/06/27/families-florida-condo-collapse-496636.

CHAPTER 9

Media

In Dan's case, the media was present from the beginning, when we were highly traumatized. We made the choice not to "go public," our family term for media requests, which had already surfaced before any arrests due to this highly sensational murder. The media propelled the case in many different formats—print, television, broadcast, and social media—and kept this heinous crime in the spotlight. There was no shortage of requests for our family to work with the media.

As mentioned, we were very privileged with TV shows, such as the *20/20* episode "In-Laws and Outlaws," on September 17, 2016. We also appeared on *Dateline NBC*: "Cold-Blooded," on April 12, 2018. Investigation Discovery had a show: *People Magazine Investigates: Marked for Murder*, on December 18, 2017. *Over My Dead Body* by Wondery was a very well received podcast started on January 29, 2019. Later on, the ABC and NBC productions created second episodes.

Although Dan was well known as a legal scholar, he was a talented writer and speaker in non-academic environments. He had a long list of contributions in print and TV, speaking engagements, and blogging. We now followed Dan's path in working with the media.

The public has always had an insatiable appetite for true crime. Ask anyone, and they will tell you exactly where they were during the O.J. Bronco car chase. From Ted Bundy and Pamela Smart to the Menendez Brothers and Casey Anthony, it seems that we as a society cannot get enough of these stories, and lately this passion for crime and murder has all but exploded. Media outlets are crowded with podcasts (*Dirty John, Joe Exotic, Crime Junkie, Serial, My Favorite Murder*), television specials (*Dateline, 20/20, Making of a Murderer*), and scripted shows (*Law & Order, CSI, Sherlock*). Entire networks have been created around the topic of violent crime (ID, Oxygen, Court TV).

Our culture is obsessed with murders, victims, law enforcement, and the FBI. It is inescapable. At times, this has made my family's life unimaginably hard, seeing as we've been given a starring role in a sensational case.

The circumstances surrounding Dan's death are, unfortunately, a true-crime addict's dream. As such stories go, at least the ones that reach the entertainment world, this one has it all: money, fast cars, hitmen, beautiful people, sandy beaches, plastic surgery, and dueling families. Even Samantha Magbanua, Katherine's sister-in-law, paid major money to a faith healer in an embezzlement scheme she would be arrested for. As it was also the focus of two episodes of *20/20* and two episodes of *Dateline*, both shows are preparing follow-up coverage as the trials resume. As much as it's been hard for me to endure all these retellings, I realize that this kind of attention is in fact a type of privilege. So many cases lose steam in the criminal justice system. This media attention might help keep the heat on Dan's case until the mystery of those who had him murdered is solved.

But the truth of my life is defined by my son's murder and is far from glitzy. I am seventy-seven years old and will likely die before reaching the small satisfaction of any kind of meaningful justice.

I often feel like the most intimate details of my private life are being played out and dissected in public. Like the families of victims of mass shootings, crimes of passion, drive-by killings, gang violence, domestic abuse, and other horrifying tragedies suffered by innocents, I have found that everything I ever knew about my day-to-day reality has been flipped on its head. Since the moment Dan's trial began, my every waking moment has been dominated by preparing for, enduring, or analyzing days, weeks, and months in court, seeking to convict Dan's killers.

True-crime stories often disproportionally focus on the criminal, pushing the victims and their families aside. In the excitement of scrutinizing villains and ascertaining guilt, the terrible suffering that these stories create for those left behind goes all but unnoticed. Media productions often forget the truth of true crime, the real flesh-and-blood survivors who are left with ruptured lives. So, the consumers of true crime get everything they want. But me? I had no manual to guide me on such things as helping the police collect evidence, writing a victim impact statement, or knowing the best way to take care of myself to maintain my stamina during this lengthy process. That is why I wanted to write this book. So that I can show others.

I have uncovered the human dimensions of standard words in criminal proceedings—evidence, verdicts, sentencing, victim rights, and victim impact statements. But we are still waiting for other events such as *plea bargaining* by any other co-conspirators, and words such as *guilty*.

Another reason for writing this book is to highlight issues and problems involving the legal rights of grandparents in Florida. Five years ago, Phil and I were unceremoniously blocked from seeing Dan's children, our grandchildren, while the family of Wendi, our ex–daughter-in-law, has unlimited access to them. Shelly and her family have also been kept from seeing Benjamin and Lincoln connected to their father's family and friends. The parental rights laws in Florida are strongly predisposed toward the natural parents. On behalf of our family, advocates are working to change Florida law to allow grandparents greater ability to access courts to petition for visitation rights. These efforts have so far received support from Florida lawmakers, including a unanimous passage through the Senate Children, Families, and Elder Affairs Committee. Advocates are working on a revised bill for the 2022 session.

After the unveiling in 2015, I had to return to my shadow existence of the trial life, with the media becoming an essential alliance. Now that Dan's murder is seven years old, our hope is that the case does not trail off. The amount of time, energy, money, and mindset required to live inside a trial is enormous. Most people cannot just abandon their immediate families, jobs, and homes to focus solely on what is happening in a courtroom. But my family has been able to participate fully in this process.

Even so, we have our own limits. For example, we were told it would be better for the case if we lived in Tallahassee, not Toronto. The presence of our family would put more pressure on law enforcement and the state attorney, which would keep this case in the public eye. As much as we love Dan, and even with all the time, energy, and resources we've invested in this situation, it would just be too hard for us. Shelly, Phil, and I all have commitments back in Canada. Already, it is not simple to be in Florida for long stretches. But moving full time, to the murder site, for this trial that we've already dedicated our lives to, would feel like a full-time job, juggling the unpredictable schedule of the criminal system.

Justice for Dan launched a petition signed by more than nine hundred people to try to push the state attorney to prosecute Wendi Adelson's older brother, Charlie, and mother, Donna.

With the help of our gifted lawyers at Gibson Dunn, particularly Orin Snyder and Matthew Benjamin, we have released numerous family statements thanking the police and prosecutors, letting them know we hope that they persist in their diligence in Dan's case.

From the start, there has been a tremendous, almost overwhelming, amount of media interest in Dan's case. Wall-to-wall coverage of the murder and the trial in the *Tallahassee Democrat* and on local TV news started the day of the murder in July 2014 and continues to date. National media interest has also remained steady.

Released on January 29, 2019, Wondery's *Over My Dead Body: Dan Markel* had over seven million downloads and has been optioned for other programs such as a TV series. It was the first season of this series, which later followed with other crime stories. A follow-up podcast is probably in the works for when the trials resume. One episode focused on the inside perspective of a juror who spoke publicly for the first time. You can find the podcast on Apple, Stitcher, or elsewhere.

With the retrial coming up and likely additional trials for the indicted co-conspirators, there will no doubt be another firestorm of media interest.

There were other challenges early on related to facing the abundant media attention that arose due to Dan's international acclaim. At the time, my family needed privacy, and yet this media attention became welcomed and instrumental as things progressed. While prosecutors and investigators do their jobs, there are huge emotional aspects of waiting, such as turmoil and disappointment, to name a few. The impacts of these delays linger on and on.

In addition to being the subject of continual on-screen news coverage on local TV stations since July 2014, Dan's murder quickly became national news, featured on numerous network and cable channels. Long-running, high-profile investigative news programs have dedicated hours to our family's story, with continuing interest focused on the case in the run-up to the retrial of Katherine Magbanua during the first half of 2022. Previous TV programs include:

- *20/20* (ABC): "In-Laws and Outlaws," September 17, 2016
- *Dateline* (NBC): "Cold-Blooded," April 12, 2018
- *Investigation Discovery: People Magazine Investigates: Marked for Murder*, December 18, 2017
- *Court TV* on YouTube

The pending Florida legislation to grant grandparents visitation rights after a homicide also engendered TV news coverage. Phil and I appeared on *20/20* in October 2019 to discuss how we have been banned from seeing our grandsons. We have been approached to participate in follow-up interviews for both NBC and ABC.

Where Are We Now?

We have had a "silent partner,"—the media—a travel companion throughout the uphill challenges of the criminal process and our portrayals as victims of crime.

Crime coverage has always been newsworthy, but how the media covers crime impacts the victim, offender, investigation, trial, and jury.

The media have been far from silent but very present and available in this high-drama case. They have followed our quest for justice in print, social media, blogs, podcasts, group chats, and TV programs. Their attendance and visibility was even evident during COVID-19 as they attended all the hearings.

Numerous comments, posts, and videos on social media were very supportive of our family, along with some relevant criticism.

The media experience with our journey for visitation as grandparents has been very positive, sensitive, and timely. We have had considerable coverage and representation in all the legislative initiatives dealing with our attempts for reunification with our grandchildren, Benjamin and Lincoln.

The media allowed us to talk about our story of grandparent alienation and to speak out about our suffering on the very serious reality that confronts millions of people. We have a grateful heart toward the media in this high-profile case and always hope it will bring new information and insights.

We have to acknowledge that we have also been privileged to have the support of person to person reporting. There is so much informal sharing on issues both directly related to the case and tangential to it. For example, we recently learned through word of mouth that Harvey Adelson was retiring. He had sent an email to members of his circle, telling them of the sale of the Adelson Institute. This was shared with us through various channels, a wonderful network of people who stay watchful on this case. Interestingly, the email from Harvey was dated the very day the October 2021 trial was originally set to start.

From: **Harvey Adelson D.M.D.**
Date: Mon, Oct 4, 2021 at 1:25 PM

Subject: Announcement from Dr. Harvey Adelson
To: Drs. Harvey and Charlie Adelson

Dear Patients,

I would like to take this opportunity to introduce Dr. Yeganeh Rezaie, to whom I am transitioning the ownership of my practice. I wanted to be very certain that our patients continue to receive the best possible dental care. I know that Dr. Rezaie and her team possess the qualifications to do so and will bring a wealth of valuable experience and excellence to our practice.

Dr. Rezaie has been serving the Broward community for over 10 years. With her extensive clinical skills and expertise, she enjoys treating patients of all ages and takes pride in understanding and listening to the needs of her patients while making them feel comfortable. Her knowledge of routine dental care as well as cosmetic dentistry, oral surgery, dental implants, Invisalign, facial rejuvenation and more, allows her to offer excellent individualized care to each and every patient.

It has been my privilege to serve and know you over the many years I have been in this community and an honor to have been able to call each one of you, not only patients, but friends! With this transition of ownership, I can assure you a continuation of the highest quality of professional dental care. Thank you all!

If you have any questions please contact the office directly or send an email to: ______. Please save this new email for any future communication.

Most Sincerely,
Harvey Adelson, DMD

CHAPTER 10

The Endings and the Beginnings

As the COVID-19 pandemic surged again in Florida, the retrial of Katherine Magbanua was scheduled for October 14, 2021 then moved again to February 14, 2022.

On August 25, 2021, the defense team was persistent in trying to get this retrial canceled, but the judge made arrangements for the trial to move ahead. At the time of this writing, it still has not happened.

I was making plans with Shelly on what flight route and airports would be safest to travel. In 2022, I prefer one direct flight to Orlando and driving to Tallahassee rather than connecting flights through two airports.

The challenges and risks of travel would continue to be on our minds.

I was hoping for socially distanced proceedings and people wearing masks. We would need extra jurors, and hopefully they would be vaccinated.

* * *

During September 2021 in Toronto, it is the week before Rosh Hashanah, the Jewish New Year. It is my tradition, and that of many others, to visit gravesites at the cemetery. I went on August 29, 2021, and shared my private thoughts with Dan, to let him know I was still fighting for justice and the reunification with his children, my grandchildren.

We will all die someday, but forty-one is too soon. Many international memorials were organized and held. Dan did not live long enough to leave a legacy project to remember those who meant the most to him or specific support donations such as scholarships. Dan pledged a donation to Harvard University through his insurance.

Our grandchildren, Benjamin and Lincoln, will find many opportunities to listen to and learn about their father's story through recordings, social media, podcasts, TV shows, and his published work. Our greatest hope is that they will see where their father lived, visit his gravesite, and connect with his living family.

While at the cemetery, I was reflective and looked forward and backward on my life with Dan. I remembered, as I sat alone in silence, how Dan did so much and made his life count in so many ways despite passing away too young. My most vivid memory of Dan when he was a toddler was as Dennis the Menace—he played with mops and step ladders. His next favorite activities were comic books, tennis, baseball, and Trivial Pursuit. He loved to play at school, excelled at drama, and dabbled a bit with the guitar. He was unreliable for piano lessons because he seldom showed up on time. His piano teacher was a very serious instructor and canceled his lessons: "Ruth, I cannot be a babysitter." All the while, Shelly excelled in piano.

Dan as an adult had one regret—that he did not learn more music. He appreciated all kinds of music, and all his expenditures were on music discs and books. He loved to dance and was a natural.

Dan's accomplishments in his childhood and youth were not all scholarly and included hockey, baseball, tennis, and skiing. His summer jobs ranged from dishwasher and walking courier, to working in a bakery and as a receptionist in a children's haircutting salon.

Our work brought Phil and me extensive travel to Europe, New York, and California. We often took our children with us to avoid long absences. Both Shelly and Dan understood packing, suitcases, travel documents, bringing along books to read, and travel timelines. Back in Canada, we visited Montreal frequently for most of the Jewish holidays. We also had a second home for winter and summer getaways.

In his late teens, Dan spent the summer at Cambridge (England), Israel, and Tufts University. He dreamed of attending Harvard, Yale, and Princeton, and he only applied to one Canadian university to have a backup plan, as Phil begged him.

He programmed his senior high school year for leadership as well as grades; he was talented and well read. School was easy for him. He restarted the school newspaper, organized the writers, and got ads to make it a success. His newspaper leadership had some rough experiences, as Danny expected a full range of "freedom of speech" and had to learn about boundaries. This was a hard lesson, which gave him some insights into organizational accountability. Danny went to Harvard and loved Boston, particularly Cambridge, Lowell House (his residence), and Harvard Hillel and Chabad. He was in his element and stayed an extra term to pay off his debt. He already had a very strong interest in Judaism and loved all the cultural experiences, including organizing Shabbat meals with his friends. His identity was with Israel, and the Jewish community defined his being.

This turned out to be enjoyable for me, as I attended Chabad in Arizona, Hungary, and Tallahassee. Dan's closeness to the Jewish community opened up many serious friendships with rabbis in different cities and countries.

Phil and I had always loved to travel and accumulated lots of stamps on our passports. We visited Dan in London, New York, Tel Aviv, Jerusalem, Boston, Phoenix, Miami, and Florida. It allowed us great pleasure to meet his international friends and see places he lived, studied, worked, married, and started a family.

Alone at the cemetery, I came out of my daze and thought, "What would have happened if he lived longer and had more time?"

Then I had a flashback to July 18, 2014, that day in Tallahassee, Florida, when Dan was shot.

* * *

People were going about their lives, working, running errands, and taking care of their families.

Dan dropped his sons, Benjamin and Lincoln, off at their daycare, hugging and kissing them goodbye, telling them he'd see them soon. He drove to the gym and worked out, as was his routine.

He also called Montreal and wished his uncle Lazar happy birthday for his ninety-seventh celebration.

It was just another day like so many others, yet it wasn't because two men in a murder-for-hire plot had been following Dan since he left his home that morning.

At about 11 a.m., Dan turned onto Trescott Drive and drove his car into his garage as routine. Dan was on his cell phone, saw a car in the driveway, and mentioned this to the person who was on the phone with him.

The gunman got out of the passenger seat and approached the driver's side window of Dan's car.

The gunman then pulled the trigger, shooting Dan twice through the car window. The person on the phone heard the shots and, getting no response from Dan, called 911.

What could it have been like for Dan? Amid the shock, horror, and pain, did he have time to realize what was happening to him? Did he know how gravely he was hurt and that he would never see his sons again?

Dan was much more than a news headline. I remember other times in his life, some as a young boy. Dan would wander off at times; even at age four, he was a free spirit.

One time, he hid inside the shirt rack in a men's department of The Bay, and Phil lost him. As we had just moved from Montreal to Toronto, I had drilled him on our new phone number. He went to a candy kiosk in the middle of the mall and called me: "I am lost."

Dan loved and was loved. The saddest experience of Dan's growing up was the loss of his special friend Marnie Kimelman, who was killed in a terrorist attack in Tel Aviv, Israel, on July 28, 1990. Dan was asked by the Kimelman family to give a tribute and wrote:

> *We are here tonight for a common purpose, to mourn the loss and preserve the memory of Marnie Tara Kimelman.*
>
> *I knew Marnie since our first day of senior kindergarten thirteen years ago this week. I had just moved here from Montreal when I met her, my first friend, confidante, and finger painting partner. I was quickly attracted to her charming personality and warm smile. Fortunately, I spent the next nine years (seven of which were in the same class) with Marnie at Associated. We grew up together during those nine years, and I got to know Marnie very well, academically*

and socially. She would help me with Torah and Science and I would reciprocate in Talmud and French. We carpooled, ate lunch, and did the Bar Mitzvah circuit together.

It never occurred to me that my childhood friend, Marnie Kimelman, would be stripped away from me, from her numerous school, camp and Israel friends or from her loving family.

What happened on July 28th was both tragic and shocking. Tragic, because an innocent person was killed; shocking, because this innocent person was Marnie. She had her whole life ahead of her. For most people, you see, the clock of life runs twenty-four hours, until midnight. Unfortunately, Marnie's ended at 9 o'clock in the morning. It was just unnatural for the young to die before the old.

The unfairness, the injustice of it all, that is what makes it so distressing. Because it could have been anyone else on that beach. Because it could have been any other place. And because it didn't have to be July 28, Shabbos no less, that the pipe bomb exploded. But it was. And that is what is so frightening. When someone like Marnie, so sensitive, beautiful, intelligent, lively, caring (the list goes on forever), leaves the world at the gentle age of seventeen it makes me scared. Scared because it proves we are no longer untouchable, no less vulnerable than the person sitting next to you.

Until that fateful day, I saw myself as a shaper of my own destiny, and along with so many other bright eyed teenagers about to conquer the world, we thought we were in control. But Marnie's death forces us to confront all our repressed fears and hidden anxieties. The suffering that we, Marnie's family and friends, are experiencing now is as undeserved as the pain we felt just 45 years ago. Our faith in a just moral order is re-examined when bad things like this happen to good people. Is it God's will, we wonder, or is it a test of our faith and decency? I have found no answers. However, we must try to find comfort in the same values to which Jews have always clung: the importance of establishing close families and strong friendships, of celebrating our culture, of passing on our heritage, and of supporting Eretz Yisroel.

It is of paramount significance that this tragedy does not deter you from visiting Israel in the future. You should visit for the same reason Marnie went there this summer.

Danny wanted to see the positive in a negative situation. Shelly's eulogy at Dan's funeral showed us how much he was loved.

We used to tease Danny that he had a hundred BEST friends because at every turning point or new geographic destination in his life, he would form a bond with someone new, a friendship that would last and be maintained for many years. I always knew that Danny had the power to connect people, but I don't think I ever fully realized how many people he had touched and how strong the bond was. Unlike my brother, I had never been much of a social media user before, but I have become an avid and addicted reader now. The outpouring of tributes from people with such strong bonds and memories of Dan has been a source of comfort to me, my parents, and my family. I can't stop reading the posts and I know they will leave a lasting memorial for Danny's sons, Ben and Lincoln. So, thank you.

Danny accomplished so much in his forty-one years. He went from being my little brother to a renowned scholar, teacher, and mature and devoted dad.

Danny was a person of strong principles and strong opinions. Intelligent and articulate. He was proud of all his accomplishments, but there was one thing that towered above all others in his pride, commitment and love…that was his two boys, Ben and Lincoln…he loved them so much and was such an involved, dedicated and beloved Abba to them. It seems almost every Facebook posting he made (and there were many) involved pictures and references to every move made by Ben-Ben and Linky. To put it in perspective, he was a serious guy, and academic, a professor…yet he always knew his priority was his boys and wasn't afraid to let the entire world know it.

With so many wonderful family ties as well as a wide breadth of friendships it makes the loss from his untimely and tragic death so far reaching and impactful…

So, we will remember and honor him:

–His friendships
–His work
–His commitment to his heritage and community
–His love of his boys and family
–His legacy

Danny, we will miss you very much and remember you in our hearts forever.

Dan will not be forgotten. His friend, Josh Berman, and our nephew, Josh Haupt, named their babies after him. (The Ashkenazic Jews have a custom to name a child after someone who died. It is believed that the loved one's soul lives on in the children, who now bear his or her name.)

As I look forward, my looking glass is portraying wonderful images—of Dan's friends, creating the drive for Toys for Tots for his forty-ninth birthday on October 9, 2021. Karen Halperin Cyphers and Jeremy Cohen organized a toy collection in Winthrop Park in Tallahassee to make sure Dan's story is never forgotten.

"We would have been in the middle of the most recent trial just now, which was delayed, but we didn't want this day to pass by unobserved and thought you know, what better way to honor Dan Markel than to give back to the community in some way?" said Cyphers.

"I do think that he's happy to see continued conversation and people around the country remembering him," said Cohen.

Dan's friends have created such a meaningful path to justice. We will write to Judge Wheeler as victims of this terrible crime to ask that he proceed with the retrial on the current schedule, on February 14, 2022, and deny any further requests for continuance.

* * *

I promise to "keep the fire burning" inside and out.

The inside is my motivation, determination, and strength to move forward in a terrible set of circumstances.

The prosecutors and law enforcement in their search for evidence and further convictions are my external support.

We are pained as every day without justice is another day we cannot fully rest, another day estranged from Danny's two sons, who we miss dearly.

The philosopher Rousseau wrote, "Patience is bitter, but its fruit is sweet." The experience of waiting may be the most difficult lesson we have learned over the past seven-plus years. We are still learning, and still hopeful that the fruits of justice are in sight.

As I continue my journey in the courtroom, I will be hearing and viewing mounds of evidence and conflicting testimonies.

After the opening arguments, the events leading up to the murder will be described again. Experts will show footage and gunshots, and will discuss the angle and height of the shooter. There will also be medical examiner reports.

I refuse to watch this footage of the murder scene and will quietly leave the courtroom.

The jurors will need these images for their deliberations, to remind them of the murder scene.

The family, jurors, investigators, and the public will retain the crime scenes as part of their memories. For me, these memories have shaped me into the co-victim of a homicide victim.

I am seeking justice for the murder of my son, Dan, in a courtroom that holds competing forensic work and analysis, dueling expert findings, and incomplete witness reports.

The fact that there is room for interpretation makes the system and courtroom very adversarial.

I hope that my quest for justice will conclude in a courtroom verdict of the truth and reunification with my grandchildren. I will keep my fire burning until we see the evidence that is still hidden—because there will be new findings to investigate.

עדן

MASTERMIND
TROUBLE
SORRY
From 1-20

Update on Legal Proceedings

(AS OF BOOK PRINTING)

A number of breakthroughs occurred early in 2022 that pushed the Markel family out of a period of waiting and into a new phase.

The Markel story inspired Florida House Speaker Chris Sprowls to lead the state legislature to pass a grandparent visitation bill, unofficially known as the Markel Act. Republican Jackie Toledo initiated HB 1119 to pass in the House and Senator Keith Perry was successful in getting unanimous support in the Senate for SB 1408. The law creates a new access point for grandparents to petition courts for visitation with grandchildren in unique, tragic cases that relate to the natural parent.

After the passage of the bill, Wendi extended an invitation to our family in April 2022. Phil and I had a warm and loving visit in Miami and were overjoyed to reconnect with our grandsons and see how they have grown.

Katherine Magbanua's retrial never took place as scheduled in February 2022. Just as we were preparing to leave for Tallahassee, the defense attorneys and prosecutors advised us that they jointly agreed on a delay. James Keith McElveen, an expert in audio matters, needed time to complete the enhancement of the Dolce Vita restaurant audio, which was covertly captured by FBI the day after the undercover "bump" when Charlie first met with Katie to discuss what had happened.

Katie's retrial is now scheduled for May 16, 2022, with the jury listening to the now-enhanced recording of Katie talking to Charlie Adelson in the restaurant. The new audio evidence brought us closer to justice when it led to the arrest of Charlie Adelson on April 21, in the early morning, just hours after our return from the Miami visit with the grandchildren.

Georgia Cappleman, the lead prosecutor stated, "This recording included statements by Charlie Adelson which can be heard for the first time." The State Attorney, prosecutors, and law enforcement moved quickly with a grand jury indictment.

The charges were first degree murder, conspiracy to commit murder, and solicitation of murder, according to Broward County Jail records. The stunning news hit our family and the international media like an earthquake.

Our Family Statement by our attorneys Orin Snyder and Matt Benjamin was released immediately.

> "The Markel Family is deeply grateful to the State Attorney's Office, the FBI. And all members of law enforcement for their tireless pursuit of justice. Nearly eight years after Danny's tragic murder, these dedicated public servants continue to fight to honor Danny's memory and to hold all accountable for his horrific death. On behalf of Danny's family and friends in the Tallahassee community and all over the world, thank you."

Acknowledgments

Although this is my tenth book, it is like no other that I have ever written. The shock of losing my son, Dan, is a very painful story compared to writing business and management books.

The Unveiling: A Mother's Reflection On Murder, Grief, and the Trial Life, allows me the opportunity to share my experience as a homicide victim and to also share the weight of the journey of my son Dan Markel's murder. Living the Trial Life has not been heard or valued in the criminal justice system. I am ready to be the storyteller of the victim's suffering and the hope for guilty verdicts for the offenders. Giving a voice is no guarantee, but writing a book starts the conversation. Also, I hope our challenges to reunite with our grandchildren will be taken seriously.

I am grateful to Christy Fletcher, of Fletcher and Co., and Rebecca Gradinger, who appreciated my story. Rebecca reached out in a timely manner and introduced me to Christy Fletcher who shared her interest and helped shape my story. Rebecca, my agent, sharpened the themes and provided the leading hand. She also introduced me to Susan Kittenplan who developed the proposal with her attention to detail. Rebecca shared the marketing of the book proposal with Eve MacSweeney. Thanks to Veronica Goldstein, Sara Fuentes, and Rachel Smalter Hall for steering the recording project.

Debra Englander became my editor from Post Hill Press, the publisher. Debra and Heather King kept the project moving forward. I also thank Madeline Sturgeon for her keen edits.

Dan's friends stepped up and were very active. Adam Burger and Steve Frank organized the memorial at Lowell House at Harvard

University and gave other meaningful contributions. This was where Dan stayed and spent most of his time during his university years. We were privileged for knowing Dan's girlfriend, Amy Adler, who shared her loss with us. She always wanted Dan's story to be told in the fullest detail.

Amy also introduced us to Orin Snyder and Matthew Benjamin at Gibson Dunn, who have been our greatest legal guides throughout the investigation, arrests, and trials. We are appreciative of their personal sensitivities to our grief and anguish. They have also expanded the Gibson Dunn team overtime with Sarah Kushner and Zoey Goldnick.

Gibson Dunn played a major role in legal issues, liaison with law enforcement, handling media requests, negotiations, and collaboration. They also introduced us to a public relations company, Teneo, and particularly Jimmy Asci and Daniel Strauss who arranged our TV appearances after the arrests. Orin and Matthew have taken on so many roles from working with the investigation, law enforcement, and all the way to attending the trials. Coupled with their legal expertise, they have given our family a level of emotional support and kept us on track, equal to or better than therapy.

Robert Solomon and Willa Marcus have guided me through the contract phases and showed continuous interest and input.

I am also grateful to Mireille Silcoff, who had some initial input into the early chapters. I am very thankful to June Lorraine Roberts for her insights at the end of the book and becoming a friend.

A special thanks to Karen Halperin Cyphers, who provided the leadership on the grandparent initiatives, social media, and video communications with Erin Rickards. Karen went out of her way to offer me support, information, and connections in Tallahassee. I will always treasure Karen as my 75th birthday gift. Erin and Karen continued to be a great team for all graphic and visual presentations.

Other internal supports came from Dan's writing partner, Ethan Leib, who is also a co-founder and contributor to *PrawfsBlawg*. We also benefitted from an introduction by Matt Price to Abe Anhang, whose son, Adam Anhang, was also murdered. Abe's support, wisdom, advice, and critique have been invaluable to me. I now call him my "murder coach."

Dan's cousins and friends continued to share their commitment throughout this ordeal. Jason Solomon organized and founded Justice for Dan, which became the major social media platform for Dan's community and memory. The community of followers has grown to over 5,700 at the time of this writing. The platform has been instrumental in sharing developments about the criminal process and grandparent efforts, mobilizing supporters to act on petitions and engage with one another.

Tamara Demko started the Go Fund Me campaign, and Jeremy Cohen acted as a representative of our family, and, as Dan's close friend, before the Florida Legislature. Jeremy attended hearings in the Florida House and Senate to advocate for the passage of our grandparent visitation bill. Throughout our Tallahassee visits, our friendship continued with Sam Kimelman and the late Dave Markell and his wife, Mona.

The story of the Dan Markel murder appeared in so many versions of the media from print, television, radio broadcasts, social media, blogs, and podcasts. For some, it is the shock of knowing Dan as a friend, colleague, or the cofounder of *PrawfsBlawg*. Other colleagues, such as David Lat from *Above the Law* and Paul Carron from *TaxProf Blog* and author Steve Epstein highlighted the criminal journey. Karen Cyphers was a key observer with deep knowledge of the case and was instrumental in refining the elements of the criminal journey for this book.

Others tracked the drama from the initial murder, the arrests, and the trial. In particular, Karl Etters and Sean Rossman at the *Tallahassee Democrat* and Julie Montanaro of WCTV, WTXL, WFSU, WTWC, and others. Thanks also goes to Brad Davis with *Dateline* and Matt Shaer with Wondery for their attention to the case. Peter Schorsch from FloridaPolitics.com provided excellent coverage of the case and the surrounding issues, particularly the grandparent visitation bill as it moved through the Legislature. Apologies for all of the media reporters whose numbers are too many, but we have had the privilege of their hard work and great writing.

I could not have written this book without the assistance and some very special talent that appeared behind the scenes. I thought about writing a book just after Dan died and made some notes. I shared my ideas with Nancy Houle and Paul Tobey, who have developed my website and also introduced me to great assistants. Allysha Howse came on first and provided research on some initial topics such as grandparent alienation and helped develop a chronology of events that supported the final book development. Alison Mackey became my major assistant in the development and editing of this book, *The Unveiling: A Mother's Reflection on Murder, Grief, and the Trial Life*. I am grateful to Alison and others who have gone through hoops to read my handwriting (chicken scratch), so the job of working with me became even harder. I am indebted to Antonella Galliuzzo for in-home support ranging from fixing printers to building office furniture.

Many thanks to Adele Balinsky, Ricky Belman, and Pearl and Larry Bell, who followed the updates and comments from Google Alert that kept the news flowing, and also for their personal support.

Keeping the criminal story alive involved so many players in the Tallahassee community, including law enforcement, victim support liaison, the State Attorney Office, prosecutors and their legal teams, and judges. I know they will still be reviewing evidence and reports long after this book is published.

Due to these terrible circumstances, I am indebted to Sara Franco from JAFCO for her support and ongoing availability. Allan Mishael kept me informed of Florida legislation regarding grandparent rights. On the grandparent visitation bill efforts, we have many to thank. We are grateful to Karen Cyphers for initiating the process and following through with great passion and persistence and to Jeremy Cohen for attending every bill hearing to represent our family and Dan. We thank House Speaker Chris Sprowls, bill sponsors Jackie Toledo, Keith Perry, and Jeff Brandes and their staffs. Senator Lauren Book took up our issue in her committee two years in a row, never wavering to show support, including as a co-sponsor of Keith Perry's bill. We also thank 2022 bill co-sponsors Melony Bell, Daisy Morales, Darryl Rouson, Cyndi Stevenson, and Michelle Salzman. We have deep gratitude to our lobbyists Jeff Johnston and Amanda Stewart who took up our cause with special attention. There are so many others who took action on this most meaningful quest, including ally Ron Watson, and staff in Governor Ron DeSantis' office.

My life has not turned out like a comedic family sitcom. Our family, friends, Dan's friends, coaches, colleagues, medical advisors, and clergy have traveled this painful journey with me and have shared my roller coaster experience. Their support needs a dedication book of gratitude to acknowledge their contributions. I will share a quote from my Facebook page on October 13, 2017 after my birthday.

> *"Thank you for all your kind birthday wishes. As some of you know, my birthday falls between Dan's (October 9th) and my grandson Lincoln's (October 13th). Sadly, both these dates become deeply painful for me with the loss of Dan and more recently not seeing my grandsons, Benjamin and Lincoln (for over a year and a half). I am very thankful to all my family and friends who keep me standing as I received life's punches. Thank you all for your year round support."*

My friends have stayed with me throughout this ordeal of grief and even supported me through joint visits to the cemetery (Arthur and the late Harvey and Linda Silver). Adele and David Balinsky stayed with me during shiva and drove me to the funeral.

Tallahassee was Dan's home and the place of his murder. I am indebted to Sam Kimelman, the congregation of Shomrei Torah, Chabad Rabbi Schneur Oreichman, Mya and Alex Greenberg, Tracy and Jeremy Cohen, Mona and the late Dave Markell, Tamara Demko, Sarah Butters, Craig Isom, Pat Sanford, Eric Abrahamson, Chief Michael DeLeo, Tor Friedman, Steve Webster, Jack Campbell, Helene Potlock, Georgia Cappleman, Jason Newlin, Karen Halperin Cyphers, Judge James Hankinson, Judge Robert Wheeler, and Melissa Russell.

FSU welcomed and supported us and held a very meaningful memorial that I will always treasure. Dean Donald Weidner, Manuel Utset, and others arranged an amazing roster of speakers. Dan's secretary, Derinda Kirkland, had the challenge of tiding up Dan's office for our visits and to return all his belongings to Toronto.

We would be nowhere in this criminal process without Dan's neighbor, James Geiger, who confronted the EMS and the dispatch with the late arrival on the criminal scene. James's observations of the car in the driveway was the major lead to the arrest. Where would we be without his open ears and eyes?

Another collective network back in Toronto was instrumental in arranging the funeral and burial arrangements. Beth Emeth Bais Yehuda Synagogue, Pearl Grundland was the executive director and Bernie Schwartz, the president, simplified our agony by coordinating with the cemetery and Benjamin's funeral home. We are indebted to

Rabbi Aron Flaszraich from the Beth Sholom Synagogue, for his caring, sensitive, and take charge leadership for the funeral and unveiling

Murder is very shocking, and I appreciate all the clergy, rehabilitation, and therapy advisors who I consulted with on the grandparent issues and my own grief.

Other family groups, the Isaksons, Haupts, Lapidots, Cohens, and Freedmans, suffered and supported alongside us. Friends who have dedicated support to this ongoing saga, include Adele, Ricky, Bobbi, Norma, Fern, Sheila, Sharon, Gloria, Paula, Arthur, Golda, Tammy, Judy, Helena, Muriel, Eva, Debbie, Bailey, Stephanie, Linda, and the late Harvey, and Allan, and the late Helaine.

A special thanks to Josh Haupt and Josh Berman and their families for naming a baby after Dan.

I want to thank everyone who wrote victim impact statements and allowed others to share their own stories of Dan and their sadness. Also, I organized a weekend at Harvard Hillel in Cambridge, Massachusetts. This was Dan's "drop in and hang out" for the eight years he spent in Boston. We had a Friday night Oneg Shabbat dinner. Rabbi Jonah Steinberg organized the event and the prayers. Noah Feldman was the speaker along with Orly Lobel, Steve Frank, and Adam Berger. The Hillel at Harvard was very meaningful for our family as well. Whenever we visited Dan, we joined him at Hillel for Shabbat, Saturday morning services.

Friends and family came from California, New York, Boston, Washington, Montreal, and Toronto. It was very special and cathartic. There were also many expressions of loss and opinions about the murder at the event.

Not to forget that Shelly, Ian, Phil, and I were supported by our individual and joint networks. We are thankful to all the visitors who attended the trial in Tallahassee.

I have learned everything about resiliency from my mother, Helen Isakson, who led by example with her energy and determination. My uncle, Lazar Lapidus, showed me how hope and optimism result in persistence and tenacity.

A special thanks goes to my daughter, Shelly, for not only experiencing these difficult memories, but also knowing the right moments to steer me to make this book more clear and understandable.

Acknowledgments

There are no words for Shelly, Ian, and her family members, and Dan's father, Phil, who are also suffering and waiting. Our family situation is still unfolding, and there are many challenges in living this story.

My list is endless and expands every day. Gratitude has become a buzz word in pop psychology but is a very real feeling for me. I am very grateful to my family and friends who have kept me standing in this period of waiting when I was still preoccupied with the harshest part of my grief.

This collective network has been the key to helping my family remain involved, informed, motivated, and hopeful. I have been privileged as these relationships have taught me to see the world's compassion.

Bibliography

Anderson, Curt. "3 Years Later, Parkland School Shooting Trial Still in Limbo." Associated Press, February 11, 2021. https://apnews.com/article/shootings-trials-florida-coronavirus-pandemic-school-shootings-ece0803d42d5d4c11ebadcf96d9d4399.

Anderson, Curt. "Ex-Wife of Slain Florida Law Professor Denies Role in Death." Associated Press, August 3, 2016. https://apnews.com/article/146781db9a3c49a3b48ba4f372972f3b.

"Canadian Report Blames Iranian Recklessness for Shoot-Down of Ukraine International Airlines Flight 752." Prime Minister of Canada. Accessed June 25, 2021. https://pm.gc.ca/en/news/statements/2021/06/24/canadian-report-blames-iranian-reckless-ness-shoot-down-ukraine.

Caron, Paul. "The #1 Story in Miami in 2019: Dan Markel's Murder Was A Contract Hit." *TaxProf Blog* (blog), December 17, 2019. https://taxprof.typepad.com/taxprof_blog/2019/12/the-1-story-in-miami-in-2019-dan-markels-murder-was-a-contract-hit.html.

Cheung, Helier. "George Floyd Death: Why US Protests Are So Powerful This Time." BBC News, June 8, 2020. https://www.bbc.com/news/world-us-canada-52969905.

Chowdhury, Maureen and Melissa Macaya. "Key Things to Know about the Condo Collapse Investigation so Far." CNN, June 28, 2021. https://www.cnn.com/us/live-news/miami-florida-building-collapse-06-28-21-intl/h_1a983d6cacc981d9376cb19080700719.

Christodoulou, Holly. “When Was Princess Diana’s Interview with Martin Bashir and Why Was It Controversial?” *The Sun*, November 19, 2020. https://www.thesun.co.uk/news/4095068/martin-bashir-princess-diana-panorama-interview/.

“Ethiopian Airlines: ‘No Survivors’ on Crashed Boeing 737.” BBC News, March 10, 2019. https://www.bbc.com/news/world-africa-47513508.

“Ethiopian Airlines Flight 302.” Podhurst Orseck. Accessed June 25, 2021. https://ethiopianflight302.com/.

“Faisal Hussain, Gunman in Danforth Shooting Rampage, Killed Himself: Police Source.” CBC News, July 26, 2018. https://www.cbc.ca/news/canada/toronto/danforth-gunman-suicide-1.4761775.

Hauser, Christine. “Florida Man Is Arrested in 2014 Murder of Law Professor.” *The New York Times*, May 26, 2016. https://www.nytimes.com/2016/05/27/us/dan-markel-arrest-2014-murder-of-law-professor.html.

Higgins, Tucker. “Former Police Officer Derek Chauvin Found Guilty of Murder, Manslaughter in the Death of George Floyd.” CNBC, April 21, 2021. https://www.cnbc.com/2021/04/20/derek-chauvin-trial-verdict.html.

Horwitz, Paul. “We Have Lost Our Beloved Friend, Dan Markel.” *PrawfsBlawg* (blog), July 19, 2014. https://prawfsblawg.blogs.com/prawfsblawg/2014/07/we-have-lost-our-beloved-friend-dan-markel.html.

Lamm, Maurice. “Yahrzeit: Memorial Anniversary.” *Death & Mourning*, May 22, 2005. https://www.chabad.org/library/article_cdo/aid/281636/jewish/Yahrzeit-Memorial-Anniversary.htm.

Lat, David. “Professor Dan Markel: Some Personal Recollections.” *Above the Law* (blog), July 24, 2014. https://abovethelaw.com/2014/07/professor-dan-markel-some-personal-recollections/.

Lat, David. “The Dan Markel Case: More Evidence in Newly Released Documents.” Above the Law, October 17, 2016. https://abovethelaw.com/2016/10/the-dan-markel-case-more-evidence-in-newly-released-documents/.

Lat, David. "The Dan Markel Case: The Wheels of Justice Turn Slowly." *Above the Law* (blog), June 23, 2017. https://abovethelaw.com/2017/06/the-dan-markel-case-the-wheels-of-justice-turn-slowly/.

"Mental Health and Substance Use During COVID-19." Canadian Centre on Substance Use and Addiction. Accessed June 17, 2021. https://www.ccsa.ca/mental-health-and-substance-use-during-covid-19.

Prasad, Ritu. "Coronavirus: How Bad Is the Crisis in US Care Homes?" BBC, July 13, 2020. https://www.bbc.com/news/world-us-canada-53172302.

Press, Associated. "Families of the Missing Visit Site of Florida Condo Collapse." Politico, June 27, 2021. https://www.politico.com/news/2021/06/27/families-florida-condo-collapse-496636.

Rabbi Marc Gellman & Monsignor Thomas Hartman. "Honoring Dead with Pebbles on Tombstones." *Sun Sentinel*, September 15, 2018. https://www.sun-sentinel.com/news/fl-xpm-2006-07-29-060727 0825-story.html.

Reynolds, Christopher. "Ottawa Rejects Iran Report That Blames Shootdown of Flight 752 on 'Human Error.'" CTV News, March 17, 2021. https://www.ctvnews.ca/canada/ottawa-rejects-iran-report-that-blames-shootdown-of-flight-752-on-human-error-1.5350716.

Rosenblatt, Kalhan, Winter, Tom, and Dienst. Jonathan. "11 Dead in Shooting at Pittsburgh Synagogue, Suspect in Custody." NBC News, October 27, 2018. https://www.nbcnews.com/news/us-news/active-shooter-reported-near-pittsburgh-synagogue-n925211.

Rossman, Sean. "Unsealed Markel Documents Cause Confusion at City Hall." *Tallahassee Democrat*, June 2, 2016. https://www.tallahassee.com/get-access/?return=https%3A%2F%2Fwww.tallahassee.com%2Fstory%2Fnews%2F2016%2F06%2F02%2Fconfusion-over-unsealed-documents-markel-case%2F85291512%2F.

"Sask. First Nation Announces Discovery of 751 Unmarked Graves Near Former Residential School." CBC News, June 24, 2021. https://www.cbc.ca/news/canada/saskatchewan/cowessess-marieval-indian-residential-school-news-1.6078375.

Simon, Mallory and Sara Sidner. "Decoding the Extremist Symbols and Groups at the Capitol Hill Insurrection." CNN, January 11, 2021. https://www.cnn.com/2021/01/09/us/capitol-hill-insurrection-extremist-flags-soh/index.html.

Staff, Intelligencer. "Attacks on Atlanta-Area Spas Leave 8 Dead, Including 6 Asian Women: What We Know." Intelligencer, March 21, 2021. https://nymag.com/intelligencer/2021/03/7-dead-after-shootings-at-multiple-spas-in-atlanta-updates.html.

Stevenson, Peter, Adrián Blanco, and Daniela Santamariña. "Which Senators Supported a Jan. 6 Capitol Riot Commission." *The Washington Post*, May 28, 2021. https://www.washingtonpost.com/politics/interactive/2021/january6-commission-senators-vote/.

Tallahassee Democrat. "Our Opinion: Dan Markel Deserves Justice." *Tallahassee Democrat*, July 17, 2015. https://www.tallahassee.com/story/opinion/editorials/2015/07/17/opinion-dan-markel-deserves-justice/30314111/.

Technologies, Raptor. "Florida School Districts Select Raptor Technologies as their Panic Alert Solution for Alyssa's Law Requirement." Cision, June 24, 2021. https://www.prnewswire.com/news-releases/florida-school-districts-select-raptor-technologies-as-their-panic-alert-solution-for-alyssas-law-requirement-301318906.html.

The Associated Press. "Florida Police Make Arrest in 2014 Slaying of Daniel Markel, Toronto-Born Law Prof." CBC News, May 26, 2016. https://www.cbc.ca/news/canada/toronto/florida-arrest-toronto-victim-markel-1.3602641.

"Will a New Law to Tackle Hate Crimes Make Asians in America Safer? | Pro/Con." *The Philadelphia Inquirer*, June 7, 2021. https://www.inquirer.com/opinion/commentary/asians-hate-crime-law-prevention-20210603.html.

Yun, Tom, Creeson Agecoutay, and Alexandra Mae Jones. "Tiny Shoes and Lowered Flags: Memorials Spread for 215 First Nations Children Found Buried in Mass Grave in B.C." CTV News, May 30, 2021. https://www.ctvnews.ca/canada/tiny-shoes-and-lowered-flags-memorials-spread-for-215-first-nations-children-found-buried-in-mass-grave-in-b-c-1.5448699.

Zine, Jasmin. "Muslim Family Killed in Terror Attack in London, Ontario: Islamophobic Violence Surfaces Once Again in Canada." The Conversation, June 9, 2021. https://theconversation.com/muslim-family-killed-in-terror-attack-in-london-ontario-islamophobic-violence-surfaces-once-again-in-canada-162400.

About the Author

Ruth Markel is a noted author, public speaker, and the president of RNM enterprises—a leading management consulting firm. She has worked in senior management positions in both private and public sectors for the past forty years. Ruth has lectured on issues concerning negotiation and advancement in organizations at the University of Toronto, the London Business School, and Ryerson University.

In addition to several TV and radio appearances, Ruth's published work includes:

> *L'Art De Negocier* (La Presse, 1988), *Une Place Au Sommet* (Les Editions La Presse, 1986), *Le Defi D'une Carrier* (La Presse, 1987), *S'affirmer Pour Evoluer* (La Presse, 1988), *Comment Gerer* (La Presse, 1987), *Karriere 1st Weiblich* (Rowohlt, 1989), *Moving Up: A Woman's Guide to A Better Future at Work* (HarperCollins Publishers, 1988), *Room At The Top: A Woman's Guide To Moving Up In Business* (Penguin Books Canada, 1985), and *Der Weg Nach Oben* (Econ, 1987).

Due to the unforeseen murder of Ruth's son, Dan Markel, she and her family have appeared on 20/20 ABC, Inside Edition, CourtTV, and Dateline NBC, and participated in the hit podcast Over My Dead Body by Wondery. With support from Dan's friends and extended networks, Ruth has engaged in efforts to change Florida's restrictive grandparent visitation statutes to provide access to courts for other families facing terrible circumstances.

She lives in Toronto with her family.